Whole-Class
Inquiry

Whole-Class Inquiry
Creating Student-Centered Science Communities

Dennis W. Smithenry
Joan A. Gallagher-Bolos

NSTApress

National Science Teachers Association

Arlington, Virginia

National Science Teachers Association

Claire Reinburg, Director
Jennifer Horak, Managing Editor
Judy Cusick, Senior Editor
Andrew Cocke, Associate Editor
Betty Smith, Associate Editor

ART AND DESIGN
Will Thomas Jr., Director
Tim French, Senior Designer, cover and interior design

PRINTING AND PRODUCTION
Catherine Lorrain, Director

NATIONAL SCIENCE TEACHERS ASSOCIATION
Francis Q. Eberle, Executive Director
David Beacom, Publisher

LIBRARY OF CONGRESS CATALOGING-IN-PUBLICATION DATA
Smithenry, Dennis W.
  Whole-class inquiry : creating student-centered science communities / Dennis Smithenry, Joan Gallager-Bolos.
    p. cm.
  ISBN 978-1-933531-34-2
  1. Science--Study and teaching (Secondary)--United States. 2. Inquiry-based learning--United States. 3. High
school students--Education--United States. 4. High school teaching--United States. I. Gallager-Bolos, Joan. II.
Title.
  Q183.3.A1S645 2009
  507.1'273--dc22
                          2008054595

Contents

Foreword

This book is all about teenagers involved in inquiry in a chemistry class-room. For us teachers and for board members, teacher educators, and researchers, this resource brings a powerful imagining to life. One simply has to watch one of the DVDs and listen as Craig, Frank, Maria, Nick, and Mark try out their can-crush experiment to know and understand what inquiry can be in a classroom. There is no doubt that this is truly their experiment; they have creative and conceptual control of it. These teens own what they are doing, why they are doing it, and what they expect to find. Beginning with some as-yet fuzzy notion of why they will be able to see some different results, they develop their ideas in a process toward a deeper understanding. They mount the argument as an explanation, connecting cause to evidence and in so doing exhibit trust in their knowledge. They amend process as they see the tests unfold; error means something real and tangible to them; and their interest is vested in these tests. Their full physical, conceptual, and emotional engagement is undeniable. They are doing science, and they are into it.

I do not know of any science classroom enterprise like this one, engaged in whole-class inquiry across the year. Inquiry is a term very much in vogue in science education circles, especially since the National Science Education Standards (NSES) placed it centrally. As usually happens with an in-vogue term, however, there are now a large number of descriptions, definitions, and interpretations for it. Inquiry has become a buzz word; a meme with myriad, conflicting understandings. The word gets mixed up with discovery, another word problematic in its usage. I have often heard teachers express misunderstandings, such as "I'm confused because I don't know what I am supposed to do when the students are confused. I know I am not supposed to tell them anything in an inquiry/discovery lesson." But the authors are not confused; they offer a clear, practical, sound, and innovative approach to the fundamental idea of inquiry in science classes.

For me, the foundation of inquiry in schools is that students engage in scientific knowledge making. Knowledge making involves students in creating increasingly secure arguments from evidence, arguments that result in deep understanding. The students own these arguments and have a strong stake in producing arguments that make sense. The teens in the classrooms depicted in this book construct chemical knowledge about, for example, particle behavior and interactions. It is scientific knowledge. They are not doing "product testing" on which coffee cup keeps coffee hot longer or which diaper holds the most water. This product-testing kind of activity often passes for inquiry in science classrooms. These students are building chemical understandings as they do inquiry. That's the point of it. The work of inquiry is integral to the year-long chemistry course; it is not an add-on nor is it a minor topic to be addressed in a few days at the beginning of the course.

The authors push this concept of inquiry to include another dimension, to "whole-class" inquiry. The whole-class piece of the practice for the authors is as important as the inquiry. This is an interesting addition and new direction from several perspectives. We now understand that science itself proceeds via the human connections among and within the scientific community, so this classroom example of whole-class inquiry has students mirroring that aspect of real science.

The sense of community the students get from working together as a class extends connections in another way. The frame of these whole-class inquiry projects connects the teens and their work to a business and a firm. We need young people who are ready for the world of work, and these projects push an explicit connection from chemistry class to possible avenues to work and employment in a useful way.

As well as building secure and accurate chemical knowledge, these young folks gain confidence and competence in their chemistry classroom. As we watch them on the DVDs, we see young people who trust others, themselves, and themselves working with others in the classic science lab setting. One reason for the call for a foundation of inquiry in science classrooms is the need to develop young people adept at working in groups, at solving problems together, and at developing their own knowledge and strengths along with those of others. The projects in this book embrace many roles and interests, from the chemistry and the product to marketing and finance. It seems as though there is a place for everyone's gifts and interests. In the end, knowledge making—i.e., inquiry—is synergistic.

As we read about the perspectives of the teacher for every video scene, we understand all of the ways in which she holds the edges of safety, deadlines, and student freedom. As we watch a teacher who pays very little overt attention, we find that her attention is focused relentlessly; she just works hard at seeming invisible. One large and persistent misunderstanding about inquiry is that the teacher is not allowed to be "present." Joan shows how critical it is to be truly present, and when and how. We understand how her understanding of adolescents, chemistry, curriculum, sequence, pacing, implementation, assessment, and self-awareness promotes this work. Joan makes her thinking wonderfully transparent. We get the force of her decision to play her roles fully in this whole-class inquiry work and see how playing those roles to the hilt allows her to be present but absent at the same time.

I love Joan's musing with respect to Craig and company: "They really care about the outcome of their work ...." Because we can see in the videos exactly what Joan is talking about, we are persuaded by the classroom evidence, just as she is. We see work across the year, warts and all. The frank and self-aware openness of this teacher-author is helpful, accessible, and useful. Her writing predicts readers' questions, and she adds details from the most practical of standpoints. It is as though we have been invited into her classroom for the full range of class sessions that the whole-class inquiry projects and assessments cover. There is no hint that the authors think this is a perfect kind of chemistry class or that a perfect chemistry class is even the goal. The point is for a group of young folks to progress, to get better at doing something important in chemistry class, and to make themselves effective and independent learners.

Some readers may not be persuaded that this approach can inform their own teaching. One issue may be a lack of well-stocked, well-designed lab classrooms such as those seen in the DVDs. Many teachers and students don't have such resources, and to pretend that lack of resources doesn't affect teaching and learning is ludicrous. But there are processes in this book that can be modified for and adapted to poorly resourced classrooms without losing the essential core of whole-class inquiry. Some readers might feel that the ethnic and socioeconomic homogeneity of the student groups in the videos reduces the potential for successfully transferring the whole-class inquiry process to their own classes. I would argue, to the contrary, that the empowerment that whole-class inquiry offers to and inculcates in students might be especially applicable to any students who are under-resourced. Those who know adolescents strongly advocate that teens be offered choices in their course work to allow them a sense of ownership over their studies. A short time spent with the students in the classrooms portrayed in this book provides incontrovertible evidence that these teens own their projects and their understandings.

Other readers may feel that their English language learners would be disadvantaged in this setting. Many, however, are persuaded that if students are to construct meaning, real understanding, there must be interstudent conversations about the real-world phenomenon at hand. In fact, whole-class inquiry is a particularly important strategy to use with English language learners, and whole-class inquiry should serve them well.

Perhaps the biggest worry science teachers might have is that they have enough time for their students to take on such lengthy projects in science. A common view holds that the standardized tests our students must take determine that teachers have to cover an enormous amount of material. The results of not doing so are thought to be that students will not perform well and that teachers and schools will suffer consequences. The authors, however, have made this more than a story of an unusual chemistry classroom by asking what the costs and benefits for their students were when a teacher took the time for whole-class inquiry. They asked the hard question about how well their students did on standardized tests compared to other students. Most research on inquiry has focused on outcomes of attitude, interest, and motivation. It is as though everyone expects a certain outcome: If we work on promoting better attitudes and more enjoyment in science, then we have to give up real content achievement in high school science. But the authors found that Joan's chemistry students had improved attitudes and enjoyed science more because of whole-class inquiry. They also had an unwavering focus on the question of how well the students built chemistry understandings. They found evidence that these students' standardized test scores, or achievement, did not suffer; their scores were comparable to those of other students. Further, we see that these teens gained much as learners. This is a solid foundation on which to build impressive edifices. We do not have to succumb to the trap that our chemistry students can either enjoy science or score high on the tests, but not both.

Science classroom teaching is a challenge for all teachers. It can be hard to hold on to one's imagination of what could be in the face of what is. The challenge of thinking about teaching science differently and moving toward inquiry is especially difficult for beginning teachers whose visions reflect their own lack of experiences with inquiry as students.

I am looking forward to using this book with my own teacher candidates. This well-told story of a chemistry class, a class that worked for its students, is pure inspiration for all of us who care about science teachers and science teaching. Not just because we should immediately try whole-class inquiry—although many might do exactly that—but because whole-class inquiry stimulates our imagination of the magic that can happen in our own science classrooms, and to and for our own science students.

Jean Lythcott
Stanford Teacher Education Program

Acknowledgments

We would like to thank the Spencer Foundation for supporting the development of this book through a generous research grant, Joan's students for participating in the project, Deborah Stipek and Richard Shavelson for providing valuable input during the initial planning stages, and Clare Kosnik and Jean Lythcott for offering extensive encouragement and advice throughout all phases of the project. Most important, we would like to thank our families for their sacrifice and support, without which this book would never have been created.

About the Authors

Dennis W. Smithenry is an assistant professor of education at Santa Clara University, Santa Clara, California, who teaches methods courses for new science teachers and conducts science education research. He has worked as a chemical engineer, taught high school chemistry, obtained a doctorate in chemistry, and conducted research in environmental engineering. He uses these experiences as a lens to conduct science education research that explores how to transform the typical science classroom into one in which the students and their teacher participate in a community of scientific practice.

Joan A. Gallagher-Bolos is a teacher at Glenbrook North High School in Northbrook, Illinois. For the past two decades, she has had the privilege of teaching all levels of high school chemistry in seven different school districts around the state of Illinois. She has used these opportunities as a foundation for developing and implementing a curriculum that teaches students how to become a self-sufficient scientific community of learners. Within this community, all members find value in their contributions to the class and have a better understanding of what it means to think as scientists. For the past seven years, she has had the pleasure of sharing this curriculum with teachers from all over the world.

Online Transcript

A transcript of the video cases on the accompanying DVDs can be found at *www.nsta.org/wholeclassinquiry*.

Chapter 1
Introduction

Imagine a high school science classroom in which two student managers orchestrate activities at the front of the room, sixteen students purposefully gather data in the laboratory for experiments they have designed, three students prepare computer graphs for a class presentation, two students debate what homework should be assigned to the class, three students record information in journals, and one teacher quietly types on a laptop at the back of the room as she observes and assesses. Her recorded observations will be used as a tool for prompting discussion with students about their experiences with this project and will also provide them with feedback to be used as a guide for future similar projects.

The above vignette portrays what occurs in our classrooms when we give our students the periodic opportunity to work together as a whole class and solve a problem that we have posed. It also illustrates the level of collaborative independence our students are able to achieve and exhibit in a multiday problem-based project that occurs about one-third of the way into a school year. In a recent book (Gallagher-Bolos and Smithenry 2004) intended for teachers who were interested in science education reform, we provided an anecdotal account of our whole-class inquiry (WCI) teaching strategies that have enabled us to transform our classrooms into student-led scientific communities such as the one portrayed above. A National Science Teachers Association review (Baca 2004) of this book said it was "the first...for high school chemistry teachers that aligns with the idea of inquiry as defined by the National Science Education Standards" (NRC 1996). This endorsement has been backed up by the hundreds of science teachers who have responded to our book and other related publications (Bolos and Smithenry 1996; Smithenry and Bolos 1997) with repeated requests for more systematic details on how we implement the WCI curriculum.

The student-led scientific communities we have created represent a transformation of the typical science classroom (Smith 2002) and align with the vision of science education reformers (AAAS 1993; NRC 1996, 2000; NSTA 1992) who have been urging educators "to provide students with inquiry experiences that allow students to participate in a community of scientific practice" (Anderson and Helms 2001). According to the National Research Council, inquiry in the classroom should be concerned with both the product (scientific ideas) and the process (how scientists study) of science (NRC 2000). To help students focus on the process side of science, we allow our students to periodically inquire together as a whole class (thus the term *whole-class inquiry*) on its own through multiday WCI projects. Much like real scientists, our students must consult with one another, make decisions for themselves, and carry out their own investigations as they seek to solve the challenging scientific problems we pose for them in our projects. Although the core of our innovative curriculum arises from these projects, students still experience a wide range of teaching strategies, such as lecture, collaborative group work, journaling, demonstrations, labs, and tests.

THE NEED FOR VIDEO CASES

Teachers who read our first book were inspired by these stories and wanted to apply these ideas in their classrooms, but we found they needed more information. Through a host of experiences, we realized that the information they needed could not adequately be provided through dialogue or more writings. We realized these avenues were limiting and that teachers wanted a literal look into our classrooms. An infinite number of subtle combinations of details go into making the mental shift necessary to implement WCI. And defining and accepting new teacher and student roles is difficult to convey through the written word; it implies that there is a formula or correct way to go about it. As evidence that more information is needed, teachers who are familiar with our publications on the WCI curriculum still ask us questions like the following:

- What do you do if a student in a class does not contribute?
- How do you give feedback to each class, even those that fail?
- How do you assess community work?
- How do the students decide who does what?
- What do you (the teacher) do while the students are working on the project on their own?
- How can you do these lengthy projects without sacrificing content?
- How do you know that the students are learning the chemistry concepts?

These questions indicated to us that our audience would benefit from observing our classrooms in action. They also suggested that teachers wanted to see some of the fine-grained details that occur as WCI projects are enacted rather than only to read retrospective descriptions of past events. At science education conferences, teachers have asked us if they could view video footage recorded in our classrooms, implying that this video would help them imagine themselves and their students in the new roles that must be assumed in the WCI classroom. In effect, these teachers were asking for video cases that document the particulars of teaching and learning in the WCI classroom. They were also asking for images of what is possible in the high school science classroom (L. S. Shulman 1992). Like other teachers and researchers (Ball and Cohen 1999; Lampert 2001; Putnam and Borko 2000; J. H. Shulman 1992b), they believe these video cases hold the potential for them to experience vicariously, explore, and learn about the complexities involved in enacting the WCI curriculum.

During the 2005–2006 school year, with generous funding from the Spencer Foundation, we embarked upon a research study to catch the WCI curriculum in action and develop several sets of video cases. The study focused mainly on documenting and analyzing the events that occurred as Joan Gallagher-Bolos implemented several WCI projects over the course of the school year in one of her chemistry classes. With data collected through structured field notes, classroom videotapes, teacher interviews, student interviews, and a teacher journal, Dennis Smithenry's research was guided by the following questions:

- How does an expert teacher introduce, implement, and assess a WCI project?
- What path of inquiry does the class take and how is the work distributed among individual students during a project?
- How do students respond to and utilize the teacher's feedback after each project?
- How does the WCI curriculum, when compared to a more conventional chemistry curriculum, affect learning outcomes?

The main product of the study has been the four sets of video cases that illustrate the events that occurred in Joan's classroom as her students experienced the WCI curriculum. We expect these video cases will be useful to both inservice and preservice teachers as they build a clearer image of what the WCI curriculum looks like and come to a better understanding of how to apply it in their classrooms. As mentioned, these videos also provide a clearer response to the questions formulated by teachers who want to implement our innovative WCI methodology and demonstrate the benefit of making these changes. In separate chapters dedicated to each video case, prompts for viewing video segments are interspersed with text that introduces the case or analyzes it from both the teacher's (Joan) and the researcher's (Dennis) perspectives.

THE GOAL—AN IMAGE OF WCI

In the remainder of this chapter, we describe the separate roles each of us assumed that allowed us to develop the four sets of video cases. We also outline the layout of the rest of the book. Before we do so, we would like you to watch a brief video that brings to life the vignette at the beginning of this chapter. This video segment documents a wonderful classroom moment that occurred in February during the third WCI project of the school year. For us, this video clip represents the overarching goal that we as teachers keep in mind throughout the school year. It contains the answer to the following questions: "Where do we want our students to be?" "How should they be interacting with one another by the end of the year?" It illustrates exactly what our goal is—to create a self-sufficient scientific community of learners.

In the clip, you will see the students discussing their plans for a lab procedure and deciding how the data they collect will help them solve the problem. You'll notice that Joan is not facilitating the discussion and is not in charge of the classroom; her students are. (In fact, we challenge you to find Joan in the video clip—she is there!) You'll see that the class is engaged and working constructively together. The students say some very intelligent things, and they say some very humorous things. It's an enjoyable conversation to observe. We think these students are working beautifully together. The discussion is unscripted; they own it. And our goal has been reached in these moments. How does this happen? How did we get our classes to behave this way? This footage will provide you with a starting point for the book, and perhaps help formulate some questions as to what WCI really is and how it is best implemented.

Video: You should now watch the GOAL video on the DVD labeled "Video Cases for Chapters 1–3."

The classroom shown in this video clip is at an affluent suburban high school. The students in the video are enrolled in an honors chemistry class, facilitated by an experienced teacher. These demographics may lead some readers to question if the WCI teaching approach can be applied effectively to classrooms with differing demographics. We can alleviate this concern by telling you that both of us—and others—have successfully implemented the WCI teaching approach in classrooms with a range of demographics, grades, academic levels, and science subjects. We have brought the WCI curriculum to life in eight different school districts that include a full spectrum of high schools (inner city, rural, and suburban), and academic levels (honors, regular, and advanced placement). Because of these experiences, we feel confident in saying that the WCI teaching approach will greatly benefit any class, no matter the demographics.

Now that you have seen an actual image of the WCI classroom in action by watching the GOAL video, please keep this image in your mind as you progress through the book. We would like you to use it as a mental guidepost for understanding all the steps Joan and her students take to create the self-sufficient scientific classroom community portrayed in the vignette and the video clip.

In the remaining sections of this chapter, we would like to introduce ourselves as authors, discuss our previous and current collaboration, and describe the separate roles that we each assumed in the research project.

JOAN'S INTRODUCTION— OPENING MY CLASSROOM TO RESEARCH

Dennis and I have been working together for 15 years. We taught together for only one year but have continued our collaboration because we have found we make a wonderful team. Dennis's science background and passion for teaching, along with my long-term, multiple-districts experience and instinct for the whole child, have allowed us to create innovative, meaningful, and beneficial teaching strategies. Along the way, we have developed a close friendship, and we have had a great deal of fun.

Completing our first book (Gallagher-Bolos and Smithenry 2004) was a very long journey. But the second book seemed predestined. Once we started presenting our WCI ideas at national and regional conferences, attendees told us what they needed: "I'd love to be able to come visit your classroom." "I wish I could see this in action." We knew there was no formulaic answer that would provide a blanket response to the questions they had. The WCI strategy involves a mental shift and an ability to work without a script.

During the time between publication of our first and second books, Dennis took a small break from the world of education to obtain a PhD in chemistry. He then started postdoctoral work in environmental engineering. But I knew he would eventually come back to education, and, luckily for me, it happened right at the time when we were ready to embark on this book. Dennis decided to apply his research skills to science education. The Spencer Foundation awarded him a grant to do a study on my classroom and the WCI approach. I was overjoyed when he told me, mostly because I would be working so closely with Dennis again. On a more practical level, I was also excited about the project because both of us were confident this research would provide the tangible information that so many teachers were requesting.

I love my job. I whole-heartedly believe this is what I am supposed to be doing. The more I work, the more fulfilled I feel. I enjoy working with high school students and teachers, and I am passionate about improving science education. I must be one of the luckiest people in the world. But, as anyone who knows me will attest, I work very hard at my job. I know what needs to go into every day's plan to make it a success. I spend an inordinate amount of time reflecting on things that have happened in my class in order to improve or move forward during the next class. Because I have many years of experience, I can apply these thoughts instinctually without recording them, and I have a firm understanding of the teaching profession.

When Dennis approached me with this research project, I knew it would require even more time than I was already dedicating to my job. The details that had become second nature to me in years past would have to be brought to the forefront of my thinking. The reasons I was taking a certain approach with a given student, with a group of students, with a particular class, or with given content would have to be put into words and recorded, not just internalized and approved. I would need to make certain that all the ideas that Dennis and I wanted to share with other teachers actually took place during the projects that were filmed. With each lesson plan I would have to record every detail from the start of a given period to the end for the entire school year.

So why did I agree to do this? I have a family who needs me, I have a life outside of school, and I already work 12- to 16-hour days, not including weekends. My colleagues regularly turn to me for help with science content; classroom management; parent communication; departmental, school, and district concerns; managerial problems; and, most often of all, curricular implementation questions. I enjoy the occasional keynote speaking opportunity. My time is more than booked.

The answer to why I decided to take on the added responsibility of working with Dennis on his research is simple. I knew the results would provide us with a product that would help improve science education. As an educator, I have always tried to give each of my students the science experience I would want my own children to have. And, if the ideas that Dennis and I had developed might inspire other science teachers to feel as passionate about improving science education as we do, then the work would be more than worth our time.

It was a packed year, but I enjoyed the work. I learned a great deal about what has to be considered when doing an in-depth research project. I revisited and reaffirmed those things that I hold true in teaching and science education, and I found revisiting those things that have become second nature to be an extremely rejuvenating process. Also, as I said before, Dennis and I always grow as professionals whenever we're given the opportunity to work together.

When Dennis gave me the videos to analyze, it was at first a little disconcerting to watch myself on the screen. Vanity raced through my head during the first video: "Do I really look like that? Boy, my daughters are right; I need some new clothes! What's with my posture? Etc." But it took only a couple of minutes to get drawn into the interactions of the students with me and with one another. Overall, I enjoyed writing about the behind-the-scenes deliberations for each of these projects and sharing my thoughts about why my students were doing the things they were doing. I felt good about the outcome of the year. I was able to see my students' growth rather than just reflecting on my memories of their growth. It was reassuring to see the benefits my students got from learning science by experiencing whole-class inquiry.

Dennis and I have realized just how important it is for the different science education arenas to come together to make constructive improvements in the classroom. Too often the findings from science education researchers are completely removed from the decisions being made within a school or district. Similarly, too often the reality of the life of a teacher, the lives of our students, and the mechanics of the classroom are missing from science education programs and the thoughts of researchers. And too often the knowledge of or access to science content or current scientific events is not part of a science curriculum. But I feel the connections among the worlds of research, academia, and education happened in this project. And I truly believe those connections are the way to make meaningful reform for our students.

DENNIS'S INTRODUCTION— CREATING THE VIDEO CASES

Developing the video cases presented in this book was a huge, complex task that took me three years to complete. I take great pride in the completion of this task because the video cases seem to tell adequately and accurately the story of how Joan leads her students into becoming a self-sufficient classroom community. Developing this image of successful inquiry teaching is what drove me to do the research project in the first place and is what sustained me as I edited the video into the forms that you find on the DVDs.

Before Joan and I began the research project in 2005–2006, we coordinated our schedules so that I could come to her school and document the events that occurred during several separate WCI projects. We also outlined parameters for how we would interact while I was in the classroom. We decided that it would be important for us to maintain our separate roles as teacher and researcher during the entire school year. For the most part, I did not help Joan with teaching activities, and Joan did not help me carry out research activities. When Joan was teaching, we did not talk or interact.

When the school year began, I randomly selected one of Joan's three honors chemistry classes to be my focus class. I asked the students (and their parents) in this class for permission to allow me to videotape them during the WCI projects or assessments and use their images in this book and the accompanying DVDs. As part of my request, I told the students that, when I was in the classroom videotaping, I would assume the role of a nonparticipant observer. I explained that this role meant that I would not interact with them or their teacher other than to capture the class's actions on film. I told the students that they should try to think of me as an invisible presence. Even though the students had only just met me and had met with Joan for only a few class sessions, all of them and their parents gave their permission. This made it possible for me to create clean video cases of the entire class without having to add any distracting blurs over the images of students who did not give permission. We owe these students and their parents a debt of gratitude for placing their trust in us.

While explaining the purpose of the research project, I talked with Joan's classes about how she and I had taught together at another school for one year and had continued our collaboration, even though our career paths had veered apart. I wanted the students to understand that, although Joan and I are collaborators, we now wore different hats. I explained that I was working as a postdoctoral researcher at a major university and had just received a grant to conduct research in the students' classroom. This information seemed instrumental in causing the students to view me in the distinct role of researcher who was interested in documenting the workings of the WCI classroom.

True to my researcher role of nonparticipant observer, I did not talk with Joan before, during, or after class. I also minimized my dialogue with the students during class sessions. During the rare instances when students did approach and try to talk with me, I ignored them, put my finger to my lips (indicating that I would not talk), or gave a terse response. My overall goal was for the students to sense that I did not want to influence any of the classroom events that occurred while I was filming. I wanted the students to allow my cameras and me to blend into the background.

While watching the video cases, you may notice that there are a few times when the students take quick glances at me (and the camcorder). The glances indicate that the students are aware of my presence but that they are trying to be respectful of my attempt to capture them acting as normally as possible. They are neither hamming it up for the camera nor constantly making reference to it. There are times when the students forget that they are being filmed and realize after the fact that something they did may be funny or embarrassing. I think that these instances suggest the students lost track of me and became comfortable with my presence. I should note that I assured the students at the beginning of the project that their teacher would not be able to view any of the video until the entire school year was completed. This helped the students know that any actions captured on film could not inadvertently affect their grades or their teacher's perception of them.

It is important to note that I did talk with some students outside the classroom session. Over the course of the year, I conducted focus-group interviews with about one-half of the students from the class. Before I began an interview, I indicated that its main point was to find out what the students were thinking about their experiences in the WCI classroom. I told them then that Joan would not be allowed to view the interview transcripts until after the school year was over. This seemed to allay the students' concerns, because they opened up and spoke freely during the interviews. You will hear more about what the students had to say in chapter 6. I bring up these interviews now, however, because the first round of interviews in October seemed to cement how the students viewed my role as a researcher. Because I provided an avenue for them to talk about their WCI experiences, they knew I cared about their ideas too. My research was not just about Joan; it was about them too. I think that this knowledge helped them understand why I would not talk with them in the classroom. It helped them see me as a researcher who was trying to capture the essence of the WCI phenomenon without changing it in any way.

In total, I videotaped the focus classroom in about 15 of the 85 class sessions that occurred during 2005–2006. When I filmed in Joan's classroom, I usually used two camcorders to capture different angles of the events that occurred during the WCI projects. There were a few times during the research study when I was unable to make it to Joan's classroom and wanted particularly important events videotaped. In these instances, Joan set up one camcorder in the back of the room (e.g., CHEMCO-1).

In the video cases, you will notice me walking around the room, operating the cameras and typing notes on my laptop computer. I tried to be as unobtrusive as possible. Although I knew that the sound quality would suffer, I decided not to place microphones on Joan or any of her students because I did not want the students to feel as though they were on a set and I did not want the classroom to appear staged. Rather,

I wanted the class to proceed as close to normally as it might have if I had not been there. My decision to not use extra microphones forced me to subtitle the video cases, but I think the end result still works. At times in the video cases, you will notice that the audio cuts out for a second or two and that the audio silences occur when the students' real names are used. At the beginning of the research project, I assured the students that their real names would not be used in the final versions of the video cases. To do this, I gave each student a pseudonym and dropped out the audio portion when a student's name was clearly stated in the video. These instances do not occur too often; however, I want you to know why the audio drops out at times. My videotaping in some of the earlier video cases is jerky because I was still getting used to my new camcorder.

During each WCI project, I collected 6 to 12 hours of video footage. Once I had all of this video data, my main challenge was to condense the footage to a reasonable length so that it would adequately tell the story of what had occurred yet not overwhelm the viewer with too much information. Magdalene Lampert identified this challenge as a "problem of scale" when she was faced with a similar task of managing large amounts of classroom video data (Lampert 2001). Telling the story in an engaging manner was the main criterion I used to select the video that ended up being included in the final video cases. I did not choose the best or remove the worst video instances; rather, my method was to select key video segments that would allow the viewer to understand the chain of events and link them together. By focusing on the video segments that tell the story, I could illustrate the full range and types of activities that occurred either as Joan led or as her students took charge of the classroom.

Thankfully, Joan and I have developed such a solid working relationship over the years that she trusted me to create video cases that would capture her practice. I developed all of them with minimal input from Joan and did not allow her to view them until at least one year had passed because I wanted Joan to react retrospectively to my carefully crafted images of her practice and then write about her reactions (J. H. Shulman 1992a). I wanted her to look back at her practice and comment on what was going through her mind as she watched the video cases and on which aspects she felt were important to elaborate. I believe that Joan's point of view provides indispensable insight into how a teacher thinks through her work in enacting successful inquiry teaching.

I come to these videos with the experiences of a science teacher who was mentored by Joan during my first year of teaching back in 1994 and who was able to continue this collaboration over the years. I also bring to these videos my experiences working as a chemical engineer, chemist, and environmental engineer. Most recently, I have been working as a science education researcher. Walking in these different shoes has given me a unique perspective on why this type of classroom is important as an image of successful inquiry teaching.

At the end of the next four chapters, I analyze and discuss the video cases from the perspective of a researcher who has filmed the classroom, recorded field observations, edited the video footage, and culled the footage together into the video cases. Because I developed the video cases, I have spent countless hours observing on film the way students interact in Joan's classroom as they work together on the various WCI projects. At this point, when I sit down to review any of the video footage, I know it all by heart. I can anticipate what each student will say and what event will happen next. This level of familiarity and intimacy with the video cases has allowed me to identify major themes that speak to how and why the WCI curriculum works. Not surprisingly, I have found that these themes also tend to illustrate what the science education research literature has identified as best practices for science education. In my video analyses, I spell out these themes and, when appropriate, make connections to other research studies that have focused on real classrooms where inquiry-based and constructivist teaching strategies have been implemented.

BOOK LAYOUT

The heart of the book is housed in chapters 2 through 5; this is where the majority of the video footage is found. In chapters 2, 4, and 5, we present three sets of video cases that involve three different WCI projects. Following the GOAL video, the first set of video cases, for chapter 2, documents the Chemistry Concoctions WCI Project that occurred in September 2005. The second set, for chapter 4, documents the CanCo WCI Project of October 2005, and the third set, for chapter 5, documents the Solutions WCI Project of February 2006. We chose these particular projects to illustrate how the implementation of WCI changes as the year progresses and as students become more comfortable with each other and the WCI approach. Throughout each of these chapters, you will first read an introduction to a video, then be prompted to watch the video, and then read Joan's thoughts about what occurred in the video. At the end of each chapter, you will read Dennis's thoughts about the video from a researcher's perspective.

Chapter 3 videos illustrate how Joan uses the teaching strategy of WCI assessments to help build a strong classroom community. These WCI assessments are 30-minute class challenges that require the whole class to work together to solve a problem. Two examples of WCI assessments are presented. The first example shows the class doing a challenge at the beginning of the year. The second example shows the class tackling a challenge in the second semester.

In chapter 6, we focus on the impact and utility of the WCI curriculum, especially from the points of view of the students who experienced it. The chapter provides a different perspective on the image of the WCI classroom from that of the video cases. We present this perspective through three angles: first, an analysis of student interview data that reveals student perceptions of WCI; second, the teacher's use of role-play and feedback and its role in creating an effective student-led scientific community in the classroom; and third, a comparison of the learning outcomes of students who experience the WCI curriculum with those who experience a more conventional chemistry curriculum.

At the end of the book in chapter 7, the two of us come together to summarize some of the key elements in the book. We present our views on science education reform and propose a challenge to those who have read our book and viewed our video cases.

In addition to the seven chapters and four sets of video cases, we have created an online collaboration tool for our book at *www. wholeclassinquiry.blogspot.com*. We hope you will visit this blog frequently and participate in an online learning community of individuals who want to discuss the book further, share stories about their efforts to implement WCI, and talk about science education reform in general. Our roles on this blog are beginning the conversation, moderating the ensuing discussion, providing additional information about WCI, and connecting individuals—science teachers, science teacher educators, and science education researchers—who are interested in bringing about true science education reform. We hope you will take advantage of this blog and help build the learning community through your online contributions.

As you read through the text, watch the video cases, and contribute to the companion website, we look forward to providing you with a new and expanded view of our WCI classrooms. We hope you finish reading with not only a clearer vision of what is possible in the high school science classroom but also a firm appreciation of what students are capable of doing when given the chance. We hope our stories will help you integrate WCI projects and assessments into your own curriculum.

REFERENCES

American Association for the Advancement of Science (AAAS). 1993. *Benchmarks for science literacy.* New York: Oxford University Press.

Anderson, R. D., and J. V. Helms. 2001. The ideal of standards and the reality of schools: Needed research. *Journal of Research in Science Teaching* 38 (1): 3–16.

Baca, S. C. 2004. *A review of teaching inquiry-based chemistry: Creating student-led scientific communities.* NSTA Recommends: NSTA.

Ball, D., and D. Cohen. 1999. Developing practice, developing practitioners. In *Teaching as the learning profession: Handbook on policy and practice,* eds. L. Darling-Hammond and H. Sykes. San Francisco: Jossey-Bass.

Bolos, J. A., and D. Smithenry. 1996. Chemistry incorporated. *The Science Teacher* 63 (7): 48–52.

Gallagher-Bolos, J. A., and D. W. Smithenry. 2004. *Teaching inquiry-based chemistry: Creating student-led scientific communities.* Portsmouth, NH: Heinemann.

Lampert, M. 2001. *Teaching problems and the problems of teaching.* New Haven: Yale University Press.

National Research Council (NRC). 1996. *National Science Education Standards.* Washington, DC: National Academy Press.

———. 2000. *Inquiry and the National Science Education Standards: A guide for teaching and learning.* Washington, DC: National Academy Press.

National Science Teachers Association (NSTA). 1992. *Scope, sequence, and coordination of secondary school science. Volume II: Relevant research.* Washington, DC: NSTA.

Putnam, R. T., and H. Borko. 2000. What do new views of knowledge and thinking have to say about research on teacher learning? *Educational Researcher* 29 (1): 4–15.

Shulman, J. H. 1992a. Teacher-written cases with commentaries: A teacher-researcher collaboration. In *Case methods in teacher education,* ed. J. H. Shulman, 131–152. New York: Teachers College Press.

———. 1992b. *Case methods in teacher education.* New York: Teachers College Press.

Shulman, L. S. 1992. Toward a pedagogy of cases. In *Case methods in teacher education,* ed. J. H. Shulman. New York: Teachers College Press.

Smith, P. S. 2002. *2000 National survey of science and mathematics education: Status of high school chemistry teacher.* Chapel Hill, NC: Horizon Research.

Smithenry, D., and J. Bolos. 1997. Creating a scientific community. *The Science Teacher* 64 (8): 44–47.

Chapter 2
WCI Project 1—Chemistry Concoctions

For teachers, the start of a new school year is filled with incredible mystery—students, their parents, staff additions, policy changes, and work space. Yet there is one constant I take comfort in year after year—the anticipation. The first day back is always abuzz with teachers sharing stories of recent sleepless nights and anxious dreams. The conversations are animated, colorful, and necessary. We feel rejuvenated, creative, nervous, and energetic. Yes, the month of August speaks a universal language to the teaching profession. It is perhaps my favorite time of the year.

The mixed bag of emotions we experience as we reconvene to begin another year is similar to what our students are feeling. They typically share stories of their summer adventures and of their dread as another school year begins. Of course, some students are happy to see their peers and still others actually enjoy school. But, for the most part, they are anxious about school and their new classes. Their thoughts race: "I can't believe summer is over; where did it go?" "Will I be able to handle school this year?" "Will my classes be interesting?" "Will they be relevant?" "Will my teachers be boring?" "Will my teachers care that I'm in the room?" And most important, "Do I have friends in my classes?"

How do we handle such an emotionally sparked environment? I try to keep the enthusiasm alive at all costs. Channeling that energy in a positive direction can set the tone for the rest of the year. I have always considered the beginning of every school year a critical time. I believe it is the key to developing the trust and climate needed for successful implementation of a meaningful curriculum, namely whole-class inquiry (WCI). I therefore spend a great deal of time using the excitement to nurture interest in learning and passion for working together. My first few lesson plans appear to the students to be focused solely on chemistry content, but the true foundation of these lessons lies in creating a positive community climate. This environment allows students to slowly but surely take charge of the classroom and become a self-sufficient scientific community capable of working together and accomplishing any challenge presented to them as a class.

At my school, each class session lasts 90 minutes and meets every other day on a block schedule. As you can see in Figure 2.1, during the 2005–2006 school year my class met for 85 sessions and participated in 9 separate units. My first unit in chemistry is a 12-day unit that focuses on phases of matter, density, particulate nature of matter, significant digits, data analysis, and experimentation. My primary focus, however, is to use this content as a means for developing our yearlong class climate. For instance, on Day 1, I introduce the topic of chemistry. We have a discussion investigating the question, "What does it mean to be a scientist?" Students tell stories about times they've behaved as scientists, both in and out of school. They tell about discoveries they've made with friends about their environment—perhaps along a creek or in a museum or on a farm, the inquisitive questions they asked their parents as a child, and their adventures of impromptu experiments with candy and pop. I tell them similar stories about ways in which my children behaved as scientists as I watched them navigate their worlds as toddlers. We then have a lengthy conversation about journals and how wonderful it is to record stories. We also discuss the difference between being a professional scientist and practicing scientific behavior. It is an exciting first day. My students get a firm understanding of what it means to be a scientist, although they don't realize that my primary objective is to get them comfortable with one another and with me. Their tangled emotional states become a bit more focused, but their enthusiasm remains. They feel safe in science class and safe talking to their classmates and teacher. This is yet another example of the mental shift discussed in chapter 1 and how each layer in your lesson plans is a necessary component of WCI.

The many details of my Unit I lesson plans fall outside the scope of this book, but the information can be found in our first book, *Teaching Inquiry-Based Chemistry: Creating Student-Led Scientific Communities* (Gallagher-Bolos and Smithenry 2004). In the three paragraphs that follow, I quickly review the activities that I typically do during Days 2 through 4 that lead to our first WCI project, Chemistry Concoctions.

On Day 2 the students do their first collaborative group work activity in which we attempt to execute the community class climate we discussed on Day 1. From the students' perspective, this activity is designed to introduce observation versus interpretation. It also provides an opportunity to practice journal record keeping. My primary goals in this activity are to build trust and to keep student enthusiasm high. By the end of the day, I believe the majority of students trust that what I plan and do is in their best interests.

On Day 3, I give a safety presentation designed to prepare students for lab. During this lesson, I teach students that safety is a community responsibility. We identify a safety team and learn about the location of

Figure 2.1

2005–2006 Schedule of Unit Topics, WCI Projects and Assessments, and Feedback

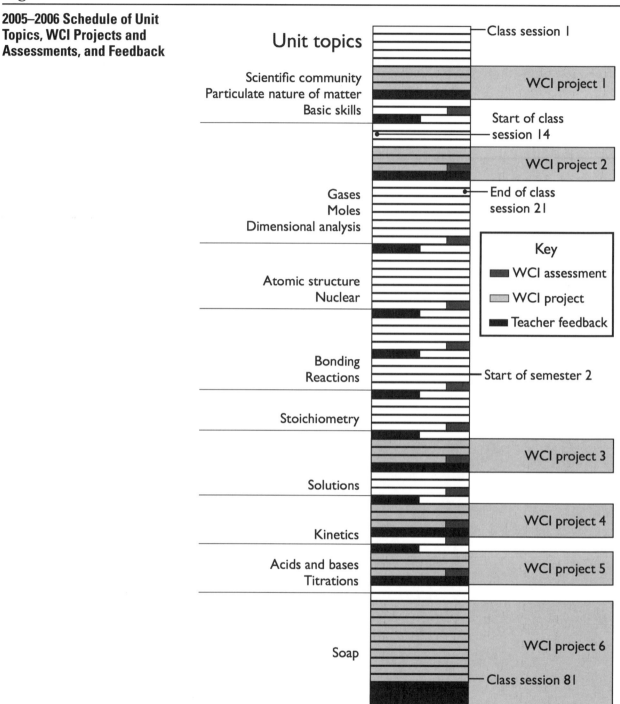

Figure 2.2

Introduction to Chemistry Lab Sheet

Introduction to Chemistry—Lab Introduction

Task: Using your powers of observation, answer the questions listed for each station described.

Safety: Always look up the safety hazards for each chemical used in lab. Use the Flinn catalog and record info. Today's chemicals are lead (II) nitrate, potassium iodide, corn starch

Lab Activity #1: States of Matter
1. Write a definition for each of the following: solid, liquid, gas
2. Now use the syringes at your lab station. For each substance that is sealed in a syringe, test the compressibility by pushing on the plunger and observing the decrease in volume for the substance. Record your findings. (Press syringes according to directions!)
3. Using words and pictures, develop and draw a model that explains the compressibility differences between a solid, liquid, and a gas based on your findings from lab.
4. Give 2 examples of each phase of matter. List at least three characteristics that classify a substance as a solid; as a liquid; as a gas.
5. Make a sample of oobleck. (2 parts corn starch and 1 part water). Investigate its properties and record your findings in words and pictures.

Lab Activity #2: Particulate Nature of Matter
6. Look at each of the reactants. What do you observe about lead (II) nitrate? About potassium iodide?
7. Follow the procedure below:
   a. Cover the petri dish with DI (deionized) water. Do NOT move the dish from this moment on. Using the dropper bottles, simultaneously add 6 drops of lead (II) nitrate and 6 drops of potassium iodide solution on opposite sides of the petri dish. Wait 12 minutes. (While waiting, start step b.) Record all observations in words and pictures.
   b. In ANOTHER petri dish, repeat step "a" but add the 6 drops of lead (II) nitrate to one side of the petri dish. Wait 8 minutes minimum and then add the 6 drops of potassium iodide on the opposite side of the dish. Record all observations in words and pictures.
   c. Dispose of all substances as instructed by your teacher.
8. Head back to your desks, shift into your lab/cooperative work groups and answer the following. What interpretations can you make about the behavior of the substances in this activity? Write them in words and pictures. (We'll go through this together, so leave lots of room!)

safety equipment in the classroom and how to use it. We also practice thinking like scientists and learning how to find and read MSDS (material safety data sheet) information.

On Day 4 students perform an introductory lab activity allowing them to explore the states and particulate nature of matter. The sheet that the students received for this introductory lab activity is shown in Figure 2.2. Although I want the lab to lead the students to a better understanding of the particulate nature of matter, my main purpose is to have students apply the safety information I introduced on the previous day. I even role-play a lab accident to have the class practice its community safety response. I can happily report that every year, the safety team has saved me from a host of potentially serious injuries.

The class is now ready to begin its first WCI Project—Chemistry Concoctions. This is the students' first experience going through the entire process of implementing a true experiment. As always, there are multiple layers to this lesson plan. The students concentrate on the science involved in the chemical reaction between baking soda and vinegar, how to best change the parameters involved with this reaction, and the apparatus used in lab. My focus is on their ability to work constructively in their small groups to share data and rely on one another, in essence, to behave as a community of professional scientists would. Setting up the project correctly is imperative because correct setup will dictate whether students take ownership of the challenge and care about the results. Depending on and supporting one another then surface as necessities within our scientific community.

CHEMISTRY CONCOCTIONS WCI PROJECT—DAY 1

Teacher's Introduction—CHEMCO-1

The first video you will view shows me reviewing the Introduction to Chemistry lab discussed previously. This is not yet part of the Chemistry Concoctions (CHEMCO) WCI Project, but it illustrates the classroom climate being nurtured so that students are more inclined to follow my lead as I facilitate their first big project. Recall that the Introduction to Chemistry lab was their first lab experience after our safety-training day. I give them feedback about their lab work for two important reasons: One is to introduce modeling reactions at the particulate level, and the other is to show them how well the class is developing in terms of following proper safety precautions and in terms of working constructively as a group.

At the start of the video, you see me using particulate models (pictures that contain dots to represent atoms) to explain the students' observations of a chemical reaction that they recorded during the Introduction to Chemistry lab. Notice that I mention information that has not yet been explored in class, such as naming compounds, predicting products, and knowing what an aqueous solution means at the particulate level. I believe that hearing bits and pieces of what is to come, both in terms of content and community challenges, helps my students adapt to our developing class climate and familiarizes them with the language of science. After demonstrating particulate modeling, I provide feedback, showing the students how well they did focusing on safety and community during this initial lab activity. This video stops at the point at which the students head back into lab to do the introductory activity that sets the stage for the Chemistry Concoctions WCI Project. (A review of this part of the day occurs in the next video.)

This video gives you a taste of how teacher-directed my classroom is at this point in the school year. There are many moments when I am asking students questions, but my focus is on directing the class toward the idea of inquiring together as a community. I am trying to give them an idea of how to reflect and grow, both as individuals and as a class. This focus requires that I model many of the skills now so that the class is prepared to accomplish community projects in the future without my direction.

Recall that what you view in this video is still the beginning of the school year, so my students are still getting used to the fact that summer is over and school is in session. Also keep in mind that we have met for only four 90-minute classes before the introduction of this first multiday WCI project.

Video—You should watch the CHEMCO-1 video on the DVD labeled "Video Cases for Chapters 1–3." This clip takes the first 60 minutes of class and compresses them into approximately 18 minutes so that you can visualize what was described.

Teacher's Analysis—CHEMCO-1

Throughout all the videos that you view in this book, one constant remains with regard to all activities in which the students participate: Feedback is the key. Without feedback, the connection from project to project and the growth made as a class over time is lost. Students think that each project is an isolated event, rather than an experience that leads to the planned conclusion of becoming a self-sufficient scientific community of learners. I want my students to apply the feedback from one activity to the next. Each block of feedback focuses on a new skill area or stimulates their thinking about individual and community improvement. Most of all, the time dedicated to feedback provides students with an opportunity to decompress individually and collectively and process what they just went through.

The feedback that you just viewed is minimal because the Introduction to Chemistry lab activity is not the focus of this chapter, but it gives you an introduction to the idea of the self-reflection and growth required of the students. A more in-depth example of feedback is shown as a conclusion to the Chemistry Concoctions WCI Project in the CHEMCO-4B video. Right now, though, I want to introduce some thoughts about feedback to give more insight into what I look for during multiday projects.

During feedback sessions, my comments always focus on three major categories—safety, accuracy, and community. Although the tasks required are unique to a particular project and sometimes change as the project progresses, a rough, skeletal design of the areas that may be assessed are listed in Table 2.1.

Table 2.1

Areas of Assessment for WCI Activities

Feedback Area	Class/Group Task Being Assessed
Safety	Lab Implementation, Lab Report, Assessment, Practical, etc.
Accuracy	Lab Implementation, Lab Report, Assessment, Presentation, etc.
Community	Lab Implementation, Lab Report, Assessment, Presentation, etc.

If part of an activity requires the students to focus on any one of the three categories—safety, accuracy, and community—feedback addresses that given area. For instance, students could potentially receive feedback in the area of safety on the lab they did, the lab report they turned in, and the assessment they are given after the project is completed. The lab safety feedback could address the following questions: Did students record safety information in their journals in order to prepare for lab? Did students remember to move the desks away from the safety equipment, providing a clear path for all? Did students remember to take their hats off and keep their goggles on? Students are also required to address safety in their lab report, so they can receive feedback on how well they detailed this information in their lab reports.

Another example of feedback includes the category of accuracy. This is the category that focuses on both the process of science (problem-solving skills) and the chemistry content. For instance, if a class is required to give a presentation outlining its findings from a multiday WCI project, it will be assessed on how accurate these findings are. Was the procedure a good approach for solving the problem? Did students analyze the data correctly and thoroughly? Were their calculations correct? Does the particulate drawing used to represent the chemical reaction make sense? Can the model be used to describe a new scenario? Were the students close to an expected or known result? All these things could also be assessed in a class lab report or a WCI assessment (see chapter 3).

This is a good time to discuss the one part of feedback that can monopolize the WCI curriculum if not carefully handled—grades. When I use the word *feedback*, I am including all aspects of the process—self-reflection, group discussion, personal and collective growth, suggestions for the future, and, of course, grades. I believe the majority of teachers would agree that some students care very little about their grades, while others care way too much, thinking the grade is everything. It is a rarity to find a student with an instilled sense of balance between grades and learning. I have found that the WCI curriculum provides a medium to help nurture that balance and teach students that when you focus on learning and working together constructively toward a common goal, the grade follows.

To put it simply, at the end of each WCI activity, each member of the class receives the same grade. This parallels our philosophy of having the WCI activities reflect those practices found in "authentic settings" in which people are accountable on both an individual and a community level. Academe and industry both function this way. As educators, we have chosen to incorporate both individual and community accountability into our assessment system. Of course, each teacher must decide on his or her own assessment system. We are unaware of how assigning unique grades to students in these activities might affect the dynamic of the community's growth, but we do have evidence (see chapter 6) to support that a class grade helps promote the community culture and that it does not hurt an individual's grade at the end of a semester. Keep in mind that a class assessment is never worth as much as an individual test in terms of points. Also, students are not expected to be as adept at working together at the beginning of the year as they are at the end of a year, and students' grades should reflect this.

All of the pieces of feedback that have been mentioned—safety, accuracy, and community—receive some point value. One critical piece of the grade is that each area must receive the same point value. For instance, if the class receives 30 points for lab implementation for a particular WCI project, 10 points should be assigned to safety (did all students abide by standard safety protocol?), 10 to accuracy (did the class implement a reasonable, reproducible procedure for accomplishing the outlined task?), and 10 to community (did the class work constructively together, not letting the pressure of time constraint or disagreement overshadow the task needing to be accomplished?).

As you continue to read this book and watch the videos, I hope you are able to recognize how few conversations are about points and grades. Instead the focus is on developing our class/company environment and on how students are learning about themselves and about chemistry.

In the CHEMCO-1 video segment in which I am giving feedback about their Introduction to Chemistry lab work, I am concerned mostly with the students' ability to work constructively together in a safe environment and their ability to record and communicate relevant and reliable data to one another and to me. The students, however, seem very concerned with writing down information they think might be on the test. This isn't necessarily a bad thing, but they have yet to have the experience of applying the information from my feedback to a new scenario, so the usefulness of the information is still abstract. I know, however, that they will need the ability to model a chemical reaction and the ability to follow appropriate safety guidelines in order to accomplish the next part of the Chemistry Concoctions WCI Project.

It's also important to make sure feedback captures the students' attention. As you see in the CHEMCO-1 video, I try to do a variety of things to make the feedback more personal to each student and to each class. I make sure to have a video camera ready, knowing that I will use video as part of my feedback. I film each class so that the class can decide for itself how well it did. I also show some entertaining quotes from the dialogue I overhear throughout the lab. This invariably ends up being the students' favorite part of feedback throughout the year. They love the quotes.

CHEMISTRY CONCOCTIONS WCI PROJECT—DAY 2

Teacher's Introduction—CHEMCO-2

The CHEMCO-1 video ends with me handing out the Chemistry Concoctions project sheet. To provide some background for this lab challenge, the Chemistry Concoctions WCI Project focuses on how the gas produced from the reaction of baking soda (sodium bicarbonate) and vinegar (acetic acid) can be used to displace a specific volume of liquid in the apparatus shown in Figure 2.3.

Figure 2.3

Chemistry Concoctions Apparatus

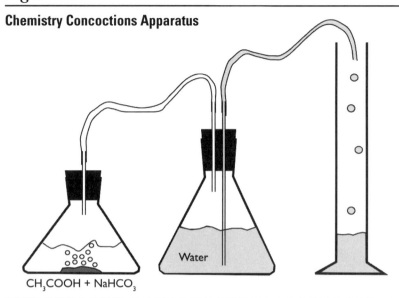

CH$_3$COOH + NaHCO$_3$

Water

After the students tape the Chemistry Concoctions project sheet (see Figure 2.4) in their journals, we read through it together. Then the students do the initial activity described on this sheet in their lab groups. (Although we don't capture the class doing this initial activity on film, you will see one group perform a similar experiment on the same phenomenon several times in the next video, CHEMCO-2.) Giving the students a chance to play with a phenomenon, one that serves as the foundation of a particular experiment, is always a good place to start. They are then better able to contribute to the planning process for whatever lab challenge is presented to them. For homework on Day 1 of the Chemistry Concoctions WCI Project, students are asked to brainstorm about what can be done in reference to technique or equipment to change the observed results of this initial activity. They record these thoughts in their journals. Before watching the video, you may find it useful to think of some of the variables that the students may come up with. I have found that putting myself in my students' position is always a beneficial piece of my planning process.

In the following video, you see five main activities that occur during Day 2 of this project. First, I have the students verbally review the initial activity from the class period before. Second, we brainstorm what variables may contribute to the observed results. We outline a control based on the initial activity and list variables. We follow that discussion by having each group choose a variable to test. I point out that each group is considered the expert for a particular variable and must later present its findings to the rest of the class. Third, I model a sample presentation

Figure 2.4

Chemistry Concoctions WCI Project Sheet

Chemistry Concoctions, Inc.
Project Sheet

Objectives:
1. To become familiar with mapping out variables.
2. To become accustomed to working in a group environment.
3. To communicate effectively group results to an audience.
4. To apply knowledge gained from lab to a practical.
5. To write a quality, formal lab report.

Safety Background:
The substances in this lab are 1.0 M acetic acid [$HC_2H_3O_2$] and solid sodium bicarbonate [$NaHCO_3$].
Task: After the initial activity, what variables do you think affected the observed results?

Chemistry Concoctions, Inc. Position:
We are in the business of developing and marketing safe, fun, and exciting chemistry kits. Background research on the provided test kits is needed, and your company has been asked to do some initial investigating. Eventually, these kits will be marketed to children 8 through 12 years old with the idea that they will be able to predict exactly how much liquid (possibly a beverage) will escape the middle flask (see drawing [Figure 2.3]) using the two chemicals provided, sodium bicarbonate and acetic acid.

Initial Investigation:
- RECORD ALL OBSERVATIONS THROUGHOUT THE LAB! DETAILS, DETAILS, DETAILS.
- PLEASE NOTE EQUIPMENT SETUP AND BE CAREFUL NOT TO BREAK ANYTHING!
- THINK BEFORE DOING!
1. Fill the 250 mL Erlenmeyer flask up to the 200 mL line with tap water. Replace stopper.
2. Place the rubber hose from the 250 mL Erlenmeyer flask into a 100 mL graduated cylinder. Make sure this hose is attached to the short glass tube! Hold or tape graduated cylinder to lab table.
3. Place 5.0 mL of 1.0 M acetic acid into the 125 mL Erlenmeyer flask.
4. Mass 0.20 g of sodium bicarbonate.
5. Quickly add the sodium bicarbonate to the acetic acid in the 125 mL Erlenmeyer flask and replace the stopper.
6. Record observations.
7. Clean up and sit with lab group and answer task question.

for the class that outlines what each group is responsible for on Day 4 of this project. Fourth, the groups prepare their journals for recording information about their specific variable. Fifth and last, the students return to lab to start testing their unique variable.

Notice just how teacher-centered this discussion is. I am leading my students through the entire process of experiencing a phenomenon, planning an experiment, delegating responsibility, and preparing to share experimental findings with a specified audience. This scaffolding serves as a model for future projects, when the class is in charge of all the above tasks.

You see me referring to a seating chart throughout our discussions. This is only the fifth time I have seen these students, and I am still getting to know their names.

Video—Watch the CHEMCO-2 video on the DVD labeled "Video Cases for Chapters 1–3." This video takes the first 60 minutes of class and compresses them into approximately 24 minutes so that you can visualize what was described.

Teacher's Analysis—CHEMCO-2

When I first watched this video, I laughed, because I had forgotten that the second day of the project was Loyalty Day at our school. Perhaps my green-and-gold costume, hat and all, is a bit distracting at first, but I am glad there is a piece of me shown in this light. I try to connect with the larger spirit of the school, and I want the students to know that all of those outside activities go hand-in-hand with classroom learning. We can be part of the big picture and still get serious about chemistry.

Regardless, this video illustrates the implementation of a lesson that took a great deal of planning. Because this lesson's primary goal is to introduce students to the model that will guide their remaining activities throughout the year, it is crucial to think through all the details. (Future lessons require planning that is focused more on impromptu decisions or follow-up plans based on a particular class's chosen path.) This is the first time I had done the Chemistry Concoctions project. Dennis and I had developed this project for my students over the summer. Because it was my first time implementing this lab, I played with the phenomenon beforehand. I had a chance to test the equipment, making sure it produced the desired initial result. I also brainstormed some of the variables the students might think up during the planning process.

The video shows that, throughout this lesson, I am the facilitator. During the planning stages, however, the students are still contributing to the procedure. In each of my three classes, a different set of six variables is chosen to test. For instance, the class that you observe in the video decides to test the different liquids in the container, whereas my two other classes do not. Keeping true to the nature of each class allows me to nurture the students' ownership of what they decide to test; regardless of my guidance, they feel it is their experiment.

As the students brainstorm, my job as the facilitator is to clarify their ideas as I write them on the board. For instance, I explain a bit about concentration when Tara suggests "concentration of vinegar" as a variable, even though learning about concentration isn't necessarily the focus of this lab. Also, I help them be more specific when offering ideas, like changing the word *amount* to *volume* of acetic acid. So we have brief discussions regarding most of the variables as I record them on the board.

We then decide on a control. It is extremely important that I go through each part of the process of selecting an appropriate control because I know how valuable it is for the students to think through this procedure. I let them know, through guided questions, that they have a good starting point already—the initial activity's directions. As we go through their brainstormed variables, however, they see that even those directions lack some guidance.

Our discussion in this class continues as we talk about how to add and mix the two chemicals together. One of my other classes thinks to question this part of the procedure, but the class in this video does not and realizes later, with my guidance, that they need to address this situation. With quite a bit of input from the class, we decide on "swirling" versus "shaking" and then add details to this idea. After reviewing this video, Dennis and I find it interesting how the addition of swirling to the group's control procedures increases the amount of water displaced into the graduated cylinder. These results appear near the end of the video when Craig's group realizes that its graduated cylinder is not large enough to catch all of the water displaced. Craig, Adam, and Michelle quickly come to the conclusion that the additional swirling caused the increased displacement of water. Because we have a chance to talk as a class about how the chemicals should be mixed, these students are able to make a probable connection between their results and changes made to the procedure. They are able to process their results and develop credible explanations on the fly.

After we decide on appropriate control conditions, I explain to my students that the class must choose from the list on the board six variables to test. Because I practiced this experiment before implementing the lab, I can guide the students as they pick variables to test. I steer them toward choices that are practical to test—based on available equipment—or that give some altered result worth investigating. There have been times, however, in other labs during previous years, when I allowed a class to choose a variable that didn't make much sense to test. Our postlab discussions in those cases helped students better understand what it means to choose variables worthy of testing.

Before beginning this lab, I challenge the students to decide if they have picked the six best variables to test. If they don't like their choices, what variable do they want to trade in? At this point, the class has a vested interest in choosing those variables it feels are the best six options because the students must share results with one another and then be challenged as a class (as I discussed at the beginning of class). Deciding on the six best variables nurtures the inquiring as a community, even though I'm doing the facilitating. My students will handle a discussion like this on their own in the near future during the CanCo WCI Project (chapter 4), so it's important that I practice with them a significant number of the potential types of discussions that might come up.

Once several students add two more variables they think should make the list, I star and circle four of the variables the students consider questionable and make them choose from those. I put a bit of time pressure on them, as well. I make them vote on the questionable variables, and we go with the rule of the majority. This doesn't happen in my other two classes. The other classes pick six variables rather quickly. So again, my experience in having similar discussions in previous years' classes helps me facilitate in this class. The more I try out these WCI projects, the better they become. Each group then volunteers to test one of the six variables. Sometimes, I assign the variables to specific groups, but, in this instance, I allow group members to raise their hands to choose their variables on a first-come, first-served basis. The variables chosen by this class are the mass of sodium bicarbonate, the volume of acetic acid, the concentration of acetic acid, the size of the first flask, the temperature of acetic acid, and the type of liquid in the middle flask.

At this point, the students are almost ready to head back into lab and test their variables. But, before having them plan their data tables and testing procedures, I demonstrate a sample presentation. Again, this presentation is a guide for presentations throughout the year. I also model how the students should listen critically during a presentation. Note that I choose a variable that doesn't make much sense only to make sure I don't use one of the variables they might choose to test.

Students then shift into their groups, plan their specific tests, and prepare a data table. I know from having seen students try to get a sample to a specific temperature in previous years' labs that I need to speak with the temperature group. So I suggest they take the temperature of each trial as they set it up rather than try to reach a specific temperature before testing. Again, sometimes I allow these glitches to happen even when I'm prepared for them. I decide which ones seem to be beneficial to experience and which ones seem to be overly frustrating. Sometimes I realize there is a glitch only during the planning stages or beginning testing stages. These instances are fun for me because I'm learning along with the students. The key is to guide students to handle the problem as scientists would in a research setting. I try to keep their frustration at an appropriate level and, at the same time, make sure I allow them to deal with the problem. The greatest benefit of these unexpected scenarios is that I'm sending the message that science is not predetermined; there's not always a ready answer or a clear path to take. Unfortunately, it seems that the science lab experiences my students have had before this class send the message that something prescribed should happen. I try to remove this notion as much as possible.

CHEMISTRY CONCOCTIONS WCI PROJECT—DAY 3

Teacher's Introduction—CHEMCO-3

The full-scale execution of an experiment requires students to think about the following: safety, journaling, procedure planning and implementation, equipment use, data collection, and group dynamics. They are also required to share their lab findings using a computer presentation program. All these requirements tend to make students focus mostly on the mechanics of the activity—what needs to be done and what needs to be known about what was done. The way this activity is designed requires that students go a bit further without realizing it. They begin to care about the problem they are investigating. They begin to take ownership, at first as a small group and then as a whole class. This sense of ownership creeps in and surprises the students as the investigation continues. Students also have some fun during the activity. They feel more comfortable with one another, particularly because they know that nobody in the room knows the answer. This collective discomfort of not knowing the answer is paradoxically comforting to students, and some smiles and jokes surface while the lab continues. Watch for signs of these behaviors as you view the next video.

In the CHEMCO-3 video, the camera focuses on Group 3 for the majority of the period during Day 3. This is the group that decided to test the type of liquid found in the middle flask. The video illustrates one lab group implementing their planned experiment from start to finish. It shows not only the mechanics listed above but also the progression of true inquiry in action—success, frustration, confusion, collaboration, and lab modifications.

As Group 3 progresses through the period, you see me walking around the room helping each group with specific requests that aid in their testing of the variables. I also stop by to check on each group's progress and to see if they have any questions. I am not only watching to make sure all of the planned experiences unfold but also checking to see whether any unplanned experiences require my intervention to keep the experience positive and safe. I am checking too to see if students appropriately apply the feedback they've received from their initial lab activity to this multiday lab.

Video—Watch the CHEMCO-3 video on the DVD labeled "Video Cases for Chapters 1–3." This video takes the entire 90 minutes of class and compresses them into 29 minutes so that you can visualize what was described.

Teacher's Analysis—CHEMCO-3

"In real science, I don't think that they work in 90-minute blocks."
—Dan

This seems to capture the tone of the day. It is fun to see students scrambling to implement their plan. I don't believe any of them had thought about whether their plan could be done in 90 minutes. I think they assume that 90 minutes is enough time simply because we talked about it together. But once the class realizes how difficult some of their trials are, they realize that science is bigger than a school schedule.

At first viewing, it may seem there is a lot of dead time for Group 3. I disagree with this wholeheartedly, because each of Group 3's experiences has unexpected but extraordinary educational moments. Their struggles mimic precisely the types of things researchers encounter. What students do with those experiences is critical for their growth throughout the year. For instance, in the beginning Group 3 realizes they might not have enough Coca-Cola for their trials. They also have a problem finding change to buy more Coca-Cola. Would they remember to come more prepared for their next lab? If I simply tell them to come prepared, it won't mean as much to them as being unprepared when the entire class is depending on them.

Group 3 also struggles with how the same chemical can have different hazards based on its form. I help them with this by bringing out the bottle of ethanol I purchased. They can then see which listing in the MSDS (material safety data sheet) is the appropriate one to use. I can then use this group as the experts on hazard listings. When another group asks me for that same type of help in the future, I refer them to Group 3 for an explanation.

Group 3's third struggle is humorous. I ask how their trials are going when they have done two of the three trials for ethanol. When their third trial for ethanol yields a significantly lower volume than the first two, Tara and Nick quickly realize why the volume is low: The stopper in the middle flask is not sealed. Nick whispers to the group that they should just make up the number. Dan realizes that this comment is caught on tape and warns Nick, "We're on film." Nick looks straight at the camera, and Jack laughs and jokes about getting spray paint to cover up the lens. Nick then says loudly enough for the video to pick up his words, "Oh, I got 44." Jack adds, "Dump it. Dump it," as if the video would register how low the volume of ethanol is and they will get caught

30

in their lie. Tara follows by recording the false data but adds with a grin, "That's naughty." And they move on to their Coca-Cola trials.

Students will always fall into the trap of mechanical completions, jumping through the hoops that teachers create without much reflection on the actual learning that might be taking place. I've seen many examples of students making up data, particularly when a few trials have been tested and one result doesn't match the others. What is exciting in these WCI projects is that students seem less willing to use that tactic as the year progresses. They know that the group will be asked to defend its position, and that, as long as they can come up with an explanation for the altered result, the data should be recorded as they witnessed it.

Another hurdle for Group 3 occurs when Dan is pouring baking soda into the flask and Tara accidentally bumps him. The baking soda spills on the lab table. So often we picture the procedure for a lab being implemented flawlessly. But when you work in an environment with other scientists, these silly frustrations happen regularly. So this is a great example of students learning to work with one another. The group immediately realizes the trial is bad and retests. They resort to laughter and camaraderie rather than anger.

During the Coca-Cola trials, the group realizes there is a significant difference in the resulting volume of displaced liquid. It takes a very long time for the Coca-Cola to stop moving into the graduated cylinder. Jack suggests that two of the group members do something constructive and go to the computer lab to start the presentation. It's great that they are taking advantage of the freedom to accomplish their tasks as they see fit. Although you don't see it on the video, other groups asked me if they could go to the computer lab and I replied that it was a great idea.

Group 3 takes quite a while to think about why the Coca-Cola continues to fill the graduated cylinder even after the sodium bicarbonate and acetic acid finishes reacting. They also have to grapple with their unexpected findings that the volume of displaced water decreases with each Coca-Cola trial. Eventually, Tara shares her thoughts about carbonation and its effect on the displaced liquid. She even adds that because the Coca-Cola had been sitting out, it is getting less carbonated over time and the lower volume in subsequent tests makes sense because of that. These students are intellectually engaged in the experiment. They are trying to develop a reasonable model that explains their data as they are collecting it.

The camera eventually pans to Group 2. I ask Frank about his data, and the conversation leads to a discussion on limiting reactants. We have barely discussed the idea of the difference between physical and chemical changes, and Frank is already thinking through modeling a chemical reaction that illustrates limiting reactants. This is one of those unexpected and wonderful results that can come from an inquiry lab.

I notice two things in Group 3 that I will address in their feedback. Tara, Dan, Jack, and Nick seem to be quite comfortable sharing their thoughts with each other. Karen, however, is mostly quiet throughout the lab. She can be heard now and then, but her thoughts are not solicited or offered. That needs to be corrected. The second thing I notice is a safety issue. The class received feedback just two days before about safety in the lab. The movie (presented within the CHEMCO-1 video) showed a student with a baseball cap on and pointed out that this should never happen. Baseball caps can block peripheral vision, and students have knocked glassware over with the bill of a cap, so no hats are allowed in lab. Students need to remind one another to take off caps. This group does not do a good job of policing itself on this point. Nick has his cap on the whole time.

CHEMISTRY CONCOCTIONS WCI PROJECT—DAY 4, PART 1

Teacher's Introduction—CHEMCO-4A

The following video highlights the presentations the students give on the fourth day of the Chemistry Concoctions WCI Project. Recall that there are six lab groups in our class. Each tests a unique variable. The six variables this class tests include mass of sodium bicarbonate, volume of acetic acid, concentration of acetic acid, the size/volume of first flask, the temperature of acetic acid, and the type of liquid in the middle flask. Only four of the six groups are shown in this video. They provide a good sampling of the types of presentations one would expect after the first class WCI project.

 Video—You should now watch the CHEMCO-4A video on the DVD labeled "Video Cases for Chapters 1–3." This video takes the first 60 minutes of class and compresses them into approximately 25 minutes so that you can visualize what was described above.

Teacher's Analysis—CHEMCO-4A

This is the first opportunity the students have to present in front of one another. It is also the first time many of them are using software to create a presentation or are using technology while presenting. So the mechanics of presenting in front of an audience, along with the details of technology, will be one part of the feedback we discuss together. But overall, the students do a fine job for their first experience.

In the beginning of class I tell the students what information they should record while listening to each other's presentations: the variable being introduced, the conclusion the group draws, and why that conclusion makes sense. If it doesn't make sense, they are to record well-formulated questions that help them understand a specific variable better. This guidance is important. It helps students focus on the big picture first and add details later. It also saves time. The first time I did presentations similar to these, students were under the impression that every detail needed to be recorded. It took us three days to get through them. So this information serves as guide for the presentations throughout the year.

As soon as I finish introducing the session, I give them one minute to finish up any last-minute details within their groups. This is not something that I do for each project. Sometimes coming to class ready to present is part of the challenge. Because this is their first time, I give them a moment to collect themselves.

Before the first group shown on the video presents, I can be heard saying, "Okay, give me a second before you start." The video shows the second group that gave a presentation on this day, and I was finishing up recording some details between the first and the second presentations. I typically have a number of things spread out on a lab table while I am watching presentations; there's a lot to record, particularly this early in the year. The students need details when I give them feedback, so I keep extensive notes. I typically record information on a rubric listing expectations for the presentation. I also keep open a file on my laptop that lists content-based questions that I ask the students either during feedback or on a quiz. I keep handy a pad of paper on which I jot down ideas I can use in a future unit to make connections to this project. I record good questions that are raised by other students, and I also record questions I want to ask the group at the end of its presentation. Because I'm juggling a number of things, I typically give myself a couple of minutes between presentations to make sure I'm ready for the next group.

In Presentation 2, the group presents the results of the experiment that examined the variable mass of sodium bicarbonate. This group of students altered the mass of sodium bicarbonate added to the vinegar and recorded the resulting volume of water displaced into the graduated cylinder. Toward the beginning of their presentation you can see the students getting used to being in front of one another. There's also a moment when Mary wows the class with her ability to move between slides by using the Smart Board. This is fun. My students and I typically learn a host of technology tricks from one another year after year.

In Presentation 2, the students provide a great visual of the lab as shown in Figure 2.5. They also do a great job during the question-and-answer session at the end of the presentation. It's amazing to hear the students having a discussion about limiting reactants without even knowing that they're having a discussion about limiting reactants. Robert and Mary both seem to have a good mental model of what was happening in the container as the amount of sodium bicarbonate is

Figure 2.5

Visual Aid in Presentation 2

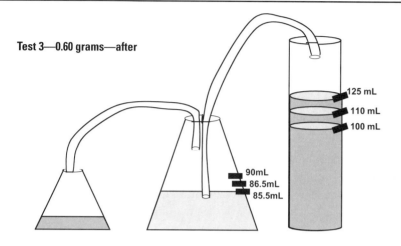

Test 3—0.60 grams—after

125 mL
110 mL
100 mL

90mL
86.5mL
85.5mL

Approximately 112 mL of water was displaced each trial.

Figure 2.6

Graph in Presentation 2

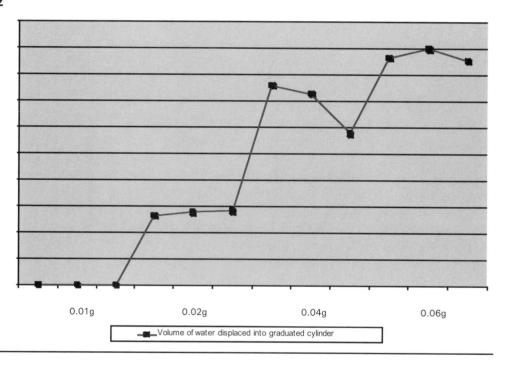

0.01g   0.02g   0.04g   0.06g

Volume of water displaced into graduated cylinder

34

changed. When Kim asks for an explanation for part of their conclusion and Robert answers, I can tell that Kim still doesn't quite understand what he means. So I ask a follow-up question about this "limiting reactant" situation to see if they can explain their data (see Figure 2.6) better. And they do. I go further to see if they have the data to support an "optimum number." I ask questions like this because I want my students to realize that they need to be able to use their own data to analyze a new situation. Their mental model needs to talk them through a story.

Interestingly, Angie and Dan follow up on my question and ask for more specific information about the optimum conditions that would displace the greatest volume of water. Dan even talks about wasting chemicals, which is a great industry-based extension of this lab. Through the course of these discussions, you can see that Mary and Kelly talk more as Robert cedes the floor to them. All three were very comfortable. Maria, however, didn't jump in. In a future presentation, I would make sure a question or two got directed to her. At the end, it's great to hear that Mary notices a difference between her lab group's equipment setup and the other groups' setups. She then applies that difference to explaining a possible data discrepancy.

Note that the majority of these moments come from allowing the group the freedom to investigate its own variable and then talk through the results together. I never bring up the idea of limiting reactants, graph interpretations, equipment discrepancies, economic restrictions on research, or testing extremes. These ideas all come out of student-student interactions with only a few interjections from me.

Throughout the presentations, there is evidence that the students know a great deal of science. Some of them go beyond what I would expect them to know in terms of chemistry content at this point in the year. They are still, however, having a difficult time communicating their thoughts. For instance, at the beginning of the Presentation 2, Kelly has a difficult time with vocabulary. She is trying to describe why the recorded volumes are not as accurate as they should be. The instrument they used was not calibrated in small enough "graduations" or increments. So you hear her fumbling over her words. This instance will serve as a great teaching moment during the later feedback session. I will talk about the importance of practicing the presentations and getting to know the science lingo.

In the next presentation (labeled Presentation 3) included in CHEMCO-4A, the group explains how the variable liquid in the center flask affects the amount of liquid displaced into the graduated cylinder. This group's graph of data is shown in Figure 2.7. I like seeing this group's presentation because I can connect it to the group's lab work captured in the CHEMCO-3 video. During the question-and-answer portion of Presentation 3, I am struck by how well this group can think on its feet when

Figure 2.7

Graph in Presentation 3

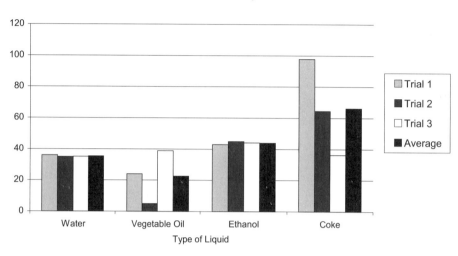

The Effect of Different Kinds of Liquids on the Amount of Liquid in Graduated Cylinder

Figure 2.8

Graph in Presentation 4

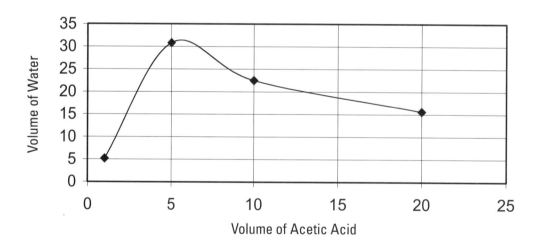

Volume of Water Versus Acetic Acid

it is sharing particulate models that explain how the viscosity of a given liquid and the excess carbon dioxide produced from the Coca-Cola affect the amount of liquid displaced. As in Presentation 2, the third group of presenters ends up discussing science concepts that go well beyond those that I had planned. I contend that these extra concepts surface because the students have taken ownership of the activities and feel the need to explain the results of an experiment that they planned. One minor flaw in this group's performance is their lack of preparedness: They failed to bring me a hard copy of their presentation to look at while the members give their talk.

In Presentation 4 shown on the video, the group presents their results from an experiment in which they varied the volume of the acetic acid that was added to a constant mass of sodium bicarbonate. The first thing I note while watching the video is that these students share the chemical equation for this reaction. I had not necessarily expected to see this balanced equation because I had not required it as part of the lab; however, the students researched this and came up with it on their own.

Figure 2.9

Graph in Presentation 6

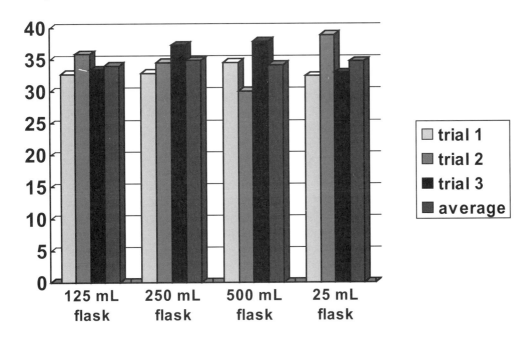

This group's presentation also illustrates how the students used the graph as a tool for analyzing and interpreting their data. As shown in this group's graph (Figure 2.8), the students used Excel to create a graph in which the data points were connected with smoothed lines. Although the quality of this smoothed-line fit is questionable in a technical sense (there are no algorithms behind it), the group interpreted the Excel line fit to mean that the maximum volume of water displaced occurred when 6 mL of acetic acid were used. Angie asks the group if it actually tested 6 mL of acetic acid. It had not. But the group does say that the maximun volume was the highest point on the line in its graph. This exchange between Angie and the presenters shows the importance of gathering enough data to support one claim. Had this group also gathered data using 3 mL and 7 mL of acetic acid, it would have been able to fill in the gaps better on their graph. This concept is typically very difficult for students to absorb, yet one that I often discuss in my feedback about data analysis.

In Presentation 6, the final group of students reports on how the size of the first flask affects how much water was displaced. As shown in the group's graph (Figure 2.9), the students found that their variable had no effect on the water displacement. Although this result is obviously not as interesting as the results obtained by the previous groups, it nonetheless answers a question the group had when planning its experiment. Note that, even though the students are getting tired and have already listened to five presentations, some students still ask clarification questions at the end. I like that, and I ask the class to clap again when the presentation is finished. This request reminds the class that it is important to support one another. I also believe it sends the signal that the class should not focus solely on the accuracy of the information each group presented but also on the community angle throughout the entire project.

CHEMISTRY CONCOCTIONS WCI PROJECT—DAY 4, PART 2

Teacher's Introduction—CHEMCO-4B

The following video highlights my feedback about the Chemistry Concoctions WCI Project and associated presentations. In this video, note the lively nature of the discussions. Students seem eager to share informally information about how their projects progressed.

I've already mentioned that I tend to give feedback in three general areas—safety, accuracy, and community. The feedback in this video focuses on safety and on a few segments of the community aspect. The remaining feedback would require time for me to process and prepare. Although we do not show the feedback given on the following class day, the video segment you see will give you insight about the climate I try to nurture during feedback days. It's a time for students to reflect, learn, and grow—and have some fun.

After you have watched this video, please keep in mind that I address all three areas of feedback with the students, even though the video focuses on just two of them. The day after, I review some chemistry content with my students in a questioning and reflecting method. For this lab, I review the concepts of chemical changes, qualitative and quantitative observations, modeling at the particulate level, and interpretations. I give my students insights into how they might improve their particulate modeling skills and how they could and should provide more evidence with experimental trials, and I point out any errors they may have made in their data collecting or analyses. My goal, once again, is to provide a balanced story for my students by giving them feedback in all three areas—safety, accuracy, and community.

 Video—Watch the CHEMCO-4B video on the DVD labeled "Video Cases for Chapters 1–3." This video takes the last 30 minutes of class and compresses them into about 20 minutes so that you can visualize what was described.

Teacher's Analysis—CHEMCO-4B

Feedback—my favorite part of a project. This is when the opportunity to learn—about chemistry and about oneself—can take place. We connect as a class, as students and teacher. I have learned something during feedback every time I've implemented one of these projects. I usually learn something about a particular class or about a student in the class. But I also learn something that enhances my teaching philosophy, from considering questions such as: Did the design of this project take too much out-of-class time? Was it worth it? How can I change it so that students will gain a better understanding of their community and of chemistry without sacrificing too much family time outside of class? Or perhaps I learn something about teenagers in general: that they do live in a technological age; that, when given the opportunity, they will fly with a project; or that there are some talented students in this class. I've learned to evaluate the purpose of some of the things I do and how these experiences affect my students' lives. Through my many years in this profession, feedback for these projects has been the second-most significant contribution to my growth as an effective, caring teacher. (The first, of course, is watching my children grow.)

The opening scene of this video shows my daughters about 10 years ago. It serves many purposes. It is a good representation of what some of the students may have been feeling throughout the course of the project, and it is a good conversation starter and attention grabber. But most important, it subtly reminds the students that I am a person, a mother with a family, and that I'm willing to share that with them. The comfort level in the room immediately changes from one of "scientific community" to "community."

I begin the feedback with some general reflective questions. I tend to keep these opening questions consistent as the year progresses, adding pertinent questions for a particular lab as needed. The questions are meant to provide the students with a means of evaluating themselves, the roles they played in taking control of their education, and the roles they played in contributing positively and constructively to the scientific community at large. I always give them a chance to write their thoughts first. Students then are more willing to share their recorded thoughts, particularly at the beginning of the year.

I have found over the years that it's wonderful to have a short, impromptu conversation with the students about their thoughts on the project. They know I'm going to read their journals, but it's important to talk as a group, at least for a little bit. They feel proud when they share accomplishments, and I congratulate them as a group. They feel validated if they share a frustration with me and I agree, giving them suggestions or reflective questions on how to improve. They realize some problems, such as technological challenges or scheduling conflicts, have no perfect solution. That I acknowledge these issues and tell them I sometimes experience similar frustrations in my job illustrates that I am not expecting perfection. They know that it is the journey they take together that matters. It's valuable to discuss these things as a class.

It is obvious that students appreciate the fact that we talk about more than just the content when we do these projects. Working together is a challenge, and they deserve the opportunity to be assessed on all aspects of the project. Discussing ways to improve community, safety, and accuracy provides a balanced reflection on what makes a research group work well. It offers them the opportunity to experience the big picture. It takes some students much longer to make the mental shift into thinking about the big picture rather than just the grade. In the video, one student asks whether a presentation sent past midnight was considered late. I say, "Yes, it's late." He presses me on the topic. You'll notice that I stick to the idea of the deadline itself and not to how missing the deadline affected the student's grades. There will be an opportunity for the class to see its grades in the three areas—safety, accuracy, and community—but this is not the time for that. I even point to the screen, indicating that there was nothing about points mentioned yet. Some students are frustrated by my vague answer. They are still getting used to our classroom climate, the WCI approach, and me. But they will get there. As a teacher, it took a lot of practice to prevent myself from being sucked into the grades discussion. But I've found the more you keep the topic on the big picture, the more rewarding it is for the students and the faster the mental shift occurs for them.

After our informal discussion, I have the students revisit the objectives listed on the project sheet. It's important to keep the broad objectives in the students' minds so they have a structure to work with. They realize that three of the five objectives have been accomplished and are now more aware of what to expect in the next class.

I then move into sharing the feedback I recorded about safety. What makes the feedback more meaningful is that I took pictures of the classroom to make the feedback real. They see some of the problems that took place from class to class. This way the feedback remains interactive instead of unidirectional. I tell the students to record the information so that they can improve the next time they're in lab. At one point I show them a picture of the lab at the end of class. The lab had not been cleaned well. One student asks, "Did we improve from last time?" She has connected feedback from the Introduction to Chemistry lab to this lab. Although the class still doesn't apply this particular feedback, it's wonderful that she remembers. I anticipate better clean-up next time as they get practice in using feedback for every WCI scenario.

The last part of the feedback shown in this video deals with community. I show some of my favorite student quotes overheard during the labs in all three classes. As I mentioned earlier, students look forward to the quotes more than anything else as the year progresses. Students want to know if the quotes are from their class or other classes. I always keep a list of quotes from all my classes, and I keep the quotes anonymous. One reason is to prevent hurt feelings or embarrassment. Another is because some classes are more serious or quiet than others, so I don't get a lot of fun or interesting quotes from them. A third reason is to provide a glimpse into the similarities and differences that exist among classes. It's a wonderful way to end feedback days. It's lighthearted, it's real, and it's fun.

RESEARCHER'S ANALYSIS—CHEMCO VIDEO CASES

As I mentioned in chapter 1, I created the video cases without Joan's help. Again, I did so because I wanted Joan to view her teaching in retrospect, reflect on it, and then write about it (Shulman 1992). I felt that a retrospective analysis would give Joan the proper distance to look objectively at her practice. I also felt this type of analysis would provide the much-needed context for situating the video cases among all of the thoughts, ideas, and decisions that go into her practice. If you have gotten this far, I imagine you would wholeheartedly agree that Joan's thoughts help you understand what occurs in her classroom, how she makes it happen, and why she thinks each piece is important. Her thoughtful analyses provide a solid thread that ties all of the video cases together and makes them come alive. They help viewers feel comfortable with what they are seeing in the video cases. Along with the video cases, Joan's analyses make viewers feel as though they have been invited to spend some quality time with her, in her classroom and in her thoughts.

Through the lengthy process of developing the video cases, I have become very familiar with the range of teaching strategies that Joan uses in her classroom. Some of her strategies mesh well with the best practices espoused in the science education research literature and in documents published by science education reformers. Others go beyond these best practices and break new ground, especially in regard to the way Joan boldly breaks with the classic notion of the teacher in charge in front of the classroom, as you will see in chapters 3 through 5. In this section and at the end of each of the next three chapters, I present you with the results of a careful analysis that examined Joan's various teaching strategies. My goal is to highlight the major types of strategies that Joan uses in her practice and to shed additional light on how and why these strategies make the WCI curriculum work.

To identify, define, and highlight Joan's teaching strategies, I again watched all the video cases and constructed an event map (Green and Wallat 1981; Kelly and Crawford 1997) containing a timeline of all the teaching strategies that Joan used. I reviewed each of the teaching strategies in the timeline and sorted them into categories using the constant comparative method (Glaser and Strauss 1967). After finding that the strategies could be grouped into 10 different categories, I reviewed the examples contained in each category and then wrote a description to summarize the key elements of each category. I also looked at the examples in each category and located the particular video case in which most

of the category's examples occurred. This process allowed me to identify which particular video case best exemplified the category's teaching
strategy. In this chapter, I present and discuss three teaching strategies
that are particularly well illustrated through specific examples found in
the CHEMCO video cases.

Teaching Strategy 1—Documenting the Community's Work

Joan often presents her students with quotes, images, or videos that she
has recorded while the class was working together as a community. She
presents this documentation about the community's work, asks the students to reflect on it, and then uses their reflections as an opportunity
to teach. In the CHEMCO video cases, several instances objectively
illustrate Joan's use of this strategy. For example, in CHEMCO-1, Joan
presents a set of student quotes that she had recorded during the previous laboratory session. In this lab, the students completed a simple
activity mixing lead nitrate and sodium iodide in a petri dish. Before
showing the first quote, Joan (Ms. G.) tells the students:

[08:49]—CHEMCO-1

Ms. G.:   As I go through the quotes, you tell me whether these are good
            quotes or bad quotes for working together in lab. Okay?

Because the source of the quotes is the students themselves, they
are intrigued. Even though the camera shows only their backs, you can
tell that the majority of the students are looking at the screen. They are
interested in seeing what it is that Joan overheard them saying. Perhaps
because of this interest, the students buy into Joan's request to analyze
the quotes as either bad or good. As part of this activity, she lets them
decide the quality of each quote and then provides her own commentary. At the very beginning of the activity in CHEMCO-1, Joan starts
with a positive quote. The students respond, and she follows up with a
bit of commentary.

[08:58]—CHEMCO-1

Ms. G.:   [reading quote] "Hey, don't forget your goggles. We're policing
            each other, you know."
Jack: That's good.
Dan: Good. There's a smiley face.
Chris: Yay.
Ms. G.:   And I don't care that you're mocking me as long as you are policing
            each other. That's fine. Okay?

Through her commentary, Joan reminds her students that safety is an important issue. It is so important that she does not mind if they make fun of her determination to get them to act safely and police one another. She indicates that having her students act in a safe manner is more important than her feelings. Joan also deals with negative quotes as shown in the two examples below.

[09:27]—CHEMCO-1

Ms. G.: "What the heck, man? Get away from me."

Students: [Laughter]

Ms. G.: And there's like a little shove right after it.

Jack: This is like an easy activity, right?

Ms. G.: It's an easy activity. Not good. Okay? Be nice.

[09:39]—CHEMCO-1

Ms. G.: "That's so gay."

Students: Whoa. No. That's weak.

Ms. G.: I'm going to respond very negatively to something like that. Okay? It's 2005. Grow up. Get that out of your vocabulary please. It is insulting and hurtful. So we don't use that kind of adjective or those descriptions in here. Okay?

In presenting the two example quotes above, Joan squarely deals with behaviors and comments that she does not want to see or hear in her classroom. By allowing the students to respond to these anonymous quotes and then providing her own critique, she indicates her wish for them to treat each other with respect. Dealing openly with these types of negative comments early on in the school year helps set up a classroom community in which there is a sense of safety and trust.

Joan uses a quote from near the end of the presentation as an opportunity to review safety procedures.

[10:02]—CHEMCO-1

Ms. G.: "Something broke!"

Jack: That's good.

Lynn: Actually, it was like nine of us.

Ms. G.: Yes. So I asked, what should you do? And immediately I get responses like:
"Take out your contacts."
"Get to the eyewash."
"Run to the nurse."
"Grab the fire extinguisher."

Students: [Laughter]

Ms. G.:   All very funny, but false. You don't do any of those things. Okay? The first thing you did was correct. You told me. Okay? But now what's our response?

Frank: Clean it up.

Kim: Let you know who's hurt.

Ms. G.:   First you check for injuries! First you check for injuries. Did anybody get hurt? Now you tell me that too. Then you clean it up. Now the "how" is important. First of all, where do we dispose of broken class?

Lynn: In the broken glass bucket.

Ms. G.:   In the broken glass bucket over by the prep room door…

In the above examples, Joan uses as a resource the dialogue that she documents when her students are working together. She pools the recorded quotes from all her classes and decides which quotes to include in the presentation. These decisions allow her to drive the agenda for what discussion the class will have and what commentary she will add. The selected quotes provide her with opportunities to teach the norms of what speech, actions, and behaviors are acceptable in her classroom.

Besides recording student dialogue, Joan often documents the community's work through multimedia and mines these images for teaching opportunities. As you saw in the CHEMCO-1 and CHEMCO-4B videos, Joan presented her students with a series of photos and videos that document the quality of their safety and clean-up efforts while working in the lab in the previous class session. In CHEMCO-1, Joan pools together images taken before, during, and after her three classes worked in the lab and asks her students to watch this video and reflect upon the images contained within.

[12:23]—CHEMCO-1

Ms. G.:   This next part is actually all of my classes put together with some feedback on how you did … with the mechanics of the room. In the beginning I took a picture of my lab. I set it up with your equipment [pointing to the picture]. Boxes are nice and straight. Chemicals here. My deionized water bottles are even standing up. You can see them. Another picture from the other side, it's all nice and dry. Soap's here. The towels are here. The lab tables only have the syringes on them. Nothing else.

Jack: I don't even see any of those wash sponges.

Ms. G.:   No, of course not. Okay? So this is you guys. All three classes. [Joan starts a movie that begins with the main caption of "So how did we do?"]

As the students watch the video that begins with images of Joan's other two chemistry classes, they make comments to one another. Because Joan is trying to make a point with the images in the video, she brings the students' comments out into the open by asking the class to analyze what is wrong with what they are seeing.

[13:53]—CHEMCO-1

Ms. G.: Okay, what's the problem with this class?

Student: No one had goggles.

Ms. G.: No one had goggles on! No one! I didn't know who to focus on! Not a single person went back and got their goggles at the beginning of class.

Jack: Did you like just say that in the class before? [referring to the fact that the class in the video had just watched themselves earlier that same morning]

Ms. G.: I said it this last class. One of the reasons that I do such a safe lab at the beginning is 'cause this kind of stuff happens.

When the movie begins to contain images of the students currently sitting in the classroom, they perk up and do not wait for Joan to ask questions. Rather they begin reacting to what they see by laughing, making comments, or even apologizing to each other. For example, the students react to a picture of their chairs blocking the pathway to the eyewash.

[14:49]—CHEMCO-1

Students: Ooooh. Aaaaah.

Jack: Sorry, guys.

Student: There's a little room.

Angie: There's someone's hat on the chair. That means they took it off.

Ms. G.: That's good.

The students continue to react to the video as the images begin to focus on the messy condition in which they left the lab. They see a series of pictures showing water all over the common lab table, powder spilled on a lab surface, and beakers and petri dishes left in random places. As they see these pictures, some more vocal students provide a running commentary with Joan picking up the thread at the end.

[15:35]—CHEMCO-1

Kelly: I think someone missed the sink.

Dan: It's supposed to be wiped down.
[new picture with powder spilled on lab bench and petri dish left out.]

46

Jack: Aaaaahhh!
Frank: My bad.
           [video with Joan squeaking her shoe on floor to indicate spilled water]
Dan: Oooooh.
Ms. G.:   I could have killed myself.
Kelly: Aaah! I almost slipped!
Ms. G.:   I could have killed myself.
Kelly: I slipped back there [confessing to another student].

In the students' critique of the images that show how safely they work and how well they clean up the lab, they give voice to what Joan wants them to say. Although it may be true that Joan is setting them up to say the things that she wants to hear, she has already informed them of proper behavior in the lab. Even though they have heard Joan describe these behavioral norms, they have not seen what these look like in practice. Students do not often recognize the products of their actions until they are confronted with them. They don't see that leaving water on the floor will cause a safety hazard. They don't see that leaving chemicals on a mass balance will cause it to corrode and stop working. They don't see that Joan has started with a relatively safe lab so that she could see how well they could apply the safety rules. She uses their own words and products as a tool to teach them. By doing so, she allows the students to critique their own work and learn from it.

In CHEMCO-4B, Joan again presents quotes that she recorded during the project and uses them to discuss the nature of scientific work. Because the students had just completed the CHEMCO project in which they were responsible for working together as a group to design an experiment and prepare a presentation to summarize their results, most of them had dealt with the typical frustrations that arise when engaging in scientific work. As you already observed in the CHEMCO-3 video, the group of students filmed had to grapple with the issue of falsifying data as they conducted their experiment. Some group members were willing to make up data when they thought a procedural error had accounted for an odd result, while others resisted and wanted to explore other possible explanations. Joan brings this tension out into the open when she presents the two quotes as shown in the dialogue below.

[17:33]—CHEMCO-4B
Ms. G.:   So you guys tell me what you think of these…
Ms. G.:   "One trial is enough. We can just make the rest up from that."
Dan: Not okay.
Kelly: Oh.
Students: [Laughter]

Jack: Ew. Yuck.
Ms. G.:   "What happened? I'm not sure. What do you think was going on? Don't know. Don't care. Let's just guess."
Dan: Triple yuck.

If you review the video right after Joan reads each of these two quotes, you will notice that the members of the CHEMCO-3 focus group (seated middle and back) look at one another sheepishly and laugh. They are likely remembering that their incidences of faking data were captured on the film, and they are reacting to the feeling of being caught. This group may have even wondered if I had gone back on my word and allowed Joan to see the film before the end of the year. The members of the focus group had a definite reaction to the quotes, but they are not alone. Look again at all of the students' reactions following the quotes, many of them giggle and look at one another knowingly. The phenomenon of faking the data is not unique to the focus group and Joan knows this. As she mentioned in her analysis, she believes that students exhibit this behavior because they have experienced so many science classroom labs where the act of obtaining data is not meant to answer a real question; it's simply a hoop to jump through. The important part here is that Joan brings this behavior out into the open. By getting her students to react negatively ("triple yuck") to this behavior, she indirectly sends the message that it is not acceptable to make up data.

Joan also uses the quotes of her students to validate the idea that science is larger than what students experience in the classroom. She also reinforces the idea that lab work is not typically straightforward, hassle free, or completed within a 90-minute class period.

[19:45]—CHEMCO-4B

Ms. G.:   "I quit. This isn't working." … That's actually a fun quote because that's the nature of science. It can actually be very frustrating. You guys had two days to do a lab. Think about someone who is doing a lab for like two years.
Dan: Who's doing a lab for two years?
Ms. G.:   Scientists typically work on experiments a lot longer than two days.
Dan: Probably more complicated than baking soda and vinegar and water.

Having spent four years working over a lab bench and in a fume hood to complete my PhD chemistry thesis, I know firsthand how tedious, frustrating, and time-consuming it can be to carry out an experiment. I could relate to the students in the focus group as they spilled chemicals, worked with imperfect equipment, and developed improvised

48

procedures. I empathized with them as their experiment dragged on, especially during the Coca-Cola trials. They went into the experiment thinking that each of the trials would last only a minute or two and then found out that each trial lasted 15 minutes. I identified with the group members' struggles to coordinate their actions in the lab and develop explanations for the data that they were collecting. I also remembered the challenges involved in simply interacting well and socializing with the human beings who happen to make up your particular research group. For me, it was gratifying to see the students in Joan's classroom engaging in scientific activities that resemble those I have experienced as a research scientist. As you will see in future chapters, the students will continue to engage in the types of scientific activities that authentically replicate both the technical and social aspects of the scientific community at large. You will also see how Joan continues to document the actual events and dialogue that occurred while her students worked in the lab; she then uses this documentation to teach her students about the nature of science and what it feels like to work as a scientist. Indeed, Joan reminds her students that she is documenting what they say and do as illustrated below.

[20:39]—CHEMCO-4B

Ms. G.: "Don't say anything stupid. Ms. Gallagher is listening."
Students: [laughter]
Ms. G.: Yes, I am listening. And don't start whispering 'cause this is a really fun part of the class, but you also don't have to say really stupid things. Just be normal. Just actually be yourselves.

Teaching Strategy 2—Asking Students to Reflect on the Community's Work

At the end of each WCI project, Joan asks the students to reflect on the quality of their community's work. In an iterative process that occurs throughout the year, Joan asks her students to process their recent experiences and think about how they could improve their work in the next project (Torrance and Pryor 2001). She pushes them to think about their work not only at the individual level, but also at the group and classroom level. By using this teaching strategy, Joan gives voice to the students. She lets them talk about their own experiences. She allows them to say what they think went well and what they think could be improved. She begins the feedback discussion with the students' ideas, not her own. This teaching strategy is illustrated in CHEMCO-4B when Joan puts up the following four questions:

[01:00]—CHEMCO-4B

What went well with this lab?

What didn't go so well?

What could you do as an individual to improve for the next project?

What could we do as a class to improve for the next project?

After giving them a few minutes to write in their journals, she asks:

[02:18]—CHEMCO-4B

Ms. G.:   Okay, what'd you think? Some of you are still writing and that's fine. I will get a chance to see what you've written when I collect your journals, but for right now, what will you share? What went well?

By starting with the positive, Joan sets the tone for the class discussion. Just as personnel in management know, it is important to begin with the positive so that employees are receptive to hearing what needs to be improved. By having her students focus on the positive, the classroom community gets to hear about what did work. In the CHEMCO project, the students worked in groups of four to five people to prepare a presentation based on their lab experiment. Because each group likely did not go down the same path or experience the same level of success, it is useful for them to hear about the positive experiences of other groups. These experiences may shed light on how other groups managed the same task. The positive experiences also help show what is possible and sets the bar for what could be normally expected. Jack is the first to respond to the question of what went well. His response conveys the idea that it is definitely possible for a group of students to put together a presentation outside of class through e-mail.

[02:30]—CHEMCO-4B

Jack: Our group had to separate the work at the end of our class period… separate out what we had to do.

Ms. G.:   Okay.

Jack: There wasn't a lot of…I mean there was a little bit of problems because they're like I really didn't want to do this…the biggest… usually when we separate work and have to bring it back together the following night, usually that just never works. Someone just doesn't follow through…someone just e-mails that this doesn't work. But it actually worked and it came out…

Ms. G.:   That is great news 'cause you're right. Usually there's some sort of glitch…

Jack: It never works well.

Ms. G.:   …so that it doesn't come together. So keep that in mind because this is the first of dozens of these things that you're going to do this year.

Dan: Dozens?
Kelly: Oh, awesome.
Students: [laughter]
Ms. G.:   So you want to keep that going…whatever made it happen.
Jack: We have a thousand batting average.
Dan: This is a solid group.
Ms. G.:   It's a solid group. It's a solid class.

In the above dialogue, Joan confirms that the group's success is "great news," and then empathizes by confirming that "usually there's some sort of glitch." Joan does not disregard the difficulty of working together with group members outside of class; rather she acknowledges that there will be glitches and that the groups will need to figure out how to deal with these glitches. She uses Jack's reflections as an opportunity to set the expectation that they will be applying what they've learned in this project to "dozens" of future projects. Although the students react to this expectation with a bit of surprise, they appear to accept it as Joan goes back to focusing on the positive and ends the dialogue with Jack by saying "It's a solid group. It's a solid class."

At the beginning of these discussions, it is typical for the students to share quite a few ideas about what went well. Not every group in the classroom, however, had a frustration-free experience or ended up with a final product of which they were especially proud. Therefore, after the initial sharing of things that went well, it is also common that some of Joan's students willingly share ideas on what could be improved. For example, in CHEMCO-4B, Frank puts forth the following idea:

[08:09]—CHEMCO-4B
Frank: I just think that, as in general it might not just be our group, but putting the whole presentation out of school, like we needed to do that better. 'Cause ours just kind of seemed like it was sloppy to me.

Think about Frank's statement from the point of view of his peers in the classroom. He is obviously taking a risk in making this suggestion for improvement. The other members of his group may not appreciate his admission that their presentation could have been more polished. Likewise, the rest of the class may not be pleased with his suggestion that all of the presentations could be done better. If you review the video, however, the students do not seem upset or displeased with Frank's suggestion. Rather, they appear to accept it as a valid critique. I believe that students like Frank are able to take risks because of the open, safe, and supportive environment that Joan has developed so quickly in her classroom. I also think that they are able to take risks because the discussion is so genuine. The discussion is not connected to the grade the students will receive; rather it is deeply rooted in a sincere, critical reflection on what went well and what could be improved. The discussion is not seen as a hoop to jump through but rather as a forum in which honest opinions are valued. This discussion (and the many more that occur throughout the year) causes Joan's students to recognize that their teacher is genuinely interested in helping them improve their work. They know that it is okay to take risks because Joan cares about them and has their best interests at heart.

Now read Frank's suggestion again and think about it from Joan's perspective. She has to listen to what Frank is saying, process it, and then respond. As Boaler and Humphreys note, "all of this thinking has to take place in an instant, in the midst of an interaction that involves a class full of students" (2005, p. 5). Joan has to make important decisions on the spot in developing a response that will appropriately use Frank's thought for the good of the classroom community. How did Joan respond to Frank's statement? As shown below, she responds by pointing out that it is difficult to create a polished presentation when collaborating as a group. She then uses Frank's comment to inform the students of a recent technology development and suggests how this development might help them collaborate more effectively in the future.

[08:21]—CHEMCO-4B

Ms. G.: Okay. Yeah, the practice part and getting the mechanics of the presentation together, that is hard. I mean, everybody usually has a very different schedule, and when you do find the time to put it together, sometimes you don't have the chance to edit it or go back and make it smooth. I will tell you, though, that the one thing you guys didn't have, that you typically do have at the beginning of the year, is computers at your lab table. So that you could actually work on it while you're doing the lab. And so that is supposed to happen by tomorrow. Those computers are supposed to be up and functioning. So that at least you could get a start on the outline of what your presentations are going to look like together, and then maybe breaking it up won't be so difficult to get it back together in the end.

Interestingly, Joan does not directly validate Frank's idea that the presentations were sloppy. Instead she focuses on two possible reasons that might explain why the presentations may have been sloppy. First, she emphasizes that the students should not expect that the coordination of tasks among group members will be easy and that it takes time, practice, and planning to get it right. Second, she suggests that the resolution of a school-related technology problem may help improve a group's efficiency in future labs. In both of the reasons offered, Joan does not dwell on the past; she provides ideas for how the students could improve their work in the future.

So how does Joan know how to respond to the students' reflections and use them as a means to teach about her expectations? I believe that the answer to this question is twofold. First, Joan actively listens to what her students are saying. You can see her writing down notes and nodding her head when the students are speaking. Through these actions alone, Joan sends the message that she wants to hear what her students have to say. Second, Joan is always thinking about the big picture. She knows that she wants to get her students to the point at which they will operate as a self-sufficient classroom community at the end of the year. She knows that it will be a lengthy process and that this worthwhile process will involve many cycles of teaching concepts, doing projects, and providing feedback. By thinking about the big picture, Joan can, on the spot, transform a student reflection into a teaching opportunity. She can use the reflections to teach her students how to improve their work in the future and what expectations she holds in terms of the quality of that work.

The teaching strategy of asking students to reflect on the community's work enables Joan to gather information about the thoughts and feeling of individual students and assess the mood and personality of the class in general. It also allows her to bring about a whole-class discussion that is grounded, first and foremost, in the students' ideas. Joan does not begin the discussion with her own thoughts and feedback; rather she waits to hear what a student has to say and then she responds. This teaching strategy is an application of conceptual change theory. Joan recognizes that the first step in bringing about conceptual change is to ascertain a student's current understanding of a particular concept. By soliciting the students' ideas and engaging in a whole-class discussion, Joan is able to informally assess the students' understanding of how they think a group should best work together to carry out a scientific inquiry. Joan and her students can then use this information to develop a common understanding of the quality of the previous bit of work and of which areas need improvement. They emerge from the discussion with a strong sense of where they have been and where they need to go. They see that they have a stake in the process of improving the community's work and that their contributions and actions toward this process matter.

Teaching Strategy 3—Developing a Strong Sense of Community

Throughout the video cases, you will notice that an overarching goal reigns. Joan wants to develop a strong sense of community in each of her classes. She wants her students to get to know one another and work together in ways that support learning. She wants them to have fun while they work together to solve challenging scientific problems and learn difficult chemistry concepts. She wants her students to participate in a community of practice where every member feels welcome and is able to make positive contributions. To achieve her goal of developing a strong community of practice, Joan is always looking for opportunities to shift the students' focus from "me" to "we." Over and over, throughout the entire year, Joan constantly asks her students to reflect upon the impact of their individual contributions in relation to the community's work. Because this teaching strategy is deeply engrained in all of the video cases, I will continue to discuss it in future chapters. Here I briefly introduce the idea and situate it in the CHEMCO video case.

As I already mentioned in my discussion around Strategy 1, at the end of the Chemistry Concoctions WCI Project, Joan presents a brief video that documents the messy condition of the laboratory at the end of the fifth class session. While she uses the video to teach the students about her expectations for cleanup, she also uses it to get her students to think about their class as a connected community. Before she starts the video, she presents a slide that poses the question "So how did we do?" She lets her students assess the answer to this question by analyzing the images in the video and informing her of what is wrong with those images. At the end of the video, Joan part jokingly says, "This class wins the prize for leaving the lab in the worst condition." In response to this statement, her students make comments using the collective pronouns of *we* and *us*.

[16:07]—CHEMCO-1

Chris: We also had it last.
Kelly: Yeah, but we win the prize for keeping our goggles on the whole time.
Frank: At least we were safe.
Kim: I was so proud of us for a while there.

Although this use of *we* and *us* may seem trivial, the students have been together in this classroom for only five class periods and they are making inclusive statements. Joan's focus on having the students examining the products of their work as a community helps them to think of themselves as a community. Joan does not assume that the students already know how to work together collaboratively, effectively, or efficiently, but rather that each class of students is at a particular point on the path of learning how to work together effectively as a community. The makeup of each class is different, and each has a unique starting point. By asking her students to view the video and reflect upon the condition of the lab they worked in, Joan forces them to confront questions that relate to the entire classroom community. At the end of the lab, did they think to check the cleanliness of the common areas that were used by all the students? Did they wipe up water spills on the floor? Did they reorganize the middle supply table? Did they clean up chemical spills on the three electronic balances that are shared by all of the students? Or did they assume that someone else would take care of these common lab areas? The video speaks for itself. When the students worked in the lab, they were not thinking about working together as a community to clean up the common areas of the lab. After the video is over, Joan points this out and then informs the class that they need to work together to ensure that the common areas are cleaned properly.

[17:38]—CHEMCO-1
Ms. G: Your cleanup. Make sure you focus on that, not just your own lab table but the middle lab table as well. That's the class's area so everybody is responsible for that.

After the video, Joan discusses how each student needs to share the responsibility of ensuring that other students are working safely while in the lab. This expectation implies that the task of maintaining a safe lab environment does not fall only on the teacher but is the community's responsibility. Joan indicates that the students should remember to police each other and that the policing should be rooted in the basic care they should exhibit toward each other.

[17:51]—CHEMCO-1
Ms. G: And then the number one thing is policing each other. So, if you're at a lab table and you've taken your glasses and my goggles are on top of my head right now and you've done this or a lot of people with the new ones seem to hang them under their chin, either one of those. The other people at your lab table should care enough about you to remind you "Hey, get your goggles over your eyes." I'm more upset with the people who don't say anything than the person who accidentally by habit does something like this or puts them on top of their head. But there's three other people staring at your naked eyes. You need to make sure you're reminding each other to take care.

In the above dialogue, Joan does not shy away from telling her students how she wants them to interact with one another. She realizes that the majority of her students have had a lifetime of classroom experiences in which a competitive, individualistic environment exists. She recognizes that the students need to be told explicitly that, in her classroom, students should care for one another, learn how to work together, and develop a strong sense of community. Joan knows that little progress will be made unless her students are on board with these expectations. Incredibly, as evidenced by the CHEMCO video case, Joan is able to instill a fledgling sense of community in her classroom after only a few class sessions.

For most of Joan's students, the experiences that they have had with the WCI curriculum so far represents a significant departure from their other, more traditional classroom experiences. As you will see in the upcoming video cases, the gap between their traditional experiences and those in Joan's classroom will continue to widen. And, as you will see in chapter 3, Joan's students are soon in for a big surprise. During the 11th session of class, Joan removes herself as the authority figure and puts the class in charge of completing a task together as a community. By dramatically changing the typical structure of the classroom, Joan gets her students to think differently about how a classroom should work.

Lave and Wenger propose that the type of knowledge that individuals construct is directly related to the goals of the practice in which the community is engaged and how its members interact to reach those goals (1991). For the classroom, this means that if students participate in a community of practice in which the main goal is to replicate the teacher's knowledge and correctly answer the teacher's questions in class discussions or tests, then they will situate their science learning within the context of doing well in class discussions or testing situations. If, however, students participate in a community of practice in which the main goal is to apply their understanding of science concepts as they collectively carry out scientific inquiries as a whole class, then they will situate their learning within the context of collaborating together as a classroom community. The students who enter Joan's classroom at the beginning of the school year are most likely familiar with the former classroom community of practice. As the year progresses, Joan's students become exposed to the latter community. Even though Joan is ultimately in charge of the classroom space throughout the year, the students take on more responsibility for the community's work as they make the transition from the traditional classroom community of practice to the WCI community of practice. During this transition, the students gain more autonomy and become members of a community in which they must make decisions for how best to organize the work of 26 students to solve a problem. They are no longer passive recipients of information but rather active members who construct and guide the community's practice, collective knowledge, and skill base. Compared to the traditional classroom's practice, the WCI classroom more closely resembles the practices of the scientific community at large. Ethnographers who have studied scientists at work have found that they typically collaborate with members of a research team. During these collaborations, scientists often engage in highly social interactions as they carry out the iterative process of clarifying a research problem, planning and conducting experiments, and reporting upon the community's results.

All three of the teaching strategies I have discussed at the end of this chapter relate to the development of a classroom community. The first strategy shows how Joan documents the community's work and uses this documentation as a teaching tool. The second strategy illustrates how Joan asks her students to reflect upon the quality of a recent piece of the community's work and think about how the community could improve its performance in the future. The third strategy demonstrates how Joan explicitly asks her students to develop a strong sense of community within the classroom. As you have already seen in the GOAL video presented in chapter 1, Joan's teaching strategies are obviously effective at getting her students to work together as a community and to take charge of the classroom. In the upcoming video cases, you will see how Joan continues to use these same teaching strategies to encourage the growth of a strong classroom community. You will also learn about several other teaching strategies that are essential in Joan's successful enactment of the WCI curriculum.

REFERENCES

Boaler, J., and C. Humphreys. 2005. *Connecting mathematical ideas: Middle school video cases to support teaching and learning.* Portsmouth: Heinemann.

Gallagher-Bolos, J. A., and D. W. Smithenry. 2004. *Teaching inquiry-based chemistry: Creating student-led scientific communities.* Portsmouth, NH: Heinemann.

Glaser, B. G., and A. L. Strauss. 1967. *The discovery of grounded theory: Strategies for qualitative research.* New York: Aldine de Gruyter.

Green, J., and C. Wallat. 1981. Mapping instructional conversations: A sociolinguistic ethnography. In *Ethnography and language in educational settings,* eds. J. Green and C. Wallat, 161–205. Norwood, NJ: Ablex.

Kelly, G. J., and T. Crawford. 1997. An ethnographic investigation of the discourse processes of school science. *Science Education* 81 (5): 533–559.

Lave, J., and E. Wenger. 1991. *Situated learning: Legitimate peripheral participation.* New York: Cambridge University Press.

Shulman, J. H. 1992. Teacher-written cases with commentaries: A teacher-researcher collaboration. In *Case methods in teacher education,* ed. J. H. Shulman, 131–152. New York: Teachers College Press.

Torrance, H., and J. Pryor. 2001. Developing formative assessment in the classroom: Using action research to explore and modify theory. *British Educational Research Journal* 27 (5): 615–631.

Chapter 3
WCI Assessments

In this chapter, Dennis and I take a break from presenting more video cases on WCI projects and discuss another extremely important facet of our curriculum: WCI assessments (Gallagher-Bolos and Smithenry 2008). At the end of each unit, I administer a two-part test. Because I teach in a 90-minute block, I typically administer a 45- to 60-minute individual, traditional test and then give the class 45 or 30 minutes to complete a WCI assessment. This assessment is a test that the entire class works on together. My expectation is that, although only one answer sheet will be turned in, the entire class will have contributed somehow to those responses.

In terms of mechanics, after collecting all individual tests, I place a one-page cover sheet containing directions and several questions for the class to answer on the front demonstration table. I include transparencies of the questions on the cover sheet so the entire class can use the overhead projector to see the questions. This WCI assessment might consist of challenging content questions unlike any my students have seen up to this point. Or it might contain lab-analysis questions, in which the class needs to use previously gathered data to answer a question or develop a model. Or it might be a lab practical, requiring the class to apply its previously collected data to a new scenario.

The purpose of administering these WCI assessments is to provide further opportunity for the class to grow as a scientific community of learners. The students see the value in working together and brainstorming to solve difficult problems. It isn't always practical or necessary to spend three to four days on a challenge as we do with WCI projects. Yet there are some valuable experiences that the class can and should have that can be accomplished within one class period. These smaller whole-class investigations also help students develop the skills necessary to work together on the multiday WCI projects.

In this chapter we show you two examples of WCI assessments being implemented. The first video presents the very first WCI assessment of the year which took place at the end of September following the completion of Unit I—Introductory Chemistry. The class met 12 times before this WCI assessment occurs. The other example WCI assessment took place at the end of February after completion of Unit VI, Solutions Chemistry.

WCI ASSESSMENT 1— UNIT I

Teacher's Introduction—WCIA-1A

The first video you watch documents what happens during the first WCI assessment, which took place at the end of September 2005. It is the end of our first unit, and the class has gone through the Chemistry Concoctions WCI Project described in chapter 2. Students had taken their individual tests on Unit I during the previous class period. Due to an altered schedule, I administered this WCI assessment the following class period and gave my students 20 minutes to accomplish the task described. The instructions for WCI assessment 1 are found in Figure 3.1.

Figure 3.1

Cover Sheet for WCI Assessment 1

WCI Assessment 1

- You may use each other, your journals, your texts (if you have them), your calculators, and any materials on the middle lab table. As always, my cart is off limits!
- I've attached an overhead of the following questions so that the class can see it.
- I must have this sheet completed and in my hands by _____ according to this clock or I will not grade it. If you fail to meet this deadline, PLACE THE SHEET ON THE FRONT LAB TABLE. DO NOT REMOVE IT FROM CLASS.
- You must submit your responses on this sheet. Attach the overhead to this sheet, as well.
- The class will be assessed on accuracy and on the effort made as a community in the process of solving the problems.
- It is assumed that everyone in the room could do this problem on his/her own once you've finished as a class.

1. Using only the materials provided on the middle lab table, perform the "Chemistry Concoctions" Lab and make it so that exactly 15.0 mL of ethanol are captured in the graduated cylinder from the tubing attached to the 250 mL flask.
   a. You have only ONE opportunity. The first try is your only try...So think before acting!
   b. Ethanol must travel through the tubes as a result of the chemical reaction between sodium bicarbonate and acetic acid.
   c. No ethanol may be poured into or out of the graduated cylinder directly. Again, it must be a result of the procedure you did during the Chemistry Concoctions lab.
   d. Show me your results before cleaning up.
2. Draw at the particulate level what happened. Make sure this drawing accurately illustrates and explains why you got the results you did.

Note that the directions on this WCI assessment state that the class is allowed to use only the equipment left on the middle lab table to accomplish the described task. The things that I left on the lab table included: five pairs of goggles, one apparatus set up like the control for the Chemistry Concoctions lab (See Figure 2.3), a balance, deionized water, a weigh boat, ethanol, a 10 mL graduated cylinder, a scoopula, a Flinn catalog (Flinn Scientific 2005), sodium bicarbonate, and acetic acid.

Near the end of the video you will notice Jack saying, "What's up, Mr. Keno?" He is speaking to another teacher who happened to walk in the room. Although it is just a brief interaction, I want to make clear that Jack is not speaking to me or another student.

Teacher's Analysis—WCIA-1A

After watching this video, I think, "Are you kidding me? What the heck were those kids doing?" I then reread the journal I wrote while observing them during this challenge, and that's exactly how I felt then. I imagine anyone watching would wonder what any respectable teacher would find valuable in an activity like this. Out of context, I would agree. But I use this experience as a starting point for yet another building block for the creation of our classroom community. The key components to this growth are reflection and feedback. And the key to valuable feedback is allowing the students to process and share their thoughts, as described in chapter 2. It is the starting point to true ownership of the opportunities presented in this class for the remainder of the year.

This is a good place to pause from analyzing the video to discuss a mental shift I had to go through as I learned to implement WCI assessments and projects 14 years ago. As I have said, it is difficult to watch the chaos that takes place during the first WCI assessment for each class every year. But I always take a step back and remember that this is a necessary starting point for my students. It is well worth the effort to endure this craziness.

The example lessons in this book cannot be implemented successfully if done in isolation from the story behind our development of the WCI approach. I think back to the challenges that I gave my classes during the first few experimental years of trying to reach my year-end goal of creating a self-sufficient scientific community of learners. I basically redefined what being a teacher meant. This took years to process and involved a 180-degree mental shift for me. For the first few years of my career, the experiences I had as a student seemed to provide a deep enough definition for what teaching meant for me. Certainly my education classes allowed me to investigate my teaching philosophy, but that philosophy was rooted in the traditional teacher-centered classroom, the type of classroom I thought I learned well in as a student.

Video—Watch the WCIA-1A video on the DVD labeled "Video Cases for Chapters 1–3." This clip takes the first 20 minutes of class and compresses them into approximately 10 minutes so that you can visualize what was described.

I made a huge shift in that definition after having children. I would watch them question their environment without prompting, create mental models without reading a textbook, and enjoy learning without the superficial result of a grade. I started to think, "What role can I take in their development without interfering or suffocating this natural magnetism for knowledge?"

I also had the added advantage of meeting Dennis during the time I was watching my children explore as toddlers, when my teaching was making this drastic shift. His experience as a professional scientist helped me envision where I wanted my children to end up in terms of their love of exploration and their joy in knowing there isn't an end to questioning. Seeing my children's curiosity at the beginning of their journey and learning about Dennis's career helped me cement the role I could take in the middle, as a parent and as a science teacher. I needed to get out of my students' way. I needed to create opportunities for them to investigate the process of science—from their perspective, with all the things that accompany a teen's world, allowing their unique life experiences to play a role in their education. So I brought the thrill of my own children's growth and what I had learned from my friendship with Dennis to my lesson-planning process.

After spending a year teaching with Dennis and trying to implement pieces of these ideas—journals, inquiry-based lesson plans, and feedback—we decided to develop a year-end, culminating lab for our classes. We called it The Soap Project; it is detailed elsewhere (Bolos and Smithenry 1996; Gallagher-Bolos and Smithenry 2004). This project serves as my guide each year; it is the challenge my students have at the end of the year. Each class is required to make two pounds of quality, packaged soap by role-playing industry-based jobs. They must work together to make this happen. The rest of the year is the time I have to prepare them for this three-week WCI project.

I finally started to understand what a "student-centered" classroom meant about 14 years ago. Students became engaged when I stopped talking and gave them the floor. Both WCI projects and assessments became my students' favorite overall activities because they were being challenged to think together toward a common goal. I think that the popularity of these redesigned lessons rests in how they allow for the whole child to be present in the room. Students consistently tell me they feel challenged by the chemistry content, but they also learn more about themselves, their strengths, and weaknesses.

My curriculum is now designed so there are periodic WCI opportunities for the students, times in which the students feel the teacher plays very little role in the classroom. As you saw in the CHEMCO video cases, I was front and center during the first unit, but, as you watch the rest of the videos, you'll see that I become more withdrawn as the year progresses. My role becomes more that of an observer. I record what my students do and then use this information during feedback to help them grow together. So my presence has shifted from being available during the beginning of an activity to being the person who helps them reflect and grow during the closing of an activity.

The hardest part of this mental shift was becoming comfortable with the idea that I had to allow my class to be unsuccessful and not intervene. Of course it's easy to allow a class to succeed. But staying quiet when you know your students are going down the wrong path is extremely difficult. This took some time. As a teacher who cares, I found it very tough to give up control of my class—an incredibly draining experience. It was like letting go of a toddler's hand. She walks sometimes and falls sometimes, but she has to figure it out for herself. As a parent, I've got to give her the struggle even though I'd much rather do the guiding. As a teacher, I feel the same way. My head and my heart are at war the whole time during any one of these WCI projects or assessments; they always are. But I'm glad I let go of my students' hands from time to time. I'm glad they walk, fall, and do just about everything in between. This is why these WCI projects and assessments are so successful, meaningful, and authentic. The students own their experiences, together. They figure it out and grow in the process.

Getting back to the video of the first WCI assessment, I have learned there are four imperatives for me to keep in mind as a class goes through a WCI assessment, especially the first:

- *Try it yourself.* During the planning of any WCI assessment, I make sure I try the task I'm asking my class to do. This way, I can see what the glitches might be and can adjust the design or parameters before implementation.
- *Follow through.* I always let my students struggle through this first unguided WCI assessment. I step in only when safety is in question. Otherwise, I intervene as little as possible. If I help, the game is over. They would ask me for help the rest of the year. They have got to get used to this new environment.
- *Record as much as possible.* Although it's difficult to record or absorb anything but total chaos and frustration during my students' first WCI assessment, I try to get it all down so that I can process it. (I now film the first WCI assessment every year to use it for feedback.) It has gotten much more instinctual for me as the years go by, but, for anyone trying this for the first time, I always advise recording everything.
- *Keep quiet until the next day.* I don't give students any immediate feedback. We all need time to process what has happened. I want to give them useful and appropriate feedback for the future, and

this takes time. Students come up and ask, "How'd we do? Did we fail?" I simply reply, "We'll talk about it next class," or "You decide for yourself, and then we'll talk next class."

Here are my specific thoughts about the students' behavior during this WCI assessment, both the good and the not-so-good moments. As soon as I walk to the back of the room, everyone in the class stands up and hurriedly grabs at the cover sheet. Jack even flails his hands in the air as if it's a race. How funny! Once he gets there, Jack begins to read the sheet to the rest of the class. Believe it or not, this is a typical response each year. I don't understand how class after class thinks this is an effective strategy. But then I remember that these are high school students who have never been through a situation like this. They've been given very little direction for a task involving the whole class.

Although typical, this is not the only reaction to the first announcement of a WCI assessment. Other classes during this year did just the opposite. Students sat bewildered for minutes in one class until finally someone stood up and grabbed the paper and read. But the full spectrum between everyone standing up and nobody doing anything has happened. All of these responses are valuable for me. They tell me something about the personality of each class. For this class, I learned that, when given little direction and a lot of freedom, it is lively with plenty of eager participants. The students seem to have very few organizational skills in a large-group setting and probably a few too many leaders. They seem happy and willing; they're able to have fun with one another. And there also seem to be quite a few friendships in the class. This is where we need to start to improve for the next WCI assessment. As I said, other classes will have a different starting point.

While viewing this video I notice a number of constructive things happening. Students are applying some of what they learned in previous feedback to this challenge, although that may not be obvious in all the chaos. As soon as the class heads back to the middle lab table, Angie yells, "Goggles! Goggles!" And Dan yells back, "Goggles are provided for us." He has obviously noticed the equipment I placed on the middle lab table includes goggles. This class knows that no one should be in lab without goggles. The students learned this from their Introduction to Chemistry lab feedback. Two students clearly, and seemingly instinctually, remove their hats as they walk to the back of the room. And last, we can hear Jack announce that the class needs to look up safety information in the Flinn catalog (Flinn Scientific 2005). Three important safety acts—wearing goggles, removing hats, and looking up safety information—have been addressed right at the beginning of their challenge, and I didn't have to say a word.

I have purposely limited their equipment and put out only five pairs of goggles. I want them to work as a class, not as 26 separate individuals. Chris comes to ask for more goggles. When I say no, he jokes in a frustrated tone that he'll "just cover his eyes." This is an okay frustration for him to have; the students all need to learn to grow in this uncharted territory of working as a class. But I would like to point out three important things that I learned from his asking me this question. One is that this particular student wants to participate. He's immediately seeking the use of goggles to get involved. That means five other people must already have goggles on.* The second thing I've learned is that this class has a number of people who dive into lab. Who chose the people to be in lab? Why isn't Chris one of them? When did the five people get picked to wear them? Was there a decision made about who was to wear the goggles and work in lab? The third thing I learned is that Chris either doesn't absorb or didn't hear the directions that Jack read at the beginning of the period. If he had, he would know that only the materials on the middle lab table were allowed. All of these things are important to discuss during feedback as we talk about organization and working together as a whole class.

As the video progresses, it's clear there is confusion about how to proceed. Some students are recalling their work during the Chemistry Concoctions WCI Project and want to apply that information to this new challenge. This is a fabulous idea, but it frustrates me that they never had a class discussion about this. They get to a point at which Angie says, "The group that used ethanol wants to talk." Certain focused students realize they have to transfer ethanol, not water, from the middle flask to the graduated cylinder, and only one group had tested that during its WCI. Again, that this realization occurs is great; but that only a few students seem to understand this and talk about it is a problem.

---

* Safety note: In my classroom, I require that each student purchase his or her own pair of goggles because I do not want my students to share goggles. I do so to prevent the spread of conjunctivitis or hepatitis. The five goggles I placed on the lab table were **CAUTION** owned by five individual students and had specific names written upon them. I expected that the students would realize that only these five students could go into the laboratory. Obviously, the students did not follow through on my expectation and decided to share the five goggles. As you can see in the video, rather than stepping in immediately to address the safety issue of goggle sharing, I chose to remain on the sideline. The risk seems minor, especially since the students were making the decision with whom to share. What is more, I knew that I could address this safety issue most effectively through the feedback that I would give in the next class session. Then I could present the scenario of sharing goggles and ask them to tell me why it was inappropriate. Another way in which I have addressed this issue (since the video was made) is by revising the WCI assessment instructions to name only five specific students who are allowed to go into the lab. This revision has removed the possibility that the students will share goggles.

Halfway through the video, we see students watching as others work in lab. Goggles regularly pass from one student to another as they allow each other a chance to help in lab. Although this is not very efficient in terms of planning (or in the safer practice of using goggles), it's a very advanced position for this class to be in terms of the social structure. The students seem to work well with one another. I am concerned that Chris seems to give up in his attempt to participate after asking me for more goggles. I will address this situation one-on-one next class. I want him to know I wasn't shutting him down.

I also hear the students asking questions such as: "Why don't we do this? Why are you doing it this way? Who has this data?" Once again, these are wonderful questions. But it's unfortunate that this didn't happen at the beginning of class during a planning session in which everyone could hear and participate.

Right before they make their attempt of transferring ethanol into the graduated cylinder, Jack shouts out, "Does anyone have any objections?" Angie says, "I say we go with it 'cause we've got 10 minutes." Kelly says, "I don't think it's going to work, but do it." Rather than ignoring her and moving on, Tom, says, "Do you have a different idea real quick?" This is phenomenal—and rare to hear at the beginning of the year. To take into consideration what others think and provide an opportunity for an individual to defend her dissenting opinion before moving forward is extremely mature. This is the point at which I hope to get my students by the end of the year. During feedback, it's important to address as many as possible specific examples like these to students, so that they know you recognize some of their greater group talents. Nothing like this happened in my other classes during the first WCI assessment.

After the lab group implements the agreed-upon procedure, the result is not what they hoped for. The interesting thing is that you notice a large number of students sincerely disappointed in the result. During the 20 minutes of their WCI assessment, they've taken ownership in this problem.

Mark absorbs the details of the procedure after it was completed by the lab group and makes a comment about a mistake in their plan. It's a bit late for that. Why didn't he jump in earlier? Perhaps he didn't hear the plan, or the plan was never shared with the larger audience, or Mark was too nervous to speak up. These are all things that need to be processed and improved upon.

During cleanup, Angie asks me how to dispose of ethanol. Because I know the entire class has used ethanol before and should know how to dispose of it, I do not respond to her question. Because I do not respond, Angie asks the class, "You guys, how do we dispose of ethanol?" When nobody seems to have a confident response, Angie and her lab partners are uncertain about what to do with their ethanol sample. Again, this is an important thing to talk about later. I hold the entire class accountable for ensuring that chemicals are properly disposed of. In my feedback, I will discuss how each student had a responsibility to find the information requested by Angie. Because each student has used the chemical before, each has the disposal information already written in his or her journal.

Finally the class turns in its response sheets. The WCI assessment is over, and I move on. I do not talk to them about it; I just say that we will discuss it next class.

What is the value in doing a WCI assessment, particularly this first one, when my students had no experience and were given little direction on how to work as a class? My main goal is to create a self-sufficient scientific community of learners. Unless I know where I'm starting—what individual and class strengths and weaknesses exist—we can't grow as a whole class. So giving the students total freedom at the beginning, and letting them fumble through it, is crucial. Intervening would remove their sense of ownership and devalue the feedback. We will continue to intersperse these WCI assessments throughout the year because they provide valuable practice for working as a whole class under time constraints. The students will get feedback and should grow together as the year progresses.

A copy of the journal I wrote while they were working on this 20-minute WCI assessment follows. I abbreviate my thoughts, and I focus on the things that need improvement, so it may appear that my journal is negative. This journal's purpose is to help me recapture the things I know need to be discussed during feedback. I have become adept at absorbing, or quickly recording, in another document those things that the class accomplishes, as well, and these too will be discussed during feedback. The purpose of sharing this journal is simply to give you a glimpse of what was going through my head during this WCI assessment for this class.

Teacher's Journal—WCIA-1A

September 29, 2005

Everyone stood up and walked up front…Are you kidding me?

Aaron read the problem out loud to the class while you all stood around the front lab table. Why? Jack also added that Dan would receive an "F."

Then, everyone walked to the back. Umm….Hello? Are you thinking?

Chaos to begin. Unbelievable.

"One person from each group should be up here," Mary says. Good idea.

I gave this class two hints as chaos was rampant. I answered the question of where the responses should go. I also told them I wouldn't open the goggle drawer to give them more goggles.

(VERY different from the other two classes.)

Kim says, "Do you want to give us some information so that we can work on it together, too?" Good—the voice of reason.

Chris, what's up with the ring stand?

And how did the five people with goggles end up as the five people with goggles? Were they the fastest? Were they chosen?

Safety pathway was finally discussed. Yikes! People have been in lab for eight minutes.

"Tara, tie your hair back," Dan says. "It's for you, not for me." Funny!

"Isn't water supposed to be in the middle one?" Angie asks. This is indicative of the class not communicating well…Oops…

"Get in there; you're the man."

Wonder what everyone else is thinking? Are they thinking? How do you get the rest involved?

Some people are up front drawing pictures. A couple people are looking at a packet. Hmmm…Those were due last class.

Tom then addresses the majority of class. This is the first conversation with the majority of class involved. And it's at the 18-minute mark. Hmmmm….

"It's over now, let's just move on…."

So what can we do? Let's wash our hands!"

"Did we write down the Flinn stuff? That'll give us some points."

I also gave Frank the make-up brush for the balance. Good that you thought to clean the balance.

"But no one would listen to me…"

No displacement was the result of the lab.

Questions asked of me, some of which had nothing to do with the test. Not a good idea.

Frank also asked what to do with the ethanol. Good for you. You're thinking.

Chris says he's used ethanol and has put it down the sink. Yes, you did. Good memory. Why aren't others listening to you?

WCI ASSESSMENT 1 FEEDBACK—UNIT I

Teacher's Introduction—WCIA-1B

The video you are about to watch was filmed the day after the students participated in their first WCI assessment. Recall that this assessment was a 20-minute challenge and it built upon the class's data obtained during the Chemistry Concoctions WCI Project. The focus of this video is the feedback given to this class on this first WCI assessment. As I said in chapter 2, the feedback I give to the class falls under three umbrellas—accuracy, safety, and community—each being given equal weight. Although I'm sure I didn't address every issue that could have been addressed after watching the WCIA-1A video, I tried to cover as much as I remembered at the time. What looks like a fuzzy cloud will appear about halfway through this video. Dennis added it to blur out the students' real names that I wrote on the white board.

Teacher's Analysis—WCIA-1B

As promised, I give the students feedback in the areas of accuracy, safety, and community. As you watch, it may seem that some of the information from this feedback could and should be told to the students before they embark on their first WCI assessment, that there doesn't seem to be a reason to withhold some of the more straightforward directions from them. But, from experience, I know giving my students the information is the exact opposite of what nurtures the growth of a self-sufficient scientific community of learners.

Video—Watch the WCIA-1B video on the DVD labeled "Video Cases for Chapters 1–3." This clip takes about 50 minutes of class and compresses them into approximately 30 minutes so that you can visualize what was described.

Although many classes are good at following directions, or will simply jump through whatever hoops a teacher gives them, doing so does not allow them to construct their own knowledge in the areas of individual and class accountability. As their teacher, I am best able to aid in student growth if I understand where we're starting from. My students can understand the reasons why some of the hints and directions they hear facilitate accomplishing a whole-class challenge only if they first know what happens when those hints and directions are missing from the scenario. The process of growth in a scientific community setting must start with students clearly understanding where the community's strengths and weaknesses lie. So, although it might seem a harmless choice to first tell them what I'm looking for during their initial WCI assessment, it undermines the reason for doing the assessment in the first place.

Although the example of this WCI assessment might appear to be an isolated lesson plan, students will quickly learn that the feedback they get from these activities is helpful for other classroom activities, such as future WCI projects and collaborative group workshops. So, because this activity is still at the beginning of the year, I am giving them a lot of information and hints for the future. My hope is that they will spend the time absorbing this information in order to apply it to their future challenges.

As I go through the information about accuracy, I remind the students what specific directions I had given for this WCI assessment. I also give them hints about how those directions might change for a future WCI assessment. After I tell them what I was looking for, I ask their opinion. Immediately, Dan says, "Not very good." And Kim and Jack both respond, looking at the slide, "Two out of three." I focus on the former response, because I don't want my students to think so quantitatively with respect to accuracy just yet. I want them to process more than just the answers to the questions on the slide. We spend a bit of time talking about their lab technique, their expectations, their results, their models, and their records. I make certain to emphasize that their performance in terms of accuracy is not only about the product (i.e., displacing the correct volume of ethanol), but also about the thinking behind their actions and their model of the phenomenon. Overall, they are surprised and happy to hear they received such a high score on their accuracy portion of the WCI assessment.

The next portion of the feedback focuses on how well the class did in terms of safety. We review safety content that should be familiar to them based on their previous lab experiences so far. Interestingly, this class seems to think that they have done fairly well in terms of safety. From my perspective, they focused on having the five students wear goggles in the lab; however, some of the students were in the lab area without goggles for quite some time at the beginning, and they should not have shared goggles. Some of them were blocking access to the eyewash. I thought the class seemed surprised that I was picky in terms of its safety performance. This class didn't apply its experiences as readily as other classes did. My students were a bit thrown by how harsh I was about their inability to determine quickly what to do with their ethanol samples. They were also surprised at how detailed I was about their inability to police the class in terms of lab safety. This sent the message that they should not cut corners in safety. Their grade was not too harsh, so they likely would be more motivated to improve in this area, rather than feel defeated and give up.

When we get to our discussion on community, I try to emphasize that each area is equally important. Most students are conditioned to believe that the accuracy of a response is the most important piece of a challenge. These students quickly realize, however, that I believe that safety and community are as important as accuracy.

After sharing these thoughts with them, I want to get their input on how well they felt they worked together toward a common goal. I am surprised at how well the class thought it did. When I was gathering material for feedback, I was shocked to notice that only Frank's eyes showed a level of disbelief at the positive perspectives that the others were sharing. Frank seemed to be the only one who had the same impression I did; I felt that the class was extremely chaotic in terms of organization. When I finally shift the discussion from only positive contributions by asking my students what they could do better, Jack offers the idea that the class should "sit down and like relax" at first. Whereupon Frank says the class should "chill." I expand on these contributions by saying, "Oh my gosh, yes. Chill." Even though my emotions are clear in this statement, it takes me quite a while to get the class to realize that they could do a much better job of planning, especially in terms of making certain that everyone is involved and has a role to play. My students finally realize this after I put forth the idea that only a few people in the room could even describe what equipment was available for use. Developing a plan that includes everyone in the class is a foundational concern that I need to get the students to absorb.

Once I give the class its score on the community section, there are a number of grumbles. This is OK. My students will definitely improve on their next whole-class challenge, especially because the class now has two class managers who can help guide the community's work. To implement the class manager system, I begin by defining the characteristics of successful class manager candidates and what I feel is the optimal number. Frank suggests having three managers, even after I say that two would be a good number. Notice that I quickly direct this conversation into a vote that results in the class agreeing with the idea of two managers. It is nice that most of this convincing comes from Jack, but I would have readily led the discussion in this direction if he had not. After Kim and Jack are chosen, with Mary as an alternate, I redefine the role of a class manager. This will definitely be revisited as the next few class challenges are implemented. The class will need guidance getting used to peers facilitating class work, but it will get there.

I then give my students mechanical suggestions for how they should begin the next WCI assessment (or project) now that they have class managers facilitating these challenges. I give them some ideas of how the class might best organize itself, based on the type of challenge given. Lastly, I make sure the class is aware that each student must be able to accurately respond to the questions asked on the WCI assessment by the next class. The best scenario for this is to leave time to reconvene as a class at the end of a WCI assessment and talk together. But time constraints can prevent that luxury. If an individual is still confused about or unaware of any part of the WCI assessment, a system is needed for communicating outside class so that students can correct possible problems before the next class period.

To finish my feedback, I share quotes with the class. As with the feedback for the Chemistry Concoctions WCI Project, the students enjoy this. Not only are the quotes a reminder that I am paying attention to what they are doing during these class challenges, but they also allow them to have some fun and bond.

To conclude Unit I and transition into Unit II, I tell the students that all of the things they learned in Unit I about working as a class, particularly in WCI assessments and projects, should be applied to the challenges experienced in Unit II. I tell them that I will start to remove my guidance and presence during these challenges, so they must be ready to depend more on one another. This is the next step in the development of our self-sufficient scientific community of learners. Unit I took a long time. Even though the content covered in it isn't particularly difficult, establishing the class climate and nurturing the skills necessary for the students to work with one another requires a lengthy experience and detailed feedback. In Unit II, I will provide a similar amount of feedback but not nearly as much guidance.

Before moving on and showing you a WCI project that took place during Unit II, Dennis and I decided that you should see another WCI assessment that occurred much later in the school year. This next WCI assessment illustrates just how much the class improves as the year progresses.

WCI ASSESSMENT 7—
UNIT V—STOICHIOMETRY

Teacher's Introduction—WCIA-7

This next video shows students going through their seventh WCI assessment for the year. Recall that these are assessments that must be completed within the same class period; they are unlike the WCI projects that require two to four days to complete. This particular WCI assessment occurred in the middle of February, about four months after the class's first WCI shown earlier in this chapter. There should be a marked improvement. My students have been working together more and more frequently as the year has progressed, receiving feedback after each challenge and applying what they've learned to all future tasks. The instructions for the WCI assessment are shown in Figure 3.2.

 Video—Watch WCIA-7 video on the DVD labeled "Video Cases for Chapters 1–3." This clip takes the first 30 minutes of class and compresses them into approximately 10 minutes so that you can visualize what was described.

Figure 3.2

Cover Sheet for WCI Assessment 7
Note: The problem included in this assessment has been modified from one found in Zumdahl's *Introductory Chemistry* (Zumdahl 2003)

WCI Assessment 7

- You can use your books, journals, calculators and room resources (other than teachers and my cart) for help.
- This must be in my hands by _____ or I will not assess it.
- Remember, you are being assessed on community work, accuracy and safety.

Nitric Acid (HNO_3) is produced commercially by the Ostwald process represented by the following equations:

$$NH_3 \quad + \quad O_2 \quad \text{---------------->} \quad NO \quad + \quad H_2O$$
$$NO \quad + \quad O_2 \quad \text{---------------->} \quad NO_2$$
$$NO_2 \quad + \quad H_2O \quad \text{---------------->} \quad HNO_3 \quad + \quad NO$$

What mass of ammonia (NH_3) must be used to produce 1.00×10^6 kg nitric acid by the Ostwald process, assuming 93% yield in each reaction? (SHOW ALL WORK!)

Teacher's Analysis—WCIA-7

The first shot in the video shows Kim reading the question of the WCI assessment to the class from the overhead transparency copy I provided. This is good; everyone needs to know the entire challenge before beginning. Once Kim finishes, you immediately hear, "Shhhh!" The class knows they should keep silent for 30 to 60 seconds to allow the managers time to determine how best to organize the class. They have been told that, during this silence, class members should reread and absorb the questions read to them by the managers so they can get a better idea of what is being asked. This processing time is extremely important.

Jack comes back to ask me, "Do we know how much time we get?" I respond, "Uh-hum." He seems perplexed. The one part of the feedback that they have heard repeatedly but that the managers do not implement here is that they are always given a cover sheet and an overhead. The overhead has only the challenge questions on it. The cover sheet also contains the parameters for the challenge. Dan asks, "What's that blank white overturned piece of paper?" Kim flips it and says, "Oh!" So it took them a while to get to this, but at least they now know the parameters for the WCI assessment. She then reads what resources the class is allowed to use.

The organization at the beginning of this WCI assessment is an improvement over what you observed in the first WCI assessment. Students quickly decide they will work in their lab groups on the challenge question. They decide to reconvene with 15 minutes left in class to compare answers.

As the groups discuss their problem-solving strategy, it's clear that the hurdle lies in how to apply the 93% yield to each reaction so that the end number makes sense. I love watching the students discuss science concepts together. And I can also see very easily which students are teaching other members of their group and that the majority of students are engaged in the problem.

After they reconvene, Sandy volunteers to write on the board. The managers go around the room to get the responses from each of the six groups. Some groups aren't done, but they use the answers they have as a basis for discussion. What a difference from the first WCI assessment—the students have planned their problem-solving strategy and have left time to check each other's work.

When the students reconvene, there seems still to be some hesitancy in grasping the content. After Jack and Kim determine that two out of the six groups have the same answer, Jack asks Sandy to write her work on the board and explain it to the class. She had earned the respect of her peers at this point in the year, evidenced by their turning to her for help many times in the past. Nevertheless, as she writes on the board, it's obvious that the class is not blindly following her lead. Kelly asks about Sandy's approach. Other students in the class start to

74

speak up. Kim reminds the class to allow Sandy to explain. These are all learned behaviors. The students have improved the way in which they conduct themselves during WCI activities as the year has progressed. And their conduct illustrates a group ownership in attempting to solve the challenge.

After Sandy's work is laid out on the board, the dilemma of how to apply the 93% yield to the problem remains. The class is discussing and debating science and math. And I am not facilitating the discussion. The class is. More impressive, their manager Kim is. She's making sure that each group's concerns are brought to the larger audience for consideration. For example, she points out, "But the thing is, guys, what a couple groups are saying is you have to divide it, not multiply it." Again, this is learned behavior that has resulted from our repeated feedback sessions after each WCI project and assessment.

The class then turns to Michelle to explain her approach to the problem (which the class appropriately identifies as the correct solution). Once she writes her conversion factors on the board, a good number of students seem to have their questions answered. But the class doesn't stop there. As a manager, Jack asks, "People understand what's going on now with this?" Sandy immediately and with comfort responds, "No. Can someone…?." Recall that Sandy was the person people originally asked to explain the problem to the class. Her response to Jack is exciting for two reasons. One is that this class started the year by keeping questions to themselves and using what seems to be the default mode for learning: simply jumping through the hoops as a teacher presents new material. This is a typical high school behavior. If students are given information, they'll either figure out the mechanics of it on their own so they can regurgitate it later or they'll fake their way through it on a future problem. Sandy, instead, wants to understand what's wrong with her approach and what's right with the approach the class seems to accept. She's thinking, questioning, and learning. And her insistence is likely aiding others in the class.

The second reason this is exciting is that Sandy feels comfortable admitting that she still doesn't understand. There is no condescending response to her confusion. The class wants to support fully each other's content growth. This supportive atmosphere has been nurtured through WCI assessments and projects experienced throughout the year. In other words, the class has bonded. This is not unique to this class. This is a universal consequence to the WCI approach, class after class, year after year.

In order for Sandy to get help, still another student, Adam is called to the board to explain the response. Michelle is recording on the master answer sheet, so Adam steps up to help the class. This is another wonderful moment to witness. Adam was very quiet at the beginning of the year. From being in classes with Adam in previous years, the students know he is quite intelligent. But he doesn't readily speak up. He is content to solve challenges on his own and listen quietly as others worked them through. One day during the first semester, I had pulled him aside and told him, "Adam, I think you'll run into some challenges in this class that will require you to focus more than you have in the past. But it won't be as challenging for you as it will be for others. You're incredibly bright. And the class needs you. You need to be more verbal. Everyone, including you, will benefit from your teaching. So given the opportunity, see what you can do." Although it wasn't easy at first, he did step up. And in this video, it's apparent that he is not just explaining the problem a third time the same way but rather using a different analogy, one he thinks the class might better understand, to help his class connect his reasoning to the WCI assessment question. This is outstanding. (It's also interesting to note that Adam took Advanced Placement Chemistry the next year and became instrumental in his class's ability to accomplish WCI assessments, WCI projects, and traditional AP labs.) Once Adam is done, Joe adds his thoughts about why this approach makes sense.

A copy of the journal I typed while observing and filming this WCIA-7 follows.

Teacher's Journal—WCIA-7

February 13, 2006

Kim read the overhead. The class was then quiet for 44 seconds while Kim and Jack made a plan. They then dealt with the time frame.

Jack came back to ask me about the time limit. "Do we know our time limit?" "Yep," I replied. He left a bit confused.

"What's that overturned piece of paper?" Dan asked.

"Oh!!!!"

So Kim reread the instructions from the cover sheet. Then they told the class to break up into rows and solve the problem. A suggestion was made to just work in cooperative work groups. Good.

Each group worked on balancing the reactions and then doing the calculations. The plan is to then reconvene. What was the time frame?

Craig, Nick, Joe, and Dan have a lively discussion about where and when to take care of the 93% yield. Good discussion; are you explaining things to one another and/or asking questions?

Kelly explains to Angie about the difference between multiplying and dividing by 93% yield.

Jack walked around at 9:35 to check the status of each group. Good.

At 9:40, Jack and Kim got the answers from each group and recorded them on the board. Sandy volunteered to write on the board.

Adam then asks about the set-up that Sandy is writing on the board. Adam, you're right.

Kim then consolidates the information by saying, "The thing is, some groups are saying we should divide by 93% instead of multiply." Great!

Michelle then heads to the board. Good. There it is!

Michelle then volunteers to write and Adam tries to explain. Excellent example!

Nicely done. Continuing to improve!

Teacher's Additional Thoughts—WCIA Video Cases

I have said this before and will continue to say it throughout this book: Carefully and accurately delivered feedback is the key to the growth witnessed from the WCIA-1 video to the WCIA-7 video. Learning to develop beneficial feedback requires the mental shift I mentioned earlier in this chapter, particularly the part about redefining teaching. This new definition places my primary role of providing guidance for students during feedback days. Although it may appear that an inordinate number of contact minutes are devoted to feedback discussions, the quality of student-student interactions and the time students spend thinking about science both soar because of it. This attention to feedback is the key to progress that this classroom community has made.

The feedback for WCIA-7 wasn't filmed, but it would have been very similar to the outline of the feedback given for WCIA-1. The class, though, was more involved in the discussion and fewer hints were given.

At this point, I give a great many journal reflection questions at the end of any class activity. After the seventh WCI assessment, I asked students to respond to the following questions in their journals:

- What went well?
- What didn't go so well?
- What will you do to improve for next time?
- What should the class do to improve for next time?
- Favorite quote?

Then we talked about it. In this case, they shared the thoughts that I had. I brought up more of the positive interactions than they remembered, and they understood why those things would be mentioned. For example, I talked about how the majority of students were involved in the problem-solving process, both in groups and as a class. And I mentioned how persistent the class was at understanding the content, using Sandy, Michelle, and Adam as wonderful teacher examples.

I asked how the class would have handled the situation had they run out of time and not had a chance to explain things in as much detail. They said they had a website on which they share information outside of class. That detail made it complete; they improved in every area mentioned from WCIA-1 to WCIA-7. Because they had met my expectations, I would have to add some new twists next time.

After this WCI assessment, I had the class renominate and vote on class managers. I like to give my classes the opportunity to change things around from time to time. This class was developing so well during the first semester that I didn't mention it until now. It ended up that the class voted for Jack and Kim to continue to facilitate future WCI assessments and projects.

RESEARCHER'S ANALYSIS—WCIA VIDEO CASES

In this chapter, I discuss three teaching strategies that are well illustrated in the WCIA video cases. Joan effectively uses each of these three strategies to change the participant structure ("who can say what, to whom, and when" [Anon. 2004, p. 389]) that exists in her classroom.

Teaching Strategy 4—Putting the Students in Charge

The first strategy that Joan uses is powerfully demonstrated in the WCIA-1A and WCIA-7 video cases; it occurs when Joan disrupts the traditional classroom structure by putting the students in charge. When she transfers this authority to her students, they become responsible for creating the participant structure that exists in the classroom. Before I further discuss this teaching strategy, which I consider to be the most important one of all the strategies that I will present in the entire book, I want to digress with a bit of history about its development.

Back in 1994, Joan and I began experimenting with putting the students in charge during the year that we taught together. Our experimentation led to the development of several classroom activities that were successful in getting the students to willingly take charge. One of these activities is the short WCI assessment that has been presented twice in this chapter. Another is the lengthier, more complex WCI project you will observe in the next two chapters. Ever since we first began placing our students in charge in our classrooms, the strategy has deeply shaped both of our teaching practices. It is so much a part of my current practice that I cannot imagine teaching without it. In retrospect, the idea of putting the students in charge seems an obvious one; and nowadays, in constructivist parlance, this phrase is almost a cliché. Figuring out how to change the structure of the classroom, however, so that students will willingly, collectively, and constructively take charge of the classroom is not a simple task. The teacher must have a clear understanding of why it is important to put the students in charge and what will be accomplished in doing so. The teacher must be willing to deal with some of the chaos that comes along with letting students make decisions. The teacher must be willing to experiment with pedagogical skills in the classroom. The teacher must also be comfortable with breaking away from the traditional classroom structure that plays out in most high school classrooms. As you have observed in the video cases in this chapter, Joan is very successful at getting her students to take charge. She has figured out how to structure her classroom and enact pedagogy that encourages her students to take charge.

Earlier in this chapter, Joan discussed the mental shift that enabled her to transform her classroom to one that was truly student centered. I made a similar mental shift; for me, however, the shift began about 25 years ago when I was a high school student. My chemistry teacher, Mr. Pasero, provided me with an early experience of what a student-centered classroom felt like. I still hold in my mind the heady, intriguing times when he would turn the classroom over to us. For example, when Mr. Pasero knew that we did not understand a given chemistry concept, he would say, "I am going to be quiet for the next 20 minutes. During that time, I want to hear you talk to each other about _____. I want you all to try to come to a better understanding." He would then sit back and wait. There was perhaps a minute or two of uncomfortable silence, but one student would always begin and the discussion would continue without our teacher's voice or guidance.

Fortunately, I entered the teaching profession with this image of a student-centered classroom in my mind. Along with the help of Joan's amazing mentorship and what I had learned in my teacher education classes, this image provided me with a foundation upon which I could build a student-centered teaching practice. After my first few months as a first-year high school chemistry teacher in a science department that espoused a traditional curriculum, I remember being deeply troubled by the classroom practice in which my students and I were engaged. I was exhausted by being in charge of everything. Although I knew it was my job to structure the learning experiences for my students, it seemed they were passively jumping through the hoops that I had set up for them, especially in terms of the time that we spent in lab. Whenever we did an experiment, I seemed to be the only person in the room who was making the intellectual decisions. I determined what equipment was needed, what procedure would be used, what data need to be recorded, what type of data table to use, and how to interpret the resulting data. Having worked for several years as a chemical engineer, I found a huge mismatch between the school science that my students were experiencing and the scientific work that I had experienced. Recognizing this mismatch gave me the momentum I needed to break away from the traditional curriculum and move toward a teaching approach that pushed my students to be engaged intellectually in all the processes that revolved around experimental lab work. It pushed me to put my students in charge of the classroom.

Luckily, Joan was my mentor at the time and she had the necessary teaching experience and strong understanding of pedagogy to make such things happen. Since then, Joan and I have continued to develop particular techniques that help with the mechanics of getting the students to truly take charge. In the video cases of this chapter, you have seen the cumulative result of more than a decade's worth of Joan's work in refining the teaching strategy of putting the students in charge of the classroom.

Now that I have discussed some of the history behind the development of the teaching strategy of putting the students in charge, I return to the context of the WCIA video cases in which you observed this strategy. Interestingly, when Joan puts her students in charge of the classroom for the first time, she does so with only a few words. She tells the students, "This is your class test. Go." By telling the students that it is a test, most of the students, especially those who care about their grades, take it seriously. Also, when she says that it is a "class" test, she implies that the whole class needs to work on it. Indeed, as you observed in the WCIA-1 video, sometimes every student runs up to the front desk. And because Joan cleverly identifies it as a test, the students easily accept the idea she will not help them solve the test's problems and will not offer much extra information. The years of conditioning that results from taking individual tests puts the students into a mindset in which they easily buy into this new concept of the "class test" (i.e., WCI assessment).

From the time that the students run to the desk to the end of the first WCI assessment, there are very few teacher-student interactions. Instead, student-student interactions dominate. When you simply look at the verbal transcript of the WCIA-1A video case, it is apparent that the students are the ones who are doing the talking. During the entire first WCI assessments, there are only seven teacher-student interactions that occur. These seven interactions collectively last for less than 1 minute of the 20 minutes allotted for the entire assessment. The high ratio of student-student interactions to teacher-student interactions that occurs in the WCI assessment is the inverse of what happens in the traditional lecture and discussion participant structure.

On average, high school chemistry teachers in the United States devote about 41% of their instructional time to whole-class lecture and discussion in which vertical, formal, and dyadic interactions occur between the teacher and students (Smith 2002). Joan also lectures to her students, but she devotes only 15% of her instructional time to this teaching strategy (see chapter 6 for further details). The 26% time difference between Joan and the average chemistry teacher frees Joan to set up WCI assessments and projects that allow her students to engage in substantial horizontal interactions with their peers. Approximately 5% of her instructional time is spent on WCI assessments and 34% on WCI projects.

From the first to the seventh WCI assessments, the number of teacher-students interactions decreases from seven to two. This decrease reflects just how self-sufficient the class has become by February. The students can now collectively work on solving a problem for 20 to 30 minutes without interacting much with their teacher. This decrease may also reflect that the students have gotten used to the idea that, during a WCI assessment, Joan would not provide information that they should be able to determine on their own. For example, in the first WCI assessment, Joan does not answer Robert's question:

[06:15]—WCIA-1A

Robert: Can't we like just have like an extra milliliter be displaced into the graduated cylinder and just pour out the rest if it goes over 15?

Ms. G.:   I can't answer your question.

In the above interaction, Robert is asking about a parameter of the WCI assessment. Joan does not answer his question because the parameters are clearly laid out in the cover sheet provided for the whole class. For Robert, the problem is that he has probably not seen this cover sheet—or no one in the class has taken the time to inform the entire class about these parameters. There is another time during the first WCI assessment when Joan chooses not to respond:

[09:41]—WCIA-1A

Angie: Wait, are you sure we put ethanol down the drain? Ms. Gallagher, how do we dispose of ethanol?

Ms. G.:   [no answer]

In this instance, Joan does not respond because her students have already worked with ethanol in the laboratory and should have the disposal information already written in their journals. In the two interactions above, Joan is trying to wean her students from being dependent upon her for information. She wants them to rely on each other, especially when it comes to information that is readily available or already provided.

In the seventh WCI assessment, there is one teacher-student interaction similar to the two interactions discussed above. For me, this interaction is quite amusing to watch because it shows how conditioned the class has become to realizing that a nonresponse from Joan means that they already have the information at their fingertips.

[01:03]—WCIA-7

Jack: Do we know how much time we get?

Ms. G.:   Uh-hum.

[Jack processes this response for several seconds and then returns to the front of the room]

Kim: Um, do you know our time limit?

Jack: Uh, we know.
Kim: Huh?
Jack: [to Ms. G.] What's our time limit?
Ms. G.:   [no response]
Dan: What's that blank overturned piece of paper?
[This piece of paper contains information about the time limit.]
Kim: Ah, excellent.
Jack: Ooooh. Very nice.

Besides getting her students to become self-sufficient as a classroom community, Joan uses the strategy of putting the students in charge to assess their current level of collaborative skills, especially during the first WCI assessment. After she conducts this assessment, Joan can then engage the class in a genuine discussion about the quality of its performance in the areas of community, safety, and accuracy as she did in the WCIA-1B video case. Rather than telling the students how they should act during a WCI assessment, she lets them work out their own method. Then when they reflect upon their work, they can focus on the positive and what could be improved. Without the perspective of what didn't go so well, the students wouldn't have a reason for (or see the relevance of) listening to ideas on how to best collaborate as a whole class. For example, when Joan asks how the students could have improved the community's work in the first WCI assessment, Jack suggests the class could have gotten "in a circle and have someone lead…like get in front of the classroom talking to everybody." Later, the students are receptive to Jack's suggestion, evidenced by their enthusiasm to Joan's idea of electing class managers. The students recognize the value of this idea because they experienced the chaos that resulted when there were no designated managers. This cycle of being put in charge, reflecting upon the experience, and receiving feedback repeats itself throughout the school year in each and every WCI assessment and project. The cycle helps the students understand why Joan puts them in charge. They see the point—each time they are placed in charge, they get the chance to apply the most recent feedback and improve their community's performance.

Teaching Strategy 5—Structuring the WCI Classroom Environment

After the first attempt the students make at working together as a class, Joan engages them in a feedback session that lasts for almost 50 minutes. As you saw in WCIA-1B, she asks her students to reflect on what went well and what could be improved. She guides this discussion and points out any mismatches between their reflections and her assessment of how they performed. Then Joan builds upon the students' ideas and thoughts by providing them with feedback in a presentation that she has prepared in advance. In this presentation, she incorporates a teaching strategy that directly affects the participant structure that will play out in future WCI assessments and projects. In using this strategy, Joan explicitly outlines a classroom structure she expects her students to utilize. She offers the idea of the classroom managers. She gives them choice in picking who the class managers are, but not if they are going to have them. She then provides a clear framework for how they should structure their work in the next WCI assessment. The key items are in boldface type.

[22:10]—WCIA-1B

Ms. G: So, now that we know who the class managers are going to be, when I might come up and give you...here's your class assessment or here's today's challenge and I walk away....here's a suggestion of how you might function for the first couple of times until there's more details to work out. OK?

Read the entire cover sheet. So one of the managers will pick up whatever it is, the piece of paper or whatever it is, and read it out loud to the class. Of course, if there's an attached overhead, it would be great to show the class as well, but all of the information will be on the cover sheet, not on the overhead. So you want to make sure that cover sheet is read out loud to the class so everyone knows. The answers to most of the initial questions you hear are answered on that sheet. What are we allowed to use? How much time do we have? Where are the materials that we're supposed to be using? All of those types of things would be answered on that cover sheet. So, one of the managers, make sure you read that cover sheet out loud to the class first.

Then, everyone shut up. Everyone sitting and looking at the problem that's on the overhead or thinking about what was just read to you, keep quiet and process it. Be thinking to yourself, "What do I know about this? How can I contribute to getting a good response to that challenge? Oh, I know where I read something in the book. I'm going to get my book out and open it up to that." Or whatever. You're processing the question individually so that you can then contribute to the group. Now a lot of people hadn't yet been given the opportunity to absorb the challenge you were supposed to do last time and that's why a lot of those questions were still going on at the end. So, during the time while everyone else is thinking, the two managers up front are organizing, "Okay, based on the way this is asked, maybe it would make sense for all of us to break up into our six groups, answer these six questions individually, and then come back and talk as a class," or "It's one lab question. We should get everyone's information from each variable and then blah blah blah." So the managers for these first 60 seconds are thinking about, together, how should we organize, what would make sense. So it's a really good idea to give your managers a minute or two. And you might think that that's just an eternity when you're sitting there, but just keep quiet the whole time so that they can actually think about what makes the most sense. And that you guys can process the question.

Then you'll plan as a class. "Here's the plan that we came up with. Any suggestions, comments, or whatever?"

And then you execute your plan. You make it happen.

And then you reconvene at the end. You leave time so that you can come back together and talk to one another about the responses you got individually or what happened in lab. Someone who was back there could actually explain it to the class. Or if you're drawing the pictures for the class, you could show it to everyone. Okay? Now if you don't have time to reconvene at the end, then you need to come...figure out some other method for communicating outside of class what went on. Okay? So somehow everyone in the room needs to know what the responses were to every question, even if you don't have that time at the end. So turn in the product on time at all costs.

In this lengthy description, Joan provides a structure for the WCI environment. She does not let the students take a trial-and-error approach to figuring out how best to structure the classroom environment. Instead she provides a framework that she expects the students to utilize and build upon. Although the framework will not guide her students through every eventuality or snafu they encounter, it provides them with a basic structure to follow. You have seen how the students apply this structure in the WCIA-7 video case, and you will see how they also apply it in the two multiple-day WCI projects in chapters 4 and 5.

Teaching Strategy 6—Holding Every Student Accountable

One of the main messages in Joan's feedback is that every student should be involved in some way during WCI assessments. She expects that every student should be aware of what's happening. She also expects that every student should end up with a similar understanding of the reasoning behind the class's actions and the chemistry concepts involved in those actions. These expectations form the basis of the third and final teaching strategy that I discuss in this chapter. Like the last two strategies, Joan's expectation that every student should be held accountable has implications for the participant structure that will develop when the students are in charge of the classroom.

When Joan uses this teaching strategy by describing her expectations for the class's work, she peppers many of her statements with "everyone in the room." In the WCIA-1B video case alone, Joan does this at least 10 times. Five example statements with the phrase "everyone in the room" are shown below:

1. Was there enough discussion before and after so that everyone in the room is confident that, if I walked in today and put one of you on the spot, could you do it?
2. So somehow everyone in the room needs to know what the responses were to every question, even if you don't have that time at the end.
3. You should be talking to one another so that everyone in the room understands the material.
4. Could everyone in the room do those models or is it just a select few?
5. If everyone in the room isn't aware of that, that's bad.

In these example statements, Joan conveys the message that she holds every student accountable for the class's work. She expects the class to ensure that every student contributes to the work and understands what the class actually did. As you will see in chapter 6, the students believe that these expectations were instrumental in helping them gain a set of collaborative skills that would be useful in the future.

Interestingly, in the WCIA-1B video case, when Joan asks the students how they did in meeting her expectations of working as a community in which everyone participates and understands, three students suggest that the class did a fairly good job and made an effort to include everyone.

[09:57]—WCIA-1B

Lynn: Well, we had like people standing in the back, watching what was going on, and then the people in lab and then we were like communicating with them, and then there were like seven or eight people in the front like looking at the directions and drawing the particulate picture. So we got it done. Like somebody in the back would always be saying like, "Who's drawing?" or whatever and we'd say, "Oh, they're in the front drawing."

Ms. G.:   Uh-hum.

Lynn: So we knew what was going on, but I don't know if we like could have done better.

Kim: Well, I think that we were able to include a lot of people into it. Like we would switch off the goggles a lot of the time, but I don't think that we discussed it enough at the very end. We did discuss it, but I don't think that everybody was paying attention.

Ms. G.: What about at the beginning?

Kim: The beginning, I think we did...we were trying to organize it, 'cause it was kind of chaotic 'cause there were only a few goggles.

Ms. G.: Uh-hum.

Kim: So we had to decide who was going to go back there and I think that turned out really well in our attempt to organize from there.

Ms. G.: Okay. Yeah.

Angie: I thought we did a really good job of making sure like everyone agreed. Even though maybe not, well, like...when we finally decided like the amounts of sodium bicarbonate we were going to use...we made sure like does anyone have a problem? Does anybody have any other suggestions? So we like made sure that it wasn't just one person who decided and then like just did the experiment.

Ms. G.: Okay.

In the above exchange, Joan responds to each of the students' thoughts with a simple "uh-hum" or "okay." Even though Joan may not wholeheartedly agree with these students' perspectives, she listens to what they have to say and gains a sense of what they are thinking. After this exchange, Joan shifts the discussion from the positives that occurred to things that might be improved. Jack and Frank then offer the idea that the class should chill, relax, and develop a plan at the beginning of the WCI assessment. Joan agrees and then pushes the class further. She points out that everyone was not involved in the WCI assessment. Several of the more vocal students resist this notion, but then relent after Joan asks a set of pointed questions that drive home her point that not everyone was fully aware of what happened in the first WCI assessment.

[13:25]—WCIA-1B

Ms. G.: So if you didn't get a chance to actually put the goggles on and see what was back there, did anyone tell you what was back there?

Dan: Well, I don't necessarily think that you needed to be up at the table to know. I mean we did it...or…and you could see...

Ms. G.: So if I asked everyone right now to write down what was at that lab table, could everyone in this room do it?

Jack: We'd basically get everything right.

Dan: I think that most people who paid attention during their...

Ms. G.: Did someone communicate what equipment was back there to the rest of the class?

Students: No.

Jack: No. We thought it was almost implied 'cause we did the lab earlier.

Ms. G.: Yeah, bad assumption.

Jack: Yeah, bad assumption.

Ms. G.: Bad assumption.

In this chapter I have discussed three teaching strategies that help shape the participant structure that develops as the students work collectively in WCI assessments. Throughout the school year, Joan continued to draw upon these three teaching strategies as she challenged her students to work together and complete tasks that are much more complex than those found in the short WCI assessments you observed in the WCIA video cases. In the next chapter, you will see how Joan's students use what they have learned from these teaching strategies in the first WCI assessment. You will observe how these students apply their new knowledge in setting up a participant structure during a multiday WCI project for which they are put in charge.

REFERENCES

[Anon]. 2004. Introduction to special issue: Investigating participant structures in the context of science instruction. *Cognition and Instruction* 22 (4): 389–392.

Bolos, J. A., and D. Smithenry. 1996. Chemistry incorporated. *The Science Teacher* 63 (7): 48–52.

Flinn Scientific. 2005. *Flinn scientific chemical & biological catalog reference manual.* Batavia, IL: Flinn Scientific.

Gallagher-Bolos, J. A., and D. W. Smithenry. 2004. *Teaching inquiry-based chemistry: Creating student-led scientific communities.* Portsmouth, NH: Heinemann.

Gallagher-Bolos, J. A., and D. W. Smithenry. 2008. Whole-class inquiry assessments. *The Science Teacher* (75) 6: 39–44.

Smith, P. S. 2002. *2000 National survey of science and mathematics education: Status of high school chemistry teachers.* Chapel Hill, NC: Horizon Research.

Zumdahl, S. S. 2003. *Introductory chemistry, fifth edition.* Boston: Houghton-Mifflin.

Chapter 4
WCI Project 2— CanCo

It is October, and we are well into the school year with an established community-oriented classroom. I finally know my students' names. I've read my students' journals a couple of times, and they describe a positive, fun environment. Students say they enjoy coming to class even though the content is challenging. They benefit from working with one another. I must keep in mind, however, that the class is still at the very beginning stages of reaching our goal of becoming an independent community of scientists, one that requires little to no intervention from the teacher. Evidence of the need for continued guidance and feedback will emerge during the student presentations shown in the videos in this chapter. This chapter's project will be the class's first opportunity to use the scaffolding I provided last month, described in the project in chapter 2, Chemistry Concoctions. I am anxious, and the students, I must say, are blissfully ignorant about what is going to happen. I know they're prepared; but they don't realize it yet.

To recap: At this point in the year, my students have experienced two whole-class, investigative activities. They've done one WCI project (Chemistry Concoctions) and one WCI assessment. I walked them through the Chemistry Concoctions WCI Project by helping them do the initial activity, discuss variables, develop a control, and prepare to collect data. Students then split into six lab groups, and each group tested one variable. Finally, they presented their conclusions about how each variable affected the outcome of the lab. I then gave them a class challenge in the first WCI assessment, which required the application of their findings from the Chemistry Concoctions WCI Project. The feedback they received from these two whole-class activities was meant to better prepare them for their next class challenges in Unit II—Gases.

Unit II is a 14-day unit, which, as mentioned, occurred during October. The focus of this chapter is on discussing the CanCo WCI Project that I implemented during days 3, 4, and 5 of Unit II. I begin by describing the first two days of this unit to provide background on the students' experiences before beginning the CanCo WCI Project. Here's what happened in Unit II.

UNIT II—DAY 1

On Day 1, we first conclude Unit I. I give the students feedback from all three parts of their Unit I test, including the WCI assessment. Then we transition into Unit II. I give students the handout shown in Figure 4.1, and they work in their collaborative work groups on answering these questions. There are six stations set up in the back of the room; students can spend about 12 minutes at each station. This takes us to the end of the period; we need part of Day 2 to finish.

As part of the planning process for the CanCo WCI Project, I give students a homework assignment of bringing in 20 clean, dry, uncrushed, pop cans. I assign this on Day 1 of the unit to ensure that enough cans

Figure 4.1

Handout for Unit II Introductory Workshop

Unit II Introductory Workshop
Gas Particles ~ Where are they? What are they doing?

Draw particulate level pictures for each of the following and use your current knowledge to explain what happens to the gas particles.

1. a. Feel the balloon and explain what keeps the balloon from collapsing. Draw a picture.
    b. What would happen to the balloon if it were 30 degrees colder? Draw a new picture.
2. Draw a picture of the "Do Not Open" 2 L bottle. Show where there are gas particles in the 2 L and surrounding the 2 L. Then, remove the lid. Draw a new picture and explain what happened.
3. Fill the jar with water. (It must be completely filled with water!). Then take a dry note card and place it on top of the jar. Holding the notecard, carefully flip the jar over. Slowly let go of the notecard. Draw a picture & explain what happens.
4. Push the 2 L bottle and observe what happens to the test tube inside. Draw a picture and explain what happens.
5. Model the following scenarios.
    a. Explain what happens to the gas particles inside an aerosol can when it is put into a fire and explodes. (You can't actually do this one!) Draw a before and after picture.
    b. A tennis ball that is made for high altitudes is different than a ball made for lower altitudes in order to obtain the same "hardness." Draw a picture showing the differences between the two types of balls.
6. Pour yourself a small drink. Place one straw outside the glass and one straw inside the glass. Place the other end of both straws in your mouth and drink. Explain your observations in words and pictures. (Finish drinking your drink, one per student. And then clean up!)

90

will be available for the start of the CanCo WCI Project, which begins on Day 3. I will remind them again at the end of the next class. Students will ask what the pop cans are for, but I will keep it a mystery.

UNIT II—DAY 2

On Day 2, I give the students the time needed to finish their stations.

I conclude by asking, "How many feel they have an accurate model to represent at least 50% of the scenarios described on your workshop?"

Most hands are raised.

"How about 75%?"

Some hands drop.

"100%?"

A few hands are left.

"Okay, write yourself a note to revisit these drawings on Day 6 of Unit II. See if you are able to correct or modify what you've recorded based on what you know by Day 6."

I then do an activity that helps the students picture a gas sample. We role-play being a gas and decide how temperature, volume, and number of particles affect the pressure of a gas sample. The handout for this activity is shown in Figure 4.2. This brings us through Day 2.

CANCO WCI PROJECT— DAY 1, PART 1

Teacher's Introduction—CANCO-1A

During the third day of Unit II, I make sure that the lab is ready for the CanCo WCI Project. Students won't get thoroughly into the project today, but I want things set up for them, just in case. Preparation is simple. Students are responsible for bringing in the cans. I put out one hot plate and one bin of water per lab table. I also put out the supply of beaker tongs, stopwatches, 10 mL graduated cylinders, 100 mL graduated cylinders, and 500 mL graduated cylinders. Students may ask for more equipment while doing the lab, but these are the basics that are needed.

As you will see in the CANCO-1A video, the third day shows me first reviewing our Day 2 Human Gas Particle activity. Next we review the definitions of P, V, T, and n. I then perform a demo in which I add hot water to an empty 2 L bottle, dump the water out, and cap the

Figure 4.2

Handout for the Human Gas Particle Activity

Human Gas Particle Activity

*Hmmmmmmm....I see humans role-playing as particles in lots of empty space...No wait--**It's a GAS!!***

Rules for role-playing as a particle:
1. Always walk in a straight line.
2. Stay within the boundaries of the box.
3. When you collide with a wall or another person, turn and walk in another direction.
4. Take one step for every "click" you hear.
5. When walking, the front foot's heel should be in line with the back foot's toe. TAKE BABY STEPS.
6. If you collide with a friend, you may not hold hands and walk together.
7. If you are approaching someone you do not know, do not change your direction before running into them.
8. The collisions should be "friendly". No rough play!! (The consequence? I bring your temperature down to absolute zero!!!!)
9. Count the number of times you collide with a wall (collisions between two people do not count!).
10. In a large open space such as a gymnasium or the hallway....
    You will become part of a collection of particles (a gas) and we'll test how changes in temperature, volume, and number of particles affect the pressure of the collection of particles.

- **Pre-Activity Questions:** How will we measure temperature, volume, number of particles, and pressure?

- **Post-Activity Discussion:** COPY DOWN THE DATA WE GATHERED...

- **Post-Activity Questions:**
    1. Come up with a hypothesis that describes the relationship between
        a. temperature and pressure.
        b. volume and pressure.
        c. number of particles in the sample and pressure.
    2. Which scenarios/trials of your data did you look at in order to formulate each hypothesis in question #1?
    3. What condition(s) must be kept constant in order for each hypothesis to hold true?
    4. Using your mind and/or your text, what relationship exists between T and V if n and P are held constant?

bottle. The students notice that the bottle begins to collapse on its own within one minute. Using this demo, I go through an example three-series particulate-level drawing that models what happens over time to the gas sample (air) in our 2 L bottle. I give the students an opportunity to process this information through a pair-share activity. Once I've assessed that the students are comfortable with modeling gas behavior, I move on to introducing the CanCo WCI Project.

I step into the prep room for a moment, throw on my tie-dyed lab coat and then reappear as "Ms. Nac," the CanCo company chemist. I am wearing a name tag so the students can easily see that I have changed roles. Because I have role-played a character before, they are not completely surprised by my "new" name. It will be a new experience for them, however, to have the teacher "absent" for a day and a half. I introduce myself to the students and hand out the project sheet shown in Figure 4.3. I read through the first three paragraphs and say, "And you should make sure to read the bottom of this sheet as it contains some important information that will help you and your company succeed."

After reading the project sheet—and in character as Ms. Nac—I perform two demos that serve as the foundation for the project. To the astute student, these demos are illustrating the control. Ms. Nac does not freely offer any information to the students. She says she will answer any questions the students have about the demos. If they want to know something, they must formulate a question and ask.

Ms. Nac places an empty can on a hot plate, heats it for two minutes, flips it into a water bath and then raises the can to show that a great deal of water falls out. (The can is not crushed.) She then puts 10 mL of water in a can, heats it for two minutes, flips it into the water bath, and then lifts the very crushed can up to show water falling out. Students ask a series of questions throughout these demos. Some example questions are:

- What is the setting of the hot plate?
- What is the temperature of the water bath?
- How much water did you place in the second can?
- How long did you heat each can?
- How exactly did you flip the can?

Ms. Nac then shows a short PowerPoint presentation that emphasizes what the company (class) must do, including the products that will be expected on the third day of the project. These products include a PowerPoint presentation that answers the questions on the project sheet and a formal lab report for any testing the company has performed to arrive at a conclusion about maximum can crushing. She reminds the company that two other companies are competing for the same contract.

Figure 4.3

CanCo WCI Project Sheet

CanCo™
Project Sheet

CanCo™ Position: CanCo™ is looking to hire a scientific community that can prove that it is able to effectively and efficiently solve our technical research problems. You can prove your community's worth by solving the problem outlined below and giving a presentation to our company representative on the assigned deadline. We will supply one of our company's chemists to act as a consultant while you perform your experiments. She will only help when asked a question. She may not be able to answer all questions, but she will try.

CanCo™ Technical Problem: CanCo™ wants to combine the cleaning and crushing operations at our plant. We have found that we can both clean and crush a can by putting some water into it, heating it, and turning the can into a bath of tap water. We are looking to install a robotics system that would do this operation, but we need to know the following:
1. What variables affect the amount of can crush (i.e., the initial can volume minus final can volume)?
2. How do each of the variables listed in #1 affect the amount of can crush?
3. What conditions should we set for the process to obtain the maximum crush?
4. Is the process (with your proposed conditions from #3) reliable enough to always give at least 75% volume crush on all cans? Provide enough data to support your claim.

Your Quality Presentation: Due to the representative's limited time, your community's presentation of results will be limited to a **maximum** of fifteen minutes on _____ (at the beginning of your class period). Your presentation needs to concisely answer the four questions outlined above (think about "effective communication" when preparing). On this date, please provide a hard copy of your community's presentation and a hard copy of your community's proposal (report) for Dr. McMurry, CanCo's company representative. Your community will be competing against _____ other companies for our future business.

Chemistry Class Stuff—Areas of Assessment
Community-Based
1. Community Effort—Working constructively and efficiently together toward accomplishing goals? Focus on Safety?
2. Community Report (not the hard copy of the presentation, but an acutal lab report...) Reliability of data (consistent? Accurate? Precise?) Completion of each task requested by representative?
3. Presentation Quality (ranked against other communities)—remember this is a competition! Make it impressive!

Individual-Based
1. Role-Play (In character? Constructive use of Class Time? Acting as Constructive Member of Scientific Community?)
2. Personal Understanding of Collected Data and Community's Presentation of Results--Quiz later

Other: You'll have the lab at your disposal for almost two days. You can ask Ms. Nac, the company chemist, about anything concerning the representative's requests and the company's future robotics operation using the "heating with water" crushing method. You are in charge of this project. Good planning!

(These are my two other chemistry classes.) The company that gives the best presentation and submits the best report will win the contract with CanCo. The company has the rest of this class period, about 25 minutes, to plan. It has the entire next class, 60 minutes, to collect data and plan its presentation and lab report for the following class. With that, Ms. Nac steps aside and turns the class over to the students. Ms. Nac walks to the back of the room to see (and record) what happens next.

CANCO WCI PROJECT— DAY 1, PART 2—PLANNING

Video—Watch the CANCO-1A video on the DVD labeled "Video Cases for Chapters 4–5." This video takes the first 60 minutes of class and compresses them into 5 minutes so that you can visualize what was described.

Teacher's Introduction—CANCO-1B

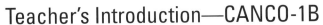

As soon as I head to the back of the room—still role-playing as Ms. Nac—I'm eager to see what happens. Based on the feedback my students received from their last WCI project, Chemistry Concoctions, and from their first WCI assessment, I know that they've received a number of hints on how to accomplish the outlined tasks. Below is a list of ideas discussed during our Unit I feedback sessions as ways to improve the students' ability to solve a challenge as a class. All of these things are important assets to building a self-sufficient, constructive scientific community of learners. I will be looking for improvements from this class in the following areas:

Safety
- Lab cleanup needs to improve. Students should leave the lab in better condition than when they found it.
- Police yourselves. Gentle reminders for wearing goggles, not sitting, and taking off hats.
- Make sure you've looked up and recorded safety information for lab chemicals and/or equipment.

Accuracy
- Does data analysis make sense? Do graphs tell a story?
- Decide whether you need to design a control/variable test or simply test a sample.
- Before conducting an experiment, make sure a procedure is outlined and data tables are prepared.
- Be able to use new class knowledge and successfully accomplish a class challenge.

Community
- Two elected class managers will stand up and facilitate discussions. (This was discussed in chapter 3.)

- Once managers stand up, there will be an immediate 30 to 60 seconds of silence so the managers can determine an organizational scheme.
- Raise hands to talk with one another. Listen when others are speaking.
- Everyone will know what's going on. The plan will be clearly communicated.
- There will be a time set to reconvene at the end of class and talk about what the class accomplished during the day.

Before you view the next video clip, showing the students planning their strategy, I'd like to point out a couple of things. In character as Ms. Nac, I tell the students that they need to review safety rules for the use of hot plates before heading into lab. When Kim, one of the newly elected class managers (see chapter 3), stands up to help facilitate class discussion, she has already found this information in her class safety contract. When she refers to "numbers 33 and 34" to the class, she is reading the two items in the safety contract that relate to the hot-plate safety information.

You might notice a clipboard being passed around the room. The students have decided they need a phone list for the class so they can contact one another outside of class, and this clipboard contains that phone list in the making.

Other than that, the focus of the class is on preparing to do the lab in the next class period. Their discussion concentrates on deciding their plan of attack.

Video—Watch the CANCO-1B video on the DVD labeled "Video Cases for Chapters 4–5." This video takes the last 25 minutes of class and compresses them into 10 minutes so that you can visualize the students planning the CanCo WCI Project on their own.

Teacher's Analysis—CANCO-1B

A typical response to watching this chaotic group of students initiating such a massive project on their own might be, "What was that?" Or a more detailed reaction might include "Okay, I watched the first set of video cases (Chemistry Concoctions), and things went pretty smoothly. I knew what was supposed to happen because you were guiding everything. But the start of this project looks completely chaotic. What was I supposed to be focusing on?"

Herein lies part of the major mental shift required to implement WCI projects. It takes practice and patience to learn to focus on the incredible triumphs rather than on some of the obvious frustrations taking place in the room. To give you some insight, the first year I started this project, I imagined that, after I handed over the reins to the class managers for the CanCo WCI Project, the class would have accomplished a minimum of the following things by the end of this first day: safety information researched and recorded, variables to test chosen and assigned, a control developed for all to use, procedure and data tables prepared for next class for each unique variable to be tested, and homework assigned of reviewing the project sheets and bringing in suggestions for further class improvement. I had thought they might even get some control testing done and information about who would do what with regard to the products. After all, these are the things they accomplished while working under my guidance in the Chemistry Concoctions WCI Project, right? So why wouldn't they use that model as they progressed?

More important, I was sure everyone would be on task. Students would be having fun, challenging one another with a positive tone and all would be contributing. As you just observed, even after all these years, the vision is far from reality. What has happened over the years, however, is that I've realized that the things that do happen in these student-led whole-class activities are far better than my dream, even during their first time through. It's real. And they own the experience.

I still have to remind myself continually to use patience to get my students to the point at which constructive flow and organized implementation occur. There are both community and content-focused skills for them to learn. The key for me is to keep in mind that my goal is to get the students to function as closely as possible to the ideal classroom by the end of the year, not instantaneously. I need to move them one step at a time. This is, after all, a mental shift for them as well.

After watching the video, I have mixed emotions. I am reminded of how I felt during this particular class and see how some things went well and some things didn't.

For this first project day, this class uses some of the feedback from Unit I to improve their community. As you can see in the video, the managers stand up and take over the planning process. This is an immediate improvement from the first WCI assessment (see chapter 3) of total chaos when everyone stood up to "lead" class. But, once the managers stand up to address the class, they unfortunately forget the suggestion of taking a moment to plan things out. They go right into their brainstorming and planning session.

Another positive is that the students remind each other to raise hands if they had a question or contribution. Kim even reins them back in when they get off task or aren't listening to one another. This is shown in the video when Frank and Craig high-five each other during a side conversation. Kim politely reminds them not to have side conversations and to listen to one another during class discussions. There are a number of moments in the video in which you can hear students shushing each other. Although the idea of listening to one another is good, there is a better way to accomplish this than shushing. When this happens during class, I type on my computer that I should teach the students to think of

Kim's voice and Jack's voice as triggers for students to quiet down, just as they do when I start to talk. The note would remind me to mention it during our feedback discussion at the conclusion of the project. That the students were trying hard to listen to one another is a tremendous improvement from their efforts in WCI assessment 1.

There is a point in this 25-minute planning period at which students head to the back of the room to test. I am a bit thrown because there is no clear decision communicated to everybody about what these people are going to do back there. Nor is there a clear assignment about what others in the room ought to be doing while these select few are in the lab. Again, I type myself a note to question this with the class during our feedback discussion.

In character as Ms. Nac, I stay accessible to the students. This class feels comfortable coming up to ask Ms. Nac questions. They ask about ice, soap, and hot plate use. This is a great sign. At least they are willing to dive into the challenge and go along with my character role-playing. This gives them a sense of making the challenge "real."

My greatest frustration, I suppose, is that things in this class do not go as smoothly as my earlier class that day—at least in appearance—in terms of planning and closure. My first period class, 2/3 B, had a very smooth transition into this WCI freedom, at least with regard to planning things as a class. By the end of the first day of the project, 2/3B seemed to be at a point at which everyone in the room was familiar with what was to happen the next class period—control, variable, and data tables determined. The focus class, 4/5 B, shown in the video, is a bit panicked by the end of its class, with people not knowing what was to happen next class. Nor do they seem clear on what happened in lab this class. However, I am more pleased with the enthusiasm of 4/5 B. In addition, 4/5 B has more willing participants. The previous class had a number of people trying to get out of work. This class has people volunteering to help right and left. Obviously, there are unique topics to focus on during feedback for each class, topics that I list in my notes to myself throughout these classes.

Why had I gotten to the point at which I believed this videotaped class was better than my ideal, imaginary class? Because I've seen the story complete itself year after year. And I know it has a positive ending. For starters, the students truly own their experiences. They are beginning a journey that they define, not by simply jumping through teacher-determined hoops. Their growth will be a result of an honest beginning. And they care about the outcome of their work. They experience the world of a realistic scientific community. And they think through the process of being a scientist, a mental activity that will help absorb what they've just learned.

CANCO WCI PROJECT— DAY 2—LAB WORK

Teacher's Introduction—CANCO-2

This second day of the project is the students' data-gathering day for the CanCo WCI Project. When they come to class, the students find they have only 60 minutes (instead of 90 minutes) to collect their data because of an unexpected shortened class schedule. As you will see in the video, the students are responsible for the outcome of this lab. I am still in character as Ms. Nac, the CanCo company chemist. I am accessible to the students, but I don't provide any direction. My role is to provide help with equipment and lab technique. I am also there to help with safety concerns. Being in character is useful because I can then control, under the guise of another person, how much or how little I am willing to tell them.

Recall that on Day 1 of this project, the class came up with variables to test in order to answer the questions on the project sheet and to determine what would give the maximum crush. The five variables this class chose to test are

- the substance in the can,
- the temperature of the water bath,
- the amount of water in the can,
- the level of the hot plate, and
- the time the can is heated.

This class decides to give the sixth group the assignment of testing the control multiple times and to have each of the other five groups testing a variable compare its data to the "control" group's average. This ill-conceived plan of having a separate control group is obviously something that I will address during our feedback discussion.

Be aware as you look at the video that a number of the clips are focused on Group 5. This group is testing how the temperature of the water bath affects the can crush. Also be aware that students are congregating in the front corner of the room at the beginning of the period because they need to sign up for a science departmental test. To stay in my role as Ms. Nac, I tell the students that Ms. Gallagher has given me an announcement about the test, and then I read it. When outside requirements interrupt project plans, I deal with them as quickly as possible to keep class disruption to a minimum.

Here is what happened on the data-gathering day of the CanCo WCI Project.

Teacher's Analysis—CANCO-2

Video—Watch the CAN-CO-2 video on the DVD labeled "Video Cases for Chapters 4–5." This video takes the entire 60-minute class and compresses it into approximately 20 minutes so that you can visualize what was described.

This video is easier to follow than the footage of the students' planning effort in the CANCO-1B video because the students are involved in accomplishing a task. There might still be a few questions on what the teacher's role is while playing a character such as Ms. Nac. My focus while I am role-playing is always to keep track of how the class is improving from the last class challenge in terms of safety, accuracy, and community. So I type myself plenty of notes in preparation for what will be helpful to tell the class during feedback, along with a host of other information that I will share below.

There are times in this video when I seem to have very little contact with the students. Remember that they were told that Ms. Nac would answer questions, not offer information. So I have to force myself to stick to that, at least for the most part. It was very difficult the first time I tried this more than 10 years ago. I had to make sure I followed through; otherwise my students would try to pull me out of character in the future, as well. This piece of my approach has become easy for me over the years because I've seen the benefit of following through. It also makes the project more fun for me. (More details on the utility and impact of role-play are discussed in chapter 6.) Please note that I am paying attention to what the students are doing, but I'm trying to make it appear that I'm not. I am constantly writing down quotes from the students; information about safety, accuracy, and community; and things I want to share with them after the completion of the project.

This role-playing piece requires practice and patience, just like everything else. Playing a character, however, also lends itself to altering my approach to a given project from year to year. I have changed the level of contact I am willing to have while in character with my students. I have changed my character to help students more with planning by offering suggestions or asking guiding questions—for instance in a lower-level class or toward the beginning of the year. Sometimes I have allowed students to ask only a given number of questions within a class period—for instance, in an advanced class or further along in the year. You can play with the character role in a host of different ways to better suit your teaching style and your classes.

I am very pleased with where the class is at this point in terms of community development. This class period occurs in October, and the students spend an entire 60 minutes implementing a plan they came up with during the previous class meeting and perhaps some outside-of-class discussions. I am there only in character. They are all engaged in this problem for the entire class.

There are moments during the class when students are crowding around Ms. Nac asking lots of questions. This is fun, because it tells me that the students are into the experience. At the beginning of class, Kim asks about using vinegar (acetic acid) as one of the alternative substances in the can. Notice I have to take a moment to make sure I don't answer the question. I then give her the task of determining what vinegar's actual concentration is and what temperature would be considered "safe" when heating vinegar. A reply such as this gives the students even more experience with how much detail goes into designing an experiment.

Ms. Nac answers Debbie's question about how long a pop can should be heated. She then leaves to get ice and salt for Frank's group. Kim thinks Ms. Nac has just disappeared and ignored her question. These brief moments of frustration for the students, of not having me or my character provide immediate feedback, is good experience for them. They learn the value of thinking on their own and depending on one another for help. After returning with the ice, I reflected on this "vinegar" dilemma and how Ms. Nac handled it. I write myself a note to talk with the students about the benefits of being "comfortable with confusion" when working together. We'll talk about this on our feedback day.

During any first student-led WCI project, I like to walk around the room once or twice while students are gathering data. They can tell I'm looking at their journals. This gives some of them the hint that they need to make sure their journals have detailed documentation of their experiences. My looking just briefly at each individual journal reminds my students of the importance of individual accountability. Watching them perform part of the lab reminds them to keep safety a priority. I even hear a couple of students reminding others to put goggles on and to watch out for the hot plate. This is great. They're policing themselves. So even though I'm in character, my presence helps keep them focused. Again, the level of direct contact I decide to have with the students can be changed from class to class, year to year, or level to level. With this class I decided to keep my contact minimal; I think they're picking up on my hints at this point quite well.

Some of my favorite moments during these WCI projects involve the unexpected hurdles the students encounter. When I first started these labs, I remember being frustrated by these hurdles simply because I hadn't planned for them. But then I realized that these are probably the most important learning moments the students will experience. For instance, when Dan comes to tell Ms. Nac that one of his cans was crushed to the point of tearing a hole in it, he says, "When the can crushed, it crushed a hole in itself. So the water's not staying in, so we can't figure out the displacement. Should we retest it or find some way to plug it?" Ms. Nac replies, "That's up to you and your group. Either one of those scenarios is doable. If you decide to do the second one, that's your engineering problem." Then he asks, "So we have to figure out what to plug it with?" Ms. Nac responds in the affirmative, and Dan goes back to his group to tell them the news. This is fabulous. They are experiencing the problems that come about when one is engaged in real lab research. Scientists have these problems, and students need to learn to solve them too. Experiments are typically not scripted and problem free.

Another one of these unexpected experiences occurred during the previous class, 2/3 B. They had too many hot plates plugged into the same outlet, and the fuse blew. Students stood around for a while thinking there was nothing to be done until finally one student said, "The maintenance guys have to know how to fix this." He left the room and found the answer to the problem. Within five minutes, they were up and running again.

In the video you see a clip of Group 5 doing their first can-crush trial. Craig first flips the can over the sink and empties out the hot water and then puts the can into the water bath. The other group members immediately tell him he is doing the procedure wrong. They work through the problem of how to fix their procedure and Craig's next flip succeeds. They're already working together to solve their own problems. More important, they start to rely on teaching each other. Again, I'm amazed, because it's only October, even if this is typical of a class at this point in the year.

I enjoyed watching the Group 5 video clips. The students exhibit a lot of enthusiasm. They're engaged. And most important, they have some conversations about the experiment they're performing. Students are making sure they get the data down, and they are discussing what their results mean. They care about the outcome of their work because they know it is going to be used for a larger purpose. One of the most rewarding moments watching this video was hearing the students bicker about who has to be the representative to leave the lab and talk to the rest of the class. No one wants to leave the lab.

The most disappointing part of watching this video was being reminded that the students had a shortened class period. Scheduling had to be inflexible because Dennis was in town to film my class only during a set period of time. The students felt so much pressure because of the shortened class that they decided to use their day off, a Jewish holiday, to prepare the products for the company representative. I expect my students to put in time outside of class, but I never want class work to interfere with family or cultural celebrations or ceremonies. I also don't want students who make the decision that the holiday comes first feeling stress or guilt. These are two situations that I would typically change, but, because of our schedule, I could not.

These WCI projects have taught me that I need to reflect constantly on how much frustration is in the room. Providing too little guidance could turn the class off and perhaps create mutiny. And providing too much guidance, preventing the students from making any mistakes or answering every question means I won't get them to what I think they could be by the end of the year—a self-sufficient, student-led scientific community. In this particular class with this particular first project, I think things are going well. But I typically assess my accuracy in that assumption during our feedback discussion. Sometimes the things that happen outside class help determine how to proceed. So I tend to wait and find out how the class feels during the feedback session and then adjust my role accordingly for the next WCI project.

I have said that I type notes to myself during these WCI projects. My computer typically has four files open during any student-led activity. One file consists of safety, accuracy, and community information that I want to share with the students after completion of a project. Another is where I keep track of a series of questions that I would like to ask the students after the project is over, as part of their self-reflection piece. A third is where I keep student quotes from all my classes for a specific project. You can view this in the feedback portions in the CHEMCO-1 and CHEMCO-4B footage of the videos.

In the fourth file I keep a journal of events that take place in the room. The text that follows shows you a copy of this last record, the journal of what I observed in the room while role-playing as Ms. Nac on Days 1 and 2. It is in my own version of shorthand, so at times it requires piecing information together. Recall, though, that Day 1 was when the class managers stood up to help plan the lab for CanCo WCI Project. Day 2 was the 60-minute data-gathering day.

There are many reasons for keeping this fourth file. I like to have a reference for what happened; it helps me remember the differences from class to class. It also helps me reflect on which students I'm noticing from project to project. Should my attention be spent elsewhere? Is there a reason the same names keep coming up? How should I address that within my role-play approach? Should I address the situation as the teacher? I do not necessarily read this journal to the class. It's mostly for me. But there have been times when reading portions of it helps the community move forward. Again, experience aids me in these decisions.

Getting a feel for what to record while in character during WCI projects was probably the most challenging mechanical piece for me when I first started out. Remember, I was typing classroom observations, recording feedback ideas so that I wouldn't forget to share them with the students, staying in character when students approached, and deciding how much or how little to tell the students when they approached me. I have gotten quite proficient at this multitasking part of the WCI projects, but it takes practice. It is, though, very rewarding and makes each class unique and fun once you've done it enough.

Teacher's Journal—CANCO-1A

October 10, 2005 (10:25–10:53 a.m.)

Jack and Kim immediately got up in front to help organize.

Kim told everyone to find hot plate info in journals. Jack wrote down info about hot plate on board. But the outlet information was not verbalized…You guys forgot that at the beginning of the year, I mentioned that only 2 hot plates could be plugged in to the same numbered outlet, otherwise you would blow a fuse. Yikes! Let's see what happens.

"Can we use her scenarios as a control and just test variables from there?" Craig asks. Jack replies, "We should do more tests to make sure." Way to go, Craig. Yes, what Ms. Nac did could be your control. But Jack is also correct; you should all do the control again and compare your data to that average.

Kim reminds the class to raise hands so that the discussion goes more smoothly. Excellent! You remembered.

The class then brainstormed variables.

Volume of water in can

Temp of water in bin

Temp of hot plate

Temp of water in can (Chris says to get rid of this one…good)

Substance in can or tub

Length of time on hot plate

Dan asks, "Does testing substances other than water make sense?"

Frank then says, "If you boil ethanol, it could light on fire!"

Hmm….Good things to think about; you certainly want to think through safety before doing anything. Plus, it's good to think through what makes sense and what doesn't. And some of this doesn't make sense!

A discussion took place about the temperature of the water in

104

the can. Did you hear the part about the temperature during boiling? I'm not sure who said it, but that's probably important. Hint! Hint!

Sandy then asks about the final volume…Good question. Did you get an answer?

Groups decided which variables to test.

Tom asks, "What if we plug the can…?"

Frank responds, "No, Tom, that would make it bigger."

The discussion continued regarding keeping particles in the can…I'm not sure some people are convinced one way or the other.

"Let's vote on 4 and 6…" The class votes.

"Well, that vote got us no where!" Jack says disgustedly.

Craig asks if the combination of variables will be tested to see a possibly even greater crush. Good question. Outstanding question. The competitive edge just kicked in.

"How will we know that a variable gets the can clean?" Karen asks…

The control group went back to test.

Mary went back to count the cans.

All of a sudden there are many people standing and working in the back.

Tom asks, "Wait, isn't the control the one with 10 mL?"

Good question. How did the class come to the idea that the 10 mL should be the control? Hmmmm…Looks like Kim changed the control to 10 mL…Does everyone know this?

Kim walked around to each group to check with them to see if they knew what to do. Excellent!

Dan asked what the cans will be used for once they're crushed. Ms. Nac said, "For recycling." Then Dan asked whether or not they should have certain substances in them or not...Ms. Nac told them to look this up on their own.

They then asked for a large beaker. I gave them a 2000 mL beaker.

The information about the hot plates has still not been determined. It's 10:47...

"Oh, gosh. This is so hard!"

You're now trying to figure out how much water to put into the bin.

At 10:50 the class tried to reconvene. Good for you...What do you need to discuss?

The hot plate didn't work for the control group...Hmmm....This is something you should discuss as a class...

Kim asked for information from each group...

Safety:

Desks were moved.

Goggles were put on.

Journals weren't prepared.

Clean-up was poor. (4 100 mL graduated cylinders left out, water on floor and lab tables, 2 cans on middle lab table.)

Teacher's Journal—CANCO-2

October 12, 2005 (10:40–11:40 a.m.)

I made an announcement regarding sophomores registering for a test. Hated doing it, but couldn't help it.

Then Jack made a couple of announcements to the class and told everyone to get busy. Looks like groups knew what they were supposed to be doing. I was asked for soap, coca-cola, salt, ice, thermometers, and stopwatches. Good. At least I know that some members of each group knew what equipment was needed.

I went around to check attendance and to ask what each group was doing.

Group 1 = Kim, Tara, Angie and Lynn = substance in can

Group 2 = Frank, Craig, Nick, Mark and Maria = T of water bath

Group 3 = Chris, Irene, Mary, Rachel, and Mary = Amt. Water in can

Group 4 = Tom, Adam, Karen, and Michelle = T of hot plate

Group 5 = Patrick, Jack, Debbie, Rita = Time on hot plate

Group 6 = Dan, Sandy, Kelly, Robert = Control … ??

"Guys, our can exploded!"*

Large pop from Group 5. "Wow, that was a winner! Let me see that one!"

Ten people around lab table 5…Yikes!

Kim and Jack take a minute to talk about time…when should people finish, what needs to be discussed. Great! Let's see what happens!

Group 1 came up and asked about a hole in the can. That's your engineering challenge. Let's see what you do.

*Safety note: The cans do not explode in this experiment; they implode.

They asked for more time. I told them Friday morning and 4/5 A would work. (A bit of a challenge…purposefully. We'll see what happens…)

At 11:35, there's a bit of a frantic clean-up mode. Journals look incomplete, except a few. Some people have detailed data tables, averages, and % crush already calculated, along with pictures of what they think might be going on. A few journals even have questions to ask the group and to ask me in order to understand the lab better. But so many people have nothing in journals; there are even a few without a journal at all in the back. What is that?

Jack then says, "It's time to wrap up, guys. If you have a representative up in front of the room, you can use the last ten minutes."

Still a bit of heightened intensity…and yet a few seem so calm, almost indifferent.

Description of a final volume being taken—water poured quickly into a LARGE graduated cylinder with water splashing in spots.

Robert and Kelly have a really clean lab table. Wow!

Mary asked if the best-case scenario would be tested by the company representative, or if they should test that as a company. They were told to test it themselves. Good thing to know; that's the type of thing you'll find on your lab sheet.

Jack threw out the idea to use Thursday as a day to get together to work, one person from each group. Good idea. You also didn't make people, particularly those observing the religious holiday, feel badly if they couldn't make it. Good for you.

"I'm presenting. I want to wear a suit!" Frank said…

Mary volunteered to have people work at her house. Great.

"Could you put your name, number, etc. up on the board?" Jack asked.

"We'll need your blood type," Dan adds.

Trying to get organized…

Information recorded on the white board:

Recommended result for each variable

	Variable	Average	What was used
Lynn	Substance in can	83 mL	vinegar
Mary	V of water in can	73 mL	5 mL
Frank	T of water	85.04 mL	Ice water w/ salt 2 L ice, 4 L water, 150 g salt
Michelle	T of plate	198.9 mL	

Things I noticed…

Safety:

Desks were moved.

Goggles were put on.

Journals still weak…This needs improving.

Clean-up was great except lab #5. Thermometer out, salt all over the balance, journal left, and graduated cylinder not replaced. (Without Frank, clean-up is lost!) The rest of the room looked great.

CANCO WCI PROJECT— DAY 3, PART 1— PRESENTATION

Teacher's Introduction—CANCO-3A

This is the day the students present their findings to the CanCo company representative. Remember that the students were given only minimal expectations for the presentation (refer back to the project sheet). Also note that students have not yet had to come up with a class presentation yet; this is their first experience working as a large group without the teacher as their guide. Not only did they plan and implement how to answer the task questions, but they also had to get both a report and a presentation together as a class.

In the video, the class enters the classroom and no adult figure is present. (I am hiding in the prep room dressed in a business suit wearing a name tag that says "Dr. McMurry, CanCo Company Representative.") The class had been told that the representative would be arriving right at the beginning of company (class) time to hear its presentation. Because this is the students' first class presentation, I give them a few extra minutes to get prepared, but I am in the prep room listening to what is happening.

To better understand what happens in the next video (CANCO-3A), here is a brief overview of what you will see. Chronologically, the video shows the students preparing for the representative (Dr. McMurry), greeting her and finding her a place to sit, having technical difficulties, and presenting their information. Then Dr. McMurry asks the students to explain their data and the meaning behind the data. Students finally exhibit a collective sigh of relief after Dr. McMurry leaves. I then return to class as Ms. Gallagher, their teacher, and give them a quiz.

A few potentially confusing things happen on the video. At the beginning, Kim is passing around a sheet of paper on which students can record their e-mail addresses. They decided as a class that communication should be better than simply making phone calls, so they're trying to fix this by setting up an e-mail list. At the end of the video, you'll notice some students flashing a white board to the presenters up front. At first, they are writing down the remaining time the students have to present. In the end, they are writing down answers to the questions Dr. McMurry asks the presenters in the hopes of helping out the "company's" presentation.

Be patient with this video portion. It is probably one of the worst CanCo presentations I've seen in nine years, but there are some valuable pieces. This video will also make you appreciate just how much a class is willing and able to improve from October to February. The improvement will be evident in chapter 5 when you watch the Solutions, Inc., presentation video. Until then, here is the CanCo company presentation.

Video—Watch the CANCO-3A video on the DVD labeled "Video Cases for Chapters 4–5." This video takes the first 40 minutes of class and compresses them into approximately 15 minutes so that you can visualize their first class presentation.

Teacher's Analysis—CANCO-3A

The first year I implemented the CanCo WCI Project, I was more nervous about seeing the class presentation and lab report than about watching the class work on its own in lab. I didn't know whether there would be a presentation to witness or a report to read. Of course I imagined what the ideal scenario would be. How wonderful it would be if the presentation day were professional, thorough, and flawless. Students would be prepared to give the presentation within the first couple minutes of class. They would all be dressed professionally, as if they had an actual contract to win or an actual job interview. They would have arranged the room in a professional manner, perhaps in a U-shape for presentation purposes. A chair would have been prepared for the company representative, with a copy of the presentation and the proposal ready. Students might have included providing name tags for all employees (students), providing food and drink for the representative, and having the PowerPoint up on the screen with presenters ready to go.

The first year that I observed my CanCo presentations, of course, not a single class pulled it all together. (To be fair, most real companies I've worked with don't have an ideally organized presentation either.) I have had some phenomenal classes come close, although that is a rarity. As I've grown as an educator, I've made a mental shift and now see the benefit of having my students go through these activities as a community, regardless of the outcome. Each class, year after year, has provided an original scientific perspective, exhibited a unique community approach, and given an innovative presentation. More important, they learn from their experiences.

It is important to mention that I never tell the students anything about my ideal presentation scenario. The only information they have about what to include in their presentation and how to act during their presentation is based on whatever class experiences they have up to this point and what is written on their project sheet. I do it this way because I believe in this open-ended approach to products. Students construct what a quality presentation means through their own experiences and through feedback.

The effort this class put into trying to make a quality presentation was apparent, particularly after I had the chance to talk to the class on Day 4 (see CANCO-4A), our feedback day. They discussed how many hours they put into the presentation, how they tried to add their creativity, and how they talked through what seemed to make sense regarding the content. Nevertheless, the result shown on this video is fragmented and chaotic. They were obviously disappointed. But everything that happened was a valuable learning experience. They needed to use the feedback from Day 4, both the positive and negative pieces, to keep morale up and improve.

As you watch the clips showing this class presentation, you may notice a strange mood before the arrival of the company representative, Dr. McMurry. The students are too calm, in my opinion, for a challenge of this magnitude. However, they are discussing relevant information. For instance, Kim announces that she is going to pass around a sheet on which to collect e-mail addresses so that the class will have better communication outside of class for the next project they might have to do. This is tremendous; they are showing how much they care about their class climate and how much they want to correct their mistakes. The best part is that I don't have to say a thing; they instigate this improvement on their own. The problem I have is that they've exhibited bad judgment in deciding that now, right before their presentation, is the appropriate time to create this list. They should spend this time preparing for the presentation and send the e-mail sheet around after the company representative leaves. It is nevertheless wonderful that they are trying to correct their own planning mistakes—getting a better method of communication system ready— even before we have had a chance to evaluate the project together.

They then continue to try to set up for Dr. McMurry. But as I watch Dr. McMurry (me) show on the video, I relive the disappointment of their not being ready. The guidelines on the project sheet said the presentation would be done "at the beginning of your [company] period," and that the class would need to provide Dr. McMurry with "a hard copy of [their] community's presentation and a hard copy of [their] community's proposal." Not one of these three things is done. I recall writing myself a note to discuss this during the feedback day. I want them to understand that when a company representative comes to hear your pitch, you need to be ready to go.

Technical difficulties will always be a part of any formal presentation students are required to give. I've learned some tricks for preventing these disasters, and I've learned to handle them when they arise. (Note that I sometimes plan for them just to see how students respond.) The way the students handle the disappointment of some files not opening correctly and some images not being present is commendable. As I watch their faces on the video, I can tell they are quite upset that their efforts aren't visible. But they move forward. This, again, is something we would discuss during feedback. And of course they would still be disappointed, so the focus during feedback must be, "How will you handle these technical setbacks? Do you have a back-up plan?"

It takes a bit of coaxing to get the students to start their presentation. After Dr. McMurry arrives and even after she mentions, "I only have 12 minutes left; whatever you can show me in the next 12 minutes would be great," the mood is still a bit too calm. Perhaps they are hiding their anxiety well. In years past students have let their panic override their ability to role-play by reverting to the student-teacher relationship and asking questions. This class stays focused on getting their materials together without the aid of a teacher.

The class then begins to present its findings to Dr. McMurry. It has chosen students who tend to feel comfortable talking about science. This happens every year. The presenters have dressed up, which is good. Their presentations model the feedback they received during our discussion that followed the first project, Chemistry Concoctions, about what to include. They share background information; data; particulate-level models (and graphs, although the graphs didn't show up due to their "technical difficulties"); and conclusions. The completeness of their presentation is a wonderful step forward.

I have learned that it is a good idea to write down as much as possible while listening to a company presentation in character. I record who presents and the order of the information they present. I record the time it takes for the students to get through the material; there is usually a time limit. I usually prepare a list of content questions that I bring with me. As they answer one of the questions during their presentation, I record it. If they don't get to something, I'll ask the question at the end. But, most important, I record questions about their scientific process and analyses as they share the information with me. They should be able to think through their work and explain their decisions from science and modeling standpoints. I record whatever responses they give and the names of those who gave the responses.

In this video I record some of my concerns while listening to the company presentation. Certainly showing graphs is a must; it's unfortunate they can't get those images to appear on their PowerPoint. Even though they are not able to share their graphs, I expect them to answer the second question on the project sheet: "How does each of the variables [tested] affect the amount of can crush?" Instead the students show a data table that apparently illustrated the greatest can-crush scenario per variable. Because this information is not what I asked for or was expecting, I become very confused. At this point, I ask several more questions because I want to see if they can provide me with specific data that shows how changes in the value of a particular independent variable (such as amount of water in the can) affect the dependent variable of percent can crush. I want to know: What tests were done? How many were done? What were all of the results that would lend support to their choices of the best-case scenarios. I find that, even after I ask them several further probing questions about their best-case choices, they present information that is still a bit vague. The information they present does not allow me to fully understand why they chose specific "best-case-scenarios" for the can-crush recommendation.

Before hearing their presentation, I hoped to see models drawn at a particulate level that would illustrate their understanding of the science phenomenon they experienced when the can crushed. We had focused on the modeling idea in the last unit, so I am thrilled to see the scanned model drawings as part of their data analysis. And I am ecstatic to hear them try to think through these drawings to explain the reasons behind the can crush. They stumble over their words at times, but many of the students are trying hard to get it. They are readily volunteering information—even when the questions are directed at someone else—to try to tell their version of the story.

The presentation on the surface, from a professional's perspective, is awkward and fragmented. They talk over one another. It is not rehearsed. They need to work on defining professionalism. But the key at this juncture is that they want to be a part of this company challenge; their presentation shows obvious signs of effort aimed at improvement. The majority of the kids try very hard to understand the concepts and contribute for the good of the class. The dedication is there. We just need to work on the mechanics.

At the very end of this video segment, I return to the classroom as Ms. Gallagher and implement a 15-minute quiz. After first using these WCI projects years ago, I learned very quickly that, upon my return to the classroom as their teacher, my students might not easily relinquish control of the classroom to allow me to reclaim the facilitator role. This is an understandable response. Sometimes they still have something to say to one another, or they need more time to unwind. Usually, though, they try to bombard me with questions. They want immediate feedback regarding their work. Most students have put a lot of time into a project of this magnitude, and they are extremely curious about what I'm thinking and how successful I thought they were. I have been "gone" for a total of two class periods. However, I have learned that, when walking into the room after a role-playing scenario, I must have a plan for the next activity to prevent the scenarios described above. When I withhold the immediate feedback they want, students learn the importance of reflecting on the activity themselves, rather than reflecting on the activity from my perspective. It's what they think that counts. And reflection takes time. It also gives me a chance to process what they have just experienced, taking a few deep breaths to let go of the frustrations and focus on their successes. So I never give feedback the same day if I can help it. This is the reason for my coming back into the classroom and immediately telling them to "have a seat, take out your journals, calculators and a writing utensil" and giving them a quiz.

CANCO WCI PROJECT— DAY 3, PART 2—WCI ASSESSMENT 2

Teacher's Introduction—CANCO-3B

The next video segment shows what happens during the second part of the third day of the CanCo WCI Project. Here is a quick chronological description for what happens during the 30 remaining minutes of class.

After giving the students the 15-minute quiz previously mentioned, I implement a WCI assessment where the students are responsible for taking their CanCo knowledge and applying it to a new, yet relevant, scenario. A copy of this class challenge is shown in Figure 4.4.

Video—Watch the CANCO-3B video on the DVD labeled "Video Cases for Chapters 4–5." This video takes the remaining 30 class minutes and compresses them into approximately 18 minutes so that you can visualize what was described.

Figure 4.4

Cover Sheet for WCI Assessment 2   **WCI Assessment 2**

- You may use each other, your journals, your texts (if you have them), your calculators, and any materials on the front lab table. As always, my cart is off limits!
- I've attached an overhead of the following question so that the class can see it.
- I must have this sheet completed and in my hands by _____ according to this clock or I will not grade it. If you fail to meet this deadline, PLACE THIS SHEET ON THE FRONT LAB TABLE. DO NOT REMOVE IT FROM CLASS.
- You must submit your responses on this sheet. Attach the overhead to this sheet, as well.
- The class will be assessed on safety, on accuracy, and on the effort made as a community in the process of solving the problems.
- It is assumed that everyone in the room could do this problem on his/her own once you've finished as a class.

In today's assessment, your community will apply what you learned in your can crushing experiments to a new, yet similar situation.

Community Task: Your community task is to make a can crush 75% by volume using the process described in the CanCo lab. (No other methods of crushing allowed.) The catch is that the can must contain 100 mL of tap water. You only have one opportunity.

Once your community chooses the conditions for the other variables in the can crushing "apparatus," alert Ms. Gallagher that you are ready. Ms. Gallagher will then randomly pick three representatives from your community to do the following. (Once the representatives are chosen, no one else may speak until called upon.)

1. Explain what conditions your community chose for each variable.
2. Show community lab data that supports these choices.
3. Explain why your community believes these conditions will make the can crush.

After these explanations, Ms. Gallagher will pick two representatives to do the can crushing test at the front demonstration desk. These representatives will also measure the amount of can crush and report this to Ms. Gallagher.

4. As a community, record your response to #1. Then draw a three-series particulate drawing of the results from the above scenario.

Good planning.

Teacher's Analysis—CANCO-3B

The WCI assessment is usually a difficult challenge for high school students, particularly when for large classes. The last time this class completed a WCI assessment was at the end of Unit I. As mentioned, one major change has occurred in the classroom's community in that the students have nominated and elected two class managers. These managers, Kim and Jack, led them through the CanCo WCI Project and now are facilitating this follow-up WCI assessment. Back when they were elected, I suggested they be sure to read aloud whatever paper I gave them. Jack does this, and then the class gets busy. (The WCI assessment is shown in Figure 4.4; in short, they need to get a can to crush by 75% of its volume, starting with 100 mL of water in it.)

Immediately after reading this challenge, the students volunteer information about what they think the class should do to accomplish the outlined task. They are using their experiences from lab to design a procedure instinctively. But, after a few initial contributions, some students look back through their journals to see what lab results might help them design a sound procedure.

Sandy eventually offers the suggestion of setting up a proportion, using the control as a known fraction between heating time and volume, and calculating the needed time for 100 mL of water. The class slowly processes this information and then is impressed with the idea. It's fun to see them give each other accolades. Jack asks Sandy to put her math up on the board so everyone can see it.

Angie then offers an idea she and some others had discussed. She thinks the class should change the known fraction to one that represents the best volume crush. She is articulate and makes sure that everyone hears the idea. I recall typing myself a note that I should mention how incredible Angie's contribution was. She reflects on Sandy's idea, she discusses it with others in the room, she offers another idea to the class that makes more sense to her, and she does it all in a professional, sincere, and polite manner. This is the type of discussion model I want the students to build upon.

Debbie then asks about whether or not the class used a proportion to solve the first class assessment a few weeks ago. She is concerned that this might not be the correct approach because the class didn't get the desired outcome the last time. Kim reassures her that the loss of points the last time was more heavily concentrated in the area of community than accuracy and that the proportion part of their attempt was not the mistake made the last time. I am impressed that they are using previous feedback and applying it to a new scenario. And they are questioning themselves and their plans.

Although the students are doing a good job at using their lab experiences in a more qualitative way to try to tackle this challenge, I now wish I had asked a different question for this class assessment. I want them to see the value of using the quantitative data gained from lab. And although this proportion idea is quantitative, it doesn't require a thorough discussion of the analyzed class data, such as looking at graphs. I think a better question would have been to ask the class to predict the percent crush with, say, 1.5 mL of water in the can. In this way, they would have had to look at the results from the "amount-of-water" variable group (see Figure 4.5) and either interpolate between or extrapolate beyond the data points in their graph. Then I would have them perform the lab and see how close they came to their prediction. Each year, I am able to assess student and community learning with new and unique

Figure 4.5

Results From "Amount of Water in Can" Variable Group

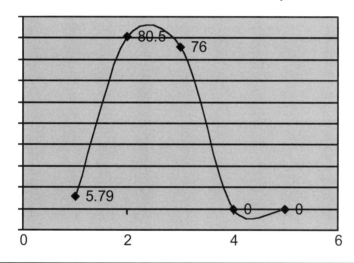

questions. And these questions tend to become better formulated and to require higher-level critical thinking skills. WCI projects have been a wonderful teaching tool in this regard. On a more philosophical level, these WCI projects help me improve my teaching: Teacher reflection happens naturally.

Once the students settle on their procedure, I call on specific students to answer the outlined questions. During this assessment, I have a grading program open on my computer that allows me to randomly select students with the click of the mouse. Patrick, Frank, Kathy, Adam, and Craig were chosen to respond. In the past I have decided who to call on during these assessments in a number of different ways—such as drawing names out of a beaker or picking students whose birthdays fall in a specific month. At the start of the year, it doesn't matter. But I try to make sure I call on each student for these WCI assessments at least once per semester.

Patrick and Frank do not do a very thorough job of answering their assigned questions. I type what they say and will address the missing pieces during feedback. Kathy stumbles over her words at first but eventually does a fairly good job of explaining why the class chose the procedure they did. Adam and Craig are fortuitous picks for performing the lab. Both are comfortable with the content, and both are enthusiastic about the lab. As a bonus, Craig is very comfortable being up in front of his peers. When I first started the WCI projects, I would make sure the students chosen to recreate lab activities had these traits. As I've learned to develop my class climate better, a climate in which students feel comfortable with one another and know that honest mistakes are okay, I find this unnecessary.

While the can is sitting on the hot plate, the class has some down time. Kim feels a sense of responsibility as a class manager to keep the rest of the class focused on something constructive. She decides to look in her journal at the feedback the class received after the first class assessment. She shares all the ideas that we went over and asks the class whether or not they think the class improved in those areas. I type myself a note that it was great that she feels this way and that the class followed her lead. I am pleased, too, that the class took the time to reflect on their implementation of these suggested methods for improvement during class assessments. I can't help but think, however, that this would have been a bit more useful earlier in the day, or even the day before. A better topic for class discussion at this point in the video is to share the responses being recorded on the class answer sheet. Students could have been drawing the particulate-level models together on the front board to make sure everyone understood them and then asking for input. I make a note to tell this to the class during feedback, as well.

When Craig is just about to flip the can, it's fun to watch the anticipation on my students' faces. They obviously want it to work. There is an incredible undercurrent of a sense of ownership in the room. They've worked hard, and this is the culminating event of the project. When the can goes into the water and is crushed, some students smile and admit they did not think that it would happen. Others are disappointed with the amount of crush but are relieved there was at least some crush as evidenced when Mary emphasizes that "Hey, it crushed." Although they don't quite get the results they hoped for, their effort and discussion help finish the project in a positive way. I make a note to share this thought with them during class feedback.

The panic of having little time left sinks in, and the class is scrambling to get all the papers together on time. Students calculate the percent crush rather quickly; but at least that tells me a number of students can do this calculation. And it's amusing how many people repeatedly ask Michelle whether or not she has all the answers recorded on the class answer sheet. She suddenly becomes a very important person.

Here again is some of what I was typing while the students were performing the above-mentioned WCI assessment. The following journal record contains most of my observations.

Teacher's Journal—CANCO-3B

October 17, 2005 (10:20–10:53 a.m.)

Jack read the entire cover sheet. Good for you. Takes a while.

Mary offers the idea that her group did amount of water and that the time needs to be increased based on their data. Good.

Chris says that even after boiling, he still didn't get it to crush.

People are raising hands and offering ideas. Jack and Kim are calling on people. That's good. The discussion is staying together, then. Jack and Kim put on goggles and Jack had the class clear the safety lane. Good.

Everyone offered Mary's services for drawing the pictures. Hmmm. Wonder if she'll ever get a break.

Sandy offers the mathematical proportion for heating for 15 minutes. More information was offered regarding this proportional response. Chris gave input on numbers.

10 mL/1.5 minutes = 100 mL/ x minutes; x = 15 minutes

Angie suggested that Kim review the variables for the class. Good idea. Reread the questions.

Frank is a bit nervous about the time, as he should be.

Patrick—boiling water for 15 minutes, 100 mL water in can

Frank—showed proportion on board

Kathy—because we have 100 mL, the control had 10 mL, we changed the time so that enough of the water evaporates to crush.

(Not good responses. Not near enough detail. We'll talk…)

Adam and Craig did the lab. They put goggles on and took hats off. Good. Craig says you need to have 93 mL for final volume to get 75% crush. Good that he figured that out. Is it correct? Did someone check that?

Kim then went through the responses to each question so that everyone in the room would understand.

Angie wrote number 1's response on the board. Kim tried to explain each variable. Michelle volunteered to write this info on the paper.

Chris went to the bathroom at 10:41. Angie asks, "Where's Chris going?" Hmm….

Craig shares that the water is boiling at the 6.5 minute mark.

Kim then shared feedback from the last class assessment. You're already giving each other feedback for this class assessment. Great. Patrick suggests underlining the important parts next time.

Mary then adds that the class needs to be quick about getting the final volume.

"Why would you need to clean a can before you crush it?" Chris asks.

"As part of the recycling process I think," Jack responds.

Walked around at 10:50 to see how detailed the journals were. Five of them looked good, others were lacking, blank or nonexistent.

"Gosh, time flies so fast when you're having fun!" Frank says.

Craig flipped it and got a crush. That's pretty impressive in and of itself. Let's see what the final crush is…

Final volume was 208 mL. Neither Craig nor Adam reported anything to me.

Kim handed me the sheets. And you were finished with a minute to spare.

"Thanks for doing this. It was a good try."

Nice finish.

CANCO WCI PROJECT— DAY 4, PART 1—FEEDBACK

Teacher's Introduction—CANCO-4A

This is the last day of the project. The students feel relieved because their required work for CanCo is complete. They have planned a lab, implemented their plan, typed a report, prepared a presentation, taken an individual quiz, and completed a WCI assessment. The students also feel a bit anxious, because they know today is the day they find out what my thoughts are on how well they did.

As I have said, whenever I give feedback, I focus my discussion in three areas—safety, community, and accuracy (see analysis of CHEMCO-1 video in chapter 2). I apply these three areas to all possible pieces of the project. For instance, safety is important when doing the lab, it is a required piece of a lab report, and students should follow safety protocol if asked to do a lab during a WCI assessment, so I will share how well they did in terms of safety in all of these areas. Students must also use efficient, effective, and constructive means of communication and organization while working as a community, so my feedback about community applies to their lab work, their presentation, and their WCI assessment. I decide how accurate the class is in terms of communicating the chemistry content and accomplishing the outlined tasks. My feedback regarding accuracy, then, applies to their lab technique, lab report, presentation information, and WCI assessment.

The next video segment shows how I provide feedback to the students for a lengthy student-led project like CanCo. The video can be broken into three main parts: (1) Students answer guiding journal reflection questions about their thoughts on the project; (2) they share those thoughts with me; and (3) I provide my feedback on both safety and community for two of the pieces of the project they did, the lab and presentation. My feedback on accuracy is covered on the same day and is shown in the next video case (CANCO-4B). We did eventually go over safety and community in reference to their WCI assessment, but this feedback occurred on the following day and was not captured on film.

Teacher's Analysis—CANCO-4A

Again, it has become apparent over the years that feedback time is extremely beneficial. I ask students guiding questions about community and content that make them reflect on their own accomplishments and tell me about them. They hear my thoughts on where they stand as a community and where they need to go. One part of feedback that

Video—Watch the CANCO-4A video on the DVD labeled "Video Cases for Chapters 4–5." This video takes the first 55 minutes of class and compresses them into approximately 19 minutes so that you can visualize what was described.

always is especially important is sending the message to the students that everything I ask them to do in this class is something that will be a beneficial experience for them and that what they put into the class dictates what they'll get out of it. When wrapping up a project, I make sure to share my thoughts on their accomplishments and trials in the three areas of safety, accuracy, and community. It has always made sense to me to make sure to spend a suitable amount of time on all three, rather than just content. Spending an appropriate amount of time on each area tells students I believe all three are important. If I were to simply give them a grade on accuracy or spend the most time on accuracy, then they would continue to believe that the right answer is the only thing that matters. And in my classes, that is not true.

At the beginning of this feedback day, I give the students some time to write down their thoughts in their journals about the project. The guiding questions that I asked this class included:

- What part of the lab planning and implementation was the most constructive? The most frustrating?
- What part of the lab report was the most constructive? The most frustrating?
- What part of the presentation was the most constructive? The most frustrating?
- What did you do as an individual to master the content and to help the community?
- What needs to happen for your community to grow? What would you like to see change?
- Suggestions, comments, questions about anything regarding the project...

After about 15 minutes of individual journal-writing time, I ask them to share their thoughts verbally. In the video, as students tell me something, you'll notice a moment of silence on my part. I don't provide the student with an immediate verbal reaction each time. A few of these noticeably quiet moments that stand out to me as I watch the video occur just after Kelly's, Jack's and Michelle's contributions. Because I am not visible in the video, the silence seems awkward. I am, however, recording what they are saying so that I can see what themes develop throughout our discussion. Because the students can see that I am writing, they don't find these moments of quiet awkward at all. They know what I'm doing.

After the first student-led WCI project, one theme that resurfaces year after year is how difficult it is to get everyone involved outside of class. I have learned how important it is to remove the students' frustration in this area because it can be very stressful. I make sure they come up with either a phone or an e-mail list to communicate with one another at any time. I teach them how to break up the work into manageable pieces and designate one person to accomplish each piece. Someone, usually a manager, must volunteer to get these pieces together into one file that will be handed in as their final product. If there is a problem with getting the pieces of information, I must be notified as soon as possible so that I can facilitate a solution. I tell my students to keep a list of who does what so the work can be spread out to new people during the next project. If possible, I give them class time to do some of these things. I have used evaluation forms to document what each person did outside of class. It takes time to develop a means for keeping track of individual accountability. I have done it all and feel comfortable with using e-mail and reading student journal reflections to help facilitate community efforts outside of class. (Since 2006, there have been a number of advances in curricular technology, namely Web 2.0 tools that allow improvements for students collaborating outside the classroom.)

I found the students' verbal responses to this project very interesting. They allowed me to put some pieces of the puzzle together. For instance, when sitting in the presentation as Dr. McMurry, I wasn't sure why there was an extra laptop computer and video projector present. I now know that it was because some of the graphics the students included in their PowerPoint were lost in the file they had sent to my classroom computer because of software differences. They had brought back-up equipment just in case.

I also found out how much time they had spent on putting this presentation and proposal together. Apparently, some of them were up until 3:00 a.m. I am now able to help them better communicate information with each other using the ideas mentioned above. I discuss how to prevent fragmented conversations—dialogue that goes off on so many tangents that students don't remember what they were originally discussing. To prevent this, I tell them to make sure to answer a given question before going on to a new one.

One of the greatest benefits in allowing the students to talk about their CanCo experiences is quite simply that they get a chance to share their stories and their perspectives with the rest of the class. They grow closer and learn each individual's strengths and weaknesses. You can see in this video how badly Kelly wanted to be at Kim's house to contribute her thoughts, but she just couldn't be there because of other obligations. Other people in the room could then understand why she couldn't be there rather than assuming she skipped out. Another example of a benefit is when Lynn tells the class how much she learned when she read the lab report. Information that people first thought was irrelevant ends up completing their understanding of the lab. She wants the class to know that reading the final product helped her put everything together. And Angie and Mary want to get to know everyone's name in the room. These moments bring the class together.

CANCO WCI PROJECT— DAY 4, PART 2—FEEDBACK

Teacher's Introduction—CANCO-4B

The last video of the CanCo WCI Project focuses on our discussion about accuracy. We talk about the chemistry behind the can-crushing lab. We discuss how well the class did in terms of accurate lab technique and accurate presentation information. (I provided feedback about the safety, accuracy, and community of the students' efforts in the WCI assessment during the next class period that was not filmed.)

I want to make sure the students conclude any activity with a well-thought-out model that logically explains the phenomenon they were studying within the project. So, through a series of guiding questions, I revisit the can-crushing phenomenon with new scenarios to see if they can describe what they think will happen. Now that they've had three days to focus on this particular phenomenon, they should be able to use their model to explain a new scenario. Through these discussions, I assess how well they understand the material.

Video—Watch the CANCO-4B video on the DVD labeled "Video Cases for Chapters 4–5." This video takes the remaining 30 class minutes and compresses them into approximately 15 minutes so that you can visualize what was described.

Teacher's Analysis—CANCO-4B

Once we have finished our discussion on safety and community, I move into a dialogue about chemistry content related to the topic of gases and phase changes. I first ask the students the following question: "With 10 mL of water in the can, hot plate on 10 and heating for 20 minutes, what happens?" I tell them to talk in their groups about what they think the results will be and why. It was fun for me to see in the video the students' immediately turning to their groups and talking about it. The majority of the students quickly conclude there will be no crushing, but it takes them a bit to decide why that's true.

During this discussion, the video focuses on the front group that includes Dan, Robert, Sandy, and Kelly. Robert seems a bit uninterested at times, but, as soon as the group sounds confused or hesitant, he jumps in with a wonderful explanation that helps the rest of them feel more comfortable with their initial hypothesis.

I refocus the class and ask for volunteers to explain their reasoning to me. As expected, all the pieces are there, the students just need some direction putting it all together. I want to give them the experience of communicating a scientific model well enough that another individual would be able to picture what they're saying. So I try not to let any comment that is inaccurate or incomplete slip by. At this point in the project, it is important that I field and repeat the responses that students

124

contribute and that I direct us toward an accurate model. Robert, from the group listed above, is the student who first gets the class on the right track. I cut him off because I feel the rest of the class is not ready for the end of the story, and he has already gotten there. He smiles when I do this; he knows that I know he gets it.

I find an appropriate place to pause while discussing their response to the initial question, and I continue with the following: "With 100 mL of water in can, hot plate on 10 and heated for 2 minutes, what happens?" On the spur of the moment I decide not to let the students discuss it in their groups. I'm afraid that the previous thoughts will be forgotten, and I want to keep them going down this path. So I ask for a response right away. Again, both their instincts and their experiences dictate that nothing will happen. Getting them to explain why is the key.

Watching the end of this dialogue is fun. There are two points in the video that show all of the students focused on me. They are curious about how all this information comes together. One of those points is when I repeat all the accurate pieces the students told me that describe a particulate model of what happened inside the can. They have been thinking about this problem for three days, and they sincerely care. The looks on their faces illustrate that they have a strong feeling of ownership in this problem and that they feel they must come to a conclusion.

I end my feedback by sharing quotes with the students, just as I did in the feedback for the Chemistry Concoctions lab. This allows us to finish on a light-hearted note. And it is fun for them later to see if anything they say will be quote-worthy during future projects and class assessments.

RESEARCHER'S ANALYSIS—CANCO VIDEO CASES

In this chapter, I discuss three of Joan's teaching strategies that are well illustrated in the CANCO video cases. The three strategies involve Joan's use of role-play, scaffolding, and engaging problems.

Teaching Strategy 7—Using Role-Play to Push Students Into New Roles

Two of the many obstacles facing teachers in implementing inquiry-based projects are understanding and playing the new roles required to enact these teaching strategies effectively (Davis, Petish, and Smithey

2006; Furtak 2006; Simmons et al. 1999). These new teacher roles are inextricable from the new roles that the students must assume. After viewing the entire set of CANCO video cases, I am struck by how much Joan's role-play as Ms. Nac affects the actions and behaviors of her students. When Joan assumes the role of Ms. Nac, she creates a reason for her students to break out of traditional student roles that tend to be passive and instead to take an active part in the classroom community. As Ms. Nac, Joan can create a ripple in the classroom environment that gives her students the cue that it is their turn to take charge. For example, as Ms. Nac finishes the PowerPoint presentation that describes what the CanCo representative will expect from the company (class) in terms of project products, she takes a few questions from the students but then quickly turns the classroom over to them. This transfer of ownership is illustrated in the classroom dialogue below that occurs right after Ms. Nac finishes her presentation.

[03:57]—CANCO-1A

Frank: When you mean 75% can crush, do you mean a 75% decrease in volume or a 25 % decrease in volume?

Ms. Nac: Um, look again at your definition for can crush, and then apply 75% to that.

Mary: Does everyone have to do the lab?

Ms. Nac: It's up to you and your company.

Angie: Wait. When you say company, you mean the whole class, right?

Ms. Nac: I answered that question.

Frank: That means our leaders should go up front.

<several students talking at once>

Mary: Kim and Jack.

Kim: What?

Angie: Yeah, you guys have to go up there.

Ms. Nac: Okay, so I'm done with all the information that I'm going to share with you. It's up to you guys to get busy now.

Kelly: Kim and Jack…

Mary: Find someone to look up the hot plate information.

Kim: Okay, um, guys I was just thinking that…

When Mary asks, "Does everyone have to do the lab?" Ms. Nac provides the clue that the students are to take charge of the planning process by responding, "It's up to you and your company." With this comment, the students begin to get restless and pick up on Ms. Nac's hint that their leaders should "go up front." A further nudge occurs when Ms. Nac states, "Okay, so I'm done with all the information that I'm going to share with you. It's up to you guys to get busy now." Along with Kelly's calling the class managers' names, Ms. Nac's last statement gets Jack and

Kim out of their seats and up to the front of the room where they begin managing the planning discussion.

By assuming another role in the classroom, Joan can place constraints on the interactions with her students, thus forcing them to take responsibility for figuring out how to proceed. Joan's character allows her to act differently than "the teacher" and pushes the students to assume their new roles. As evidenced by the limited number of questions the students ask of Ms. Nac once she goes to the back of the room, the students understand she will not answer questions they could figure out themselves. This is not to say that the students are afraid to ask her a question; but rather that the students limit their questions to those that relate to Ms. Nac's role. As stated in her Powerpoint, Ms. Nac is available to arrange for lab supplies, time, and safety. As illustrated in the following dialogue, Frank asks Ms. Nac to make available certain lab supplies that will enable them to alter the temperature and composition of the water in the tub.

[06:24]—CANCO-1B

Frank: Uh, are we gonna like have things available to help us test these variables tomorrow?

Ms. Nac: Uh, it depends on what kinds of things you want.

Frank: Like ice or a different substance.

Ms. Nac: I can give you ice. What do you mean by different substance?

Frank: Uh, to like, put in the tub.

Ms. Nac: Other than...

Frank: Water.

Ms. Nac: What other substance? You would need to tell me before I...

Frank: A cleaning agent, I guess?

Ms. Nac: Like soap? Yes, we have soap.

Frank: Like soap water?

Ms. Nac: Uh-hum.

Frank: Alright, and then, I think we just need ice.

Ms. Nac: Okay.

Frank: Ice.

Before Frank came up to Ms. Nac, he had to go through a series of steps that led him to ask such questions. First, he and his group have to think about their experimental design. Then, they have to consider the specific lab supplies and materials needed to conduct such investigations. And finally, they have to ask Ms. Nac to arrange for specific supplies. The constraints that Joan places on her role in the classroom force Frank and his group to design and plan their experiment without Joan's having to tell them to do so. The experimental design and planning that Frank's group did on its own relates directly to what scientists spend a significant amount of their time doing. It also relates to the type of work that the National Science Education Standards insist students must do to engage in true inquiry (NRC 2000). The fact that Frank's group assumes the role of "experimental designers and planners" is precipitated by Joan's assumption of her character role. By being Ms. Nac, Joan allows her students to enter into the new classroom roles required for them to take part effectively in an inquiry-based science curriculum. Her role creates a reason for them to act differently than they might if she were acting in the traditional role of teacher.

As Joan states in her video analyses, she finds it important to stay in character. Joan's dedication to playing the role of Ms. Nac is rewarded by her students' acceptance of it. This is clear when Jack asks *Ms. Nac* if he can erase the board. In this case, he is asking Ms. Nac because he knows that Ms. Gallagher (Joan, who is the teacher) probably does not want certain information on the board to be erased (i.e., her agendas), so he asks through Ms. Nac. He is working within the system created by Ms. Nac's role. Sometimes, the students forget to call Ms. Nac by her name and identify her as Ms. Gallagher. In these instances, Ms. Nac stays in character by reminding them that Ms. Gallagher is not around or by saying she is unfamiliar with that person. For example, when Kim begins to talk to Ms. Nac about the various substances that they have identified for use in their cans, Ms. Nac corrects her use of Ms. Gallagher's name.

[01:13]—CANCO-2

Kim: All right, Ms. Gallagher, we did some research on…

Ms. Nac: …is not here, but I can help.

Kim: Oh, Ms. Nac. We did some research on what we can put for substance in the can to see if it could crush better. We came up with Coke, soap…

It may seem a minor point here that Ms. Nac insists on being called by her correct name or that Joan is adamant that her students recognize her new character, but Joan knows that there can be no cracks in her role-playing performance. If there were, she would be unable to subtly convince her students to accept their new roles in the WCI projects.

Teaching Strategy 8—Using Scaffolding to Prepare Students for Their New Roles

In addition to role-playing, Joan uses the first project as a means to prepare her students for their new roles in future projects. She does this by modeling the entire process of how the whole class might go about solving a problem that she has posed. As you observed in the CHEMCO

128

video cases, Joan is in charge of the classroom and directs all of the students' activities. After proposing the problem to figure out what affects the amount of water produced in the Chemistry Concoctions apparatus, Joan directs her students to think of all the variables involved, creates a list of these variables on the board, and asks her students to identify a control condition for each variable. Once the students have looked up safety information about the chemicals involved and recorded this information in their journals, Joan asks groups to volunteer to study one particular variable and design an experiment to test its effect on the amount of water produced. Joan continues to guide her students in every step throughout the remaining two days of the project as each group collects data and presents its results through PowerPoint.

With Joan firmly in charge of the class's activities, the first project is very teacher-centered; nonetheless, Joan frequently and explicitly reminds the class that in the next WCI project they will be in charge. She reminds them so that they are aware that she is building a scaffold for them to use in the next project. As this next project unfolds one month later, Joan's scaffold reappears several times as the students take charge in the CanCo WCI Project. For example, soon after Kim and Jack walk to the front of the class to begin their roles as managers on the first day of the project, Kim refers to the scaffold when she says,

[01:11]—CANCO-1B

Kim: Alright. So last time before when Ms. Gallagher was explaining we had to come up with a control group, so I'm thinking so that to appropriately show the difference…so I think when she demonstrated that she used the one where it was just heated up and then put in the water as the control group, alright?

In this statement, Kim is referring to the project in which Joan explains that the class needs to come up with a control. Kim uses this reference as a way to inform the class that they need to have a control in their current experimental plan. She then goes on to offer a suggestion for what the control conditions should be. Kim is using her experiences with the first project as a scaffold to help the class determine what they should do in this new, yet similar situation. Her fellow classmates pick up on this cue to ensure that they have selected a control condition that makes sense as illustrated in Craig's comment below.

[02:04]—CANCO-1B

Craig: Couldn't we use the one that she crushed as our control and then change variables from there?

In Joan's scaffold, she creates a list of the possible variables, records these on the board, and then asks the class to suggest the conditions for each variable that would constitute the control. Obviously, because the class is thinking about the control before identifying the possible variables, they are not following the exact order that Joan suggested in her scaffold. It is not long, however, before Jack realizes that they need to identify the possible variables that may affect how much the can crushes.

[02:28]—CANCO-1B

Jack:　　We should probably start discussing ideas for the other variables that we could use. Obvious ideas...

This prompt from Jack has a calming effect on the classroom. Students raise their hands and patiently wait their turn to offer suggestions for the variables. In the entire set of CANCO video cases, there are probably few other activities that are more orderly and purposeful than when the students are creating this list of variables. Because Joan has scaffolded this process, the students know they need to create this list and have been waiting for this moment. In the excerpt from this orderly dialogue that follows, Kim is calling on students who have their hands up, with Angie recording the suggestions on the board.

[02:36]—CANCO-1B

Angie:　Okay, so wait, what did he just say?
Jack:　　Just different liquids in the tub.
Kim:　　Okay, Chris.
Chris:　　The length of time it's on the, uh, hot plate?
Kim:　　Okay. Yeah.
Craig:　The tub water temperature we could think about being lower and higher.
Kim:　　Right.

Once they finish creating this list, Kim asks the groups to volunteer to choose a variable around which they will design an experiment. Although Kim is continuing with the process that Joan modeled in the previous project, the process gets interrupted as Kelly (and other subsequent students) questions the validity of the variable "temperature of the water in the can" and asks the class to ponder whether it matters.

[02:57]—CANCO-1B

Kim:　　So, now we're gonna have to probably start going to volunteers for which variables they want.

Kelly: Wait. Wait. Sorry. Well, the thing about the temperature…of the water in the can is that if it's colder or hotter when we put it in, the amount that turns into a gas, uh, that evaporates, or the amount of water left in the can will affect it. I don't know if that matters.

Angie: You, guys, everybody make sure you listen.

Kim: Yeah, did you…did you guys hear, Kelly?

Frank: No.

Kim: Alright, what she said is…depending on the temperature in the can, if it's hotter, it may evaporate more when it's at its boiling point; if it's colder, it could also affect it because it would take a longer time. What do you guys think about that?

Kelly: I don't know if it matters.

Kim: Yeah, but it may not matter, but do you guys still feel that it's not important?

Even though Joan provides a scaffold, it does not provide a complete blueprint for all eventualities that her students will encounter. Because the scaffold requires that one variable be assigned to each of the six groups, listing seven variables on the board means that the students must decide which variable is not important. When Joan was in charge during the Chemistry Concoctions WCI Project and there were too many variables on the list, she asked the students to think about which variables were least important and then guided them to make a quick decision. This decision, however, is much more difficult because no one has the authority that Joan holds (the decision is not made until the end of the period); thus they must closely examine each other's logic and ideas. Kelly's question is one of the first that derails them from the scaffold that Joan provided. Even though Kelly's focus is on only one specific variable, her question causes the students to reexamine the validity of most of the variables listed, whereupon several tangential discussions ensue. For example, after examining the variable of "substance in the can," Frank wonders aloud whether it would be prudent to boil ethanol:

[03:41]—CANCO-1B

Jack: You may have a good point because ethanol doesn't clean as well.

Frank: But why would you boil ethanol? It would light on fire. It's highly flammable.

Kelly: Well, we'll need to check a Flinn catalog.

Jack: Yeah, we'll have to check with Flinn.

In her video analysis, Joan talks about how the students often diverge from her ideal of how the students should structure their work when they are in charge and that this divergence occurs more often at the beginning of the school year. Through the feedback that Joan gives her students at the end of each project, she is able to close the gap between her ideals and what happens, especially in terms of getting her students to hold discussions in which many voices can be heard and critical thinking takes place. Yet even though the discussions at the beginning of the year may be a bit chaotic, they provide the teacher with valuable information concerning her students' conceptions. The solid logic that flows through Kelly's question about the "temperature of the water in the can" variable suggests that she is thinking hard about the can-crushing phenomenon and wants the class to examine closely the decisions they are making.

What should be exciting to any science teacher reading these dialogues is that the students are having ardent discussions and lively conversations about science. They own these conversations and are grappling with the same kinds of issues that arise when a group of professional researchers try to design an experiment that will lead to useful results. In my own experiences of working as a chemical engineer, chemist, and environmental engineer, I found that most scientists spend a significant portion of their time designing experiments. While planning experiments in meetings with a group of scientists, I have often heard "garbage in equals garbage out" when someone is getting impatient with the lengthy process. Scientists understand that, if the experimental design is not well thought out, then the experimental results will be equally vague. Although the students may depart from the scaffold that Joan provides, their departure takes them in a direction in which they are trying to be thorough and thoughtful in their experimental planning. And however uncomfortable it may be to watch the messy, uncertain, and tentative discussions shown in the video, these types of discussions are important, because they indicate the students are struggling with the difficult issues that arise when designing a real experiment for which potentially meaningful and usable results are required.

Even though the students may veer from Joan's structure, they do return to it. After finishing the discussions mentioned above, the students come back to the scaffold when Kim asks each group to volunteer to design an experiment for a specific variable.

[04:03]—CANCO-1B

Kim:	So one person per group can you raise your hand to volunteer for which variable that you want. Yeah.
Frank:	We want tub.
Kim:	What, you want tub?
Craig:	The temperature of the tub yeah.

Overall, as illustrated in the student dialogues presented in this section, the chain of events that occurs when the students are in charge tends to follow the example that they experienced throughout the first project. They keep coming back to the scaffold for guidance even after their path deviates when they need to explore issues that they find important. The fact that they keep returning to the scaffold suggests they find it useful. This enables them to ease into their challenging, new, and required roles in the WCI environment.

Teaching Strategy 9—Using Engaging Problems to Sustain Student Interest and Focus

When Ms. Nac turns over the classroom on the first day of the CanCo WCI Project, her students must step into their new roles and draw upon the scaffold that she has modeled in the previous Chemistry Concoctions WCI Project. When Kim and Jack first walk to the front of the room in the CANCO-1B video case, it is interesting to note how quickly the class takes to the task at hand. There is no hesitation; in fact they seem eager to prove their capabilities. Kim and Jack stand up and the class gets going. Perhaps more important, as you have observed throughout the CANCO video cases, this level of interest and focus continues over the next few days of student-led activity.

How does Joan get her students to work willingly and purposefully together on their own for such an extended period? Is it the careful and thoughtful preparation she put into her first nine lessons that prepared her students to take charge? Is it her presence in the classroom as Ms. Nac that kept the students on task? Does her reputation as an outstanding teacher have something to do with their willingness to try? It is likely that a combination of many factors enable her to pique her students' interest over the long term; however, I propose that the key element that sustains interest can be found in the questions that Ms. Nac proposes at the beginning of the project:

1. What variables affect the amount of can crush (i.e., the initial can volume minus final can volume)?
2. How do each of the variables listed in #1 affect the amount of can crush?
3. What conditions should we set for the process to obtain the maximum crush?
4. Is the process (with your proposed conditions from #3) reliable enough to always give at least 75% volume crush on <u>all</u> cans? Provide enough data to support your claim.

These four questions provide the class with a defined problem that needs to be solved and gives structure to their future investigation. Researchers, who have studied project-based science for almost two decades, propose that a project will be effective if it starts out with a driving question that is judged to be worthwhile, feasible, contextualized, meaningful, and open-ended by the students (Krajcik and Czerniak 2007; Singer et al. 2000). In this specific case with the CanCo WCI Project, the four driving questions listed above also have the advantage of being centered on a science phenomenon that is genuinely impressive. This advantage is particularly evident in the video that focused on Group 5 in the lab. In one sequence, one of their cans crushes loudly and draws a crowd from the rest of the groups whereupon these visitors want to know more details about Group 5's procedures.

[10:31]—CANCO-2

Craig:	Hold up, everybody. We're goin' again.
Maria:	Oohh!
Frank:	Yeah!
Dan:	Let me see that!
Craig:	That was money.
Mark:	Dude, that was a nice one.
Dan:	Good form!
Mark:	Yeah, you gotta put it in fast.
Tom:	How are you guys putting it in?
Frank:	Just straight.
Patrick:	Straight or turned over?
Mark:	Straight.
Patrick:	Where did you guys get the ice?
Kelly:	That should have been a variable how we put it in.
Mary:	No, because if you don't put it in upside down the experiment doesn't work.

Note that there are eight students who take part in this quick dialogue. Judging from their descriptions, they are impressed by the can's dramatic crush. Their expressions indicate that they find this science phenomenon interesting and one that is worthwhile of their focus.

Although it is clear that all of the students are not doing the same thing or are equally involved in a similar manner throughout the project, the CANCO video cases indicates that the classroom as a whole is engaged in the problem and that they are determined to solve it. The observation that Joan's students are interested and focused for several hours of work inside the classroom (and many hours outside for some of the students) is notable. This sustained interest on the part of her

134

students is one of the rewards of incorporating a truly engaging problem with a set of driving questions into a WCI project.

REFERENCES

Davis, E. A., D. Petish, and J. Smithey. 2006. Challenges new science teachers face. *Review of Educational Research* 76 (4): 607–651.

Furtak, E. M. 2006. The problem with answers: An exploration of guided scientific inquiry teaching. *Science Education* 90 (3): 453–467.

Krajcik, J. S., and C. M. Czerniak. 2007. *Teaching Science in Elementary and Middle School: A Project-Based Approach,* 3rd ed. Mahwah, NJ: Lawrence Erlbaum.

National Research Council (NRC). 2000. *Inquiry and the National Science Education Standards: A guide for teaching and learning.* Washington DC: National Academy Press.

Simmons, P. E., A. Emory, T. Carter, T. Coker, B. Finnegan, D. Crockett, L. Richardson, et al. 1999. Beginning teachers: Beliefs and classroom actions. *Journal of Research in Science Teaching* 36 (8): 930–954.

Singer, J., R. W. Marx, J. Krajcik, and J. C. Chambers. 2000. Constructing extended inquiry projects: Curriculum materials for science education reform. *Educational Psychologist* 35 (3): 165–178.

Chapter 5
WCI Project 3—Solutions

It is February, and we are about to begin only our third WCI project. It has been a while since the students have done a multiday WCI project. In fact, it was October when we did the CanCo WCI Project. Reflecting on this school year, I'm extremely surprised at how long we have gone without a WCI project—I don't recommend this at all. I normally do three projects in the first semester, three projects in the second semester, and one culminating project in May on soap. Unfortunately, during this year, the third WCI project I typically implement during first semester lasted only one class period, a modification due to an abnormally high number of altered class days during 2005–2006. But this class has still gone through a number of WCI assessments and inquiry-based labs. The students have had a number of class periods in which I role-played a character. The class still has a wonderful community climate, and its journals still indicate that students are enjoying chemistry. I feel they are ready to continue these WCI challenges. And I know we have the time to do all three projects, plus The Soap Project, during second semester. So we dive in.

SOLUTIONS WCI PROJECT—DAY 1, PART 1

Teacher's Introduction—SOLN-1A

The students are very comfortable working with one another at this point in the year. They have completed two four-day-long WCI projects, two week-long research group projects, five single-day WCI assessments, and many single-day inquiry-based lab activities. The focus of this chapter is to highlight their third four-day-long Solutions WCI Project. A copy of the project sheet is shown in Figure 5.1.

In the video documentation for Day 1, I first appear in my normal role as teacher. I make a couple of announcements and review some content with the students. I want to check for some basic understanding of the content for the solutions project before proceeding with the next

Figure 5.1

Solutions WCI Project Sheet

Solutions
Project Sheet

Due to your ongoing, positive record regarding safety and quality control, your scientific community has been recommended to enter a contract competition. At least six companies (classes) have been challenged by Solutions, Inc. The company (class) that best completes these tasks will receive a lucrative contract with Solutions. Criteria is listed below.

Task: Calculate the percentage (by mass) of each component of a mixture containing sodium carbonate and potassium iodide. The only other chemical available for your use is 0.5 M calcium chloride, which you must make on your own. (Materials that you are allowed to use for making this solution are found on the middle lab table in the back of the room. But that's it. Get this done ASAP. Read the bottle closely!)

Parameters:
1. You will receive six identical samples of the mixture. Don't lose/destroy any! There are no replacements.
2. You are working as a company (class). You may use all room resources except the cart and other adults.
3. A list of materials you will need to complete the lab (other than the ones for making the 0.5 M $CaCl_2$ solution found on the middle lab table today) must be listed on a separate sheet of paper and submitted to the lab manager by the end of company time today! Be thorough! Not only should you think through EVERY piece of equipment, but be accurate in your description of it. For instance, don't just list "six beakers"; instead list "six 250 mL beakers."
4. You have today and next class period to work on this. If further lab time is requested, you must e-mail your lab manager, Kima, at *kimasolution@ yahoo.com*. She will only provide further lab time if given 24 hours notice AND if she is available. So get your requests in early! She will only look at one e-mail per company per day, so make sure you record your company block in the subject heading.
5. Kima is here to help you and your company today and during the next company (class) time. Her purpose is to help with equipment and lab technique. Your company can only ask her five questions each company day, so think about and formulate your questions well. She may refuse to answer should the response to your question give your company an unfair advantage over other companies.

HINTS:
1. At a minimum, think about the words *double replacement reaction, net ionic equation, solution, solubility, precipitate, molarity.*

138

Figure 5.1 (continued)

Solutions WCI Project Sheet

2. To aid you in your planning, here is a sample problem that is similar to the task asked of you above, using different chemicals. Your company managers may ask your lab manager, Kima, whether or not they have the correct answer at any time during this project. But they may only ask 3 times. (This is in ADDITION to the above-mentioned five questions.)

Example: A chemist has a 5.00 g mixture of silver nitrate and potassium nitrate. To isolate the silver, excess 1.5 M HCl is added. The dry AgCl precipitate has a mass of 3.50 g. What was the percentage of $AgNO_3$ in the original mixture. What volume (in mL) of HCl should the chemist have added to make sure all the chloride ions precipitated out? (This is a good practice problem for you to try before the lab. As you're trying to solve the problem, think through how the chemist performed the lab.)

Products:
1. You must give a maximum 10-minute presentation explaining your background, procedure, data, data analysis and conclusion to a Solutions, Inc. representative at the beginning of company (class) time on _____.
2. You must have professional-quality visual aids showing the above info. Visual aids should have MINIMAL wording. You fill in the details verbally. (If this is a PowerPoint, Keynote, etc. presenation, please send it to Kima by midnight the evening before your company's presentation.)
3. Turn in a hard copy report of the company's background, procedure, data, data analysis, and conclusion. (This is NOT simply a printout of the presentation. This is a REPORT!)
4. Company (class) managers may NOT be the presenters. They can (and should) be part of the planning. Presentations should be done by others in the company. Who you choose and the number of presenters is up to your company.
5. You will be assessed in three categories—work during company time (safety, accuracy and community effort); presentation (accuracy and professionalism); and report (accuracy, professionalism, and thoroughness).

Questions everyone should be able to answer (besides the task itself and the above example):
1. List 2 other solutions that would precipitate out one of the starting 2 chemicals from your lab. Write the net ionic equations.
2. For this lab, write out the net ionic equation. What were the spectator ions?

WCI project, which contains an investigation that is quite challenging conceptually. I also want to reconnect with my students because I haven't seen them for a week because of our alternative schedule. It takes me a bit to get their heads back into the Solutions Chemistry lingo.

I then hand out the project sheet (Figure 5.1), disappear into the prep room, and return wearing my lab coat in character as the Solutions, Inc., lab manager, Kima. And, finally, I read through the project sheet to the students. I will remain in character as the company lab manager throughout the lab.

One twist for this activity is that the company (class) is allowed to ask Kima only five questions a day. Kima reserves the right to not answer any question that might be too telling, but she will typically answer any question regarding chemistry equipment or lab technique. Notice that the project sheet also says that Kima will allow the company (class) three tries at checking its answers to the practice problem.

Video—Watch the SOLN-1A video on the DVD labeled "Video Cases for Chapters 4–5." This video takes the first 30 minutes of class and compresses them into approximately 11 minutes so that you can visualize what was described.

Teacher's Analysis—SOLN-1A

As I read through the project sheet, some students appear to need time to gear up for this. Jack, being a class manager, appears to need more time than most to get used to the idea that the class is in for another multiday lab investigation. Other students are reading along as I do, carefully trying to soak up all the details. They are familiar with the time constraints that typically plague their class during a multiday project. They are very used to the components in these projects at this point in the year, they know I won't break character, and they know that every detail and minute counts.

For this project, similar parameters are set for the students in that I have removed myself from the role as teacher. But I've added a few new ones, as mentioned earlier. The class can ask Kima only five questions per day. This will require that they use each other and carefully think through the planning and implementation of their lab. They know it will probably be necessary to use a question or two, so they want to make sure none of the questions are wasted. A second change is that the class must request the materials needed for lab. This requires that the class think through the actual lab procedure in detail to compile a complete list of materials. In the next video, you see to what extent the students implement the feedback received from the CanCo WCI Project and other class activities and grapple with these new twists.

SOLUTIONS WCI PROJECT—DAY 1, PART 2

Teacher's Introduction—SOLN-1B

This video focuses on watching the students in the planning stages of a project. Remember, it has been four months since they planned CANCO together. First, Jack and Kim immediately stand up to take charge. The class does a number of appropriate tasks to get them to a point at which they will begin lab. They work on safety, the example problem, and the list of materials needed.

Teacher's Analysis—SOLN-1B

It is evident that the students recognize quickly that this is another one of "those" labs—a four-day-long, student-led project. As soon as I exit at the front of the room, Jack and Kim stand up to take over. Even though Jack had been one of the students who required time to gear up for this, he is immediately speaking to Kim about some ideas on how to proceed. Both take a minute together to process the information, as had been suggested in previous feedback. Then Jack requests that the students look in their journals to find some suggestions from previous feedback to make sure they improve their problem-solving abilities as a company (class).

Quickly, the class moves into recording safety information, and Lynn stands up to record this information on the board. Kelly and Angie go to the back to look up the information online, and Joe looks in the Flinn manual (Flinn Scientific 2005). Lynn and the managers reiterate how important it is that the class record this information in all journals. This is wonderful because this has been routine feedback to them throughout the year, and recording is now instinctual.

Jack then has the class break into groups to solve the practice problem in order to process the challenge on a smaller scale. Not only is he using the built-in structure of the cooperative work groups, but he also is recognizing the need to follow the hints that are in the project sheets. He knows from experience that doing the things designed on these sheets will lead the company (class) in the right direction.

I walk around the room simply to absorb some of the conversations taking place within each group. I am still in character as Kima, so most students avoid looking at me. They know I won't provide verbal or body-language feedback, and time is limited. This makes the scenario fun and sends the message to them that I believe they can do this if they work together.

Video—Watch the SOLN-1B video on the DVD labeled "Video Cases for Chapters 4–5." This video takes the remaining 30 minutes of class and compresses them into approximately 19 minutes so that you can visualize what was described.

Although there appears to be a bit of disjointedness at times, the class is actually running in a very relaxed, efficient mode for this particular group of students, especially when I compare it to where they were five months ago. Each individual member has fallen into his or her comfort zone based on previous class experiences. For instance, some students are at ease getting up and walking around from group to group asking questions and keeping everyone focused. Examples include Angie, Michelle, Lynn, Mary, Sandy, Kelly, and the managers. Others are very constructive working on their assigned tasks in their small groups. They will then use what they've determined to check others' work once the class talks together as a whole. These people often include Adam, Patrick, Maria, Debbie, Craig, Joe, Rachel, Robert, Karen, Irene, Mark, and Frank. Others, including Rita, Tara, Dan, Kathy, and Nick, are listening to the traveling students as they speak with the group members. Each student in the room falls into one of these three categories throughout the day. This is an enormous and encouraging improvement from the beginning of the year in terms of participation, organization, comprehension, and communication.

One student in particular, however, starts to get a bit nervous about time. Frank approaches Jack with his concerns. Frank wants to work on the list of materials and the calculations for the lab, not the example problem. He feels they need to spend at least a little time preparing for lab for next class, and he knows they have run into problems with this in the past. This is a great example of how working together requires a balance. Both Jack and Frank have valid reasons for their plans.

In the end Jack announces to the class that four things need to happen. The students need to get the safety information into their journals, they need to get the practice problem done and explained, they need to talk through the equipment list, and they need to get the solution prepared. Not only does this announcement give the class a renewed sense of structure, but it also appeases the students who were nervous about whether or not the class would be prepared for lab for Friday.

During the course of its planning time, the class checks its practice problem answers twice with Kima. When Sandy first checks, she and her group have correctly answered the first part but missed the second part. Kima gives her a hint; the numbers determined as a result of doing the lab cannot be used for this second calculation. It makes sense to start only with numbers known before the lab began. Later Adam comes up and checks their retry. It is correct. So toward the end of class time, one whiteboard is used to share their practice problem calculations with the class.

Another whiteboard is used to list the equipment needed for doing the lab. The other class members are then able to add their thoughts to this list. And three students volunteer to make the calcium chloride solution for Friday's lab.

I love that the groups spend the time using whiteboards to share their discoveries and plans with the rest of the class. They have been using whiteboards almost daily as a part of sharing information, so they automatically know they should use this approach to sharing. More important, without the guidance of the teacher or even another adult character, they find it necessary and important to spend the time teaching one another. This is one of my primary goals for my students. I am amazed when they share relevant, self-discovered information with one another without being told.

The class has made a big change from the CanCo planning day. It has acquired the challenging skill of recognizing the tasks that need to be completed. This is something I was nervous about because of the length of time between the CanCo WCI Project and this one. Of course there are moments of frustration on my part, particularly when the conversations become fragmented. For instance, when the students start to do safety, then shift to the example problem, and then come back to safety, I wanted to scream. But they figure it all out. And, as mentioned, Jack's announcement defining the chores needing completion puts all the students at ease. For 60 minutes, the entire class is talking chemistry, planning every aspect of the lab, and no adult was facilitating the conversation. It fascinates me every year!

SOLUTIONS WCI PROJECT—DAY 2, PART 1

Teacher's Introduction—SOLN-2A

Recall that, in the last class, the students left the room with some planning left to do. They correctly calculated the answers to the example problem. They researched and recorded safety. They made an equipment list of necessary lab materials. And they made their solution of calcium chloride. They still, however, had not come up with a lab procedure to solve the main problem posed in the project sheet.

This video shows the first half of Day 2. The managers have dedicated this time to clarifying chores and developing the lab procedure. You can see the managers assigning sections of the lab report to each group. They also discuss chores for the presentation and some of the mechanics necessary for communicating this information to one another. The class finds the initial mass of the samples and then runs through the calculations and procedure. By the end of the video, the students feel ready to head back into lab.

Video—Watch the SOLN-2A video on the DVD labeled "Video Cases for Chapters 4–5." This video takes the first 45 minutes of class and compresses them into approximately 25 minutes so that you can visualize what was described.

Teacher's Analysis—SOLN-2A

After watching the planning stages for this lab that occurred during the first and second sessions, I am struck by a number of triumphs that might not be readily apparent. It is important to realize that the Solutions WCI Project is very different from both the Chemistry Concoctions and CanCo WCI Projects. Recall that I guided them through the Chemistry Concoctions WCI Project, doing an initial activity, identifying variables, testing those variables and then communicating results to one another. The class then used this example to help them through their second WCI project, CanCo, which required similar planning and execution.

The Solutions WCI Project, however, is not based upon a variable-type experiment as are the two previous projects. This difference alone forces the class to be a bit hesitant. This project is much more difficult in terms of content. The challenge lies in recognizing that the crux of this puzzle requires modeling solution behavior at the particulate level and then applying that model to the stoichiometry and lab procedures necessary to answer the task question. The triumph is that the class recognizes these changes, even though students are having a difficult time verbalizing it. These triumphs are indicative of their growth.

I am also amazed at how hard they're trying. They throw out a number of incorrect assumptions and ideas—for instance, boiling water to capture the precipitate rather than using filter paper. But the fun part of these discussions is seeing the comfort that these students feel with one another. Many ideas are offered and with great ease and an obvious feeling of safety. The students know the only way to get to an acceptable conclusion is to drain their minds of all seemingly feasible plans to see how they fit in with the big picture. And many of them feel as though their contributions are valued.

The class is very protective of the finite number of questions they are allowed to ask Kima, the company chemist. The first question that Sandy asks about the chemical reaction is excellent. Without knowing what to focus on for the chemical reaction, the calculations and lab procedure would be incorrect. As we talk through her thoughts, I finish with questions that would make her go back to a discussion with other classmates. She doesn't choose to stand there and guess in front of Kima (me). She goes to her peers to talk. Only after concluding that she and her classmates have an appropriate response does she come back to me with more information.

When Joe asks about filtering a solute from a solution, I chose to answer with a simple "no" and tell him this is something they should look up. The answer to Joe's question is basic information that the students can figure out by reading their notes or reviewing a previous lab. In role-play and with the parameters I've set, I have the freedom to pick and choose my responses, determining what challenges are appropriate from class to class, project to project.

One thing to notice is that Adam is absent this day. Adam had taken on the role of the behind-the-scenes content specialist. He and Sandy and Mary had collaborated up to this point in the year on a regular basis whenever the class faced a content challenge. They bounced ideas off one another and worked through the roadblocks. Once they figured it out, they helped the class with whatever remaining questions they had. Typically, Sandy does a very good job explaining things to the class, whereas Adam has a more difficult time. Without Adam, I think Sandy, and at times Mary, are stumped a little longer than they normally would be. This is good in one way, because Sandy has been asked to explain things to the class, so she needs to think things through. We all know that when you teach something, that's when you understand it. This is her teaching moment.

Perhaps the most rewarding time began when I saw Debbie stand to ask Sandy about her calculations on the front board. All teachers know how heartwarming it is when we're able to finally reach a student. I would describe Debbie as introverted, intelligent, and organized. She does not want attention. She would be perfectly happy with a chemistry text, chapter problems, and individual labs and tests. She has performed outstandingly on all paperwork throughout the year. The fact that she has been placed in a classroom in which the teacher uses collaborative group work on a regular basis is difficult for her. But she adjusts. And now, in February, she's going far beyond participating in simple group-work activities. She's jumping in during WCI projects, knowing that her contribution is not only accurate but is also necessary for the good of the company (class).

Another triumphant moment comes when Maria speaks up. She has been instrumental in making small-group contributions. In fact we saw her in the CanCo footage with Group 3. She made sure the four boys in her group recorded information and performed the lab accurately. But to talk in front of the whole room is unlike her. Yet, at 22 minutes into this video, she feels the need to question what's being discussed. She wants to understand. She feels her question is valuable.

The most exciting point of the year, I think, is when Kim calls on Debbie and Debbie calmly shares the answer to the class's dilemma. She says, "It's a matter of stoichiometry," and then explains how the class can use the mass of the precipitate to calculate the mass of one of the compounds in the initial mixture. The students don't know it yet, but every question the class has had up to this point is answered in this one, quiet, calm moment of explanation. I want to stand up and applaud. I wanted to hug Kim for having the sense to call on Debbie, the quiet girl in the room. I wanted to high-five Debbie and make her smile and tell her just how incredible this moment is. She has no idea how many people in the room have just had one of those "aha!" experiences. This includes Maria, who I can tell is pleased that someone has helped her with the last piece of the puzzle. But I have to wait for our feedback day. And I will most definitely tell the class about this breakthrough.

Perhaps the funniest moment is when Sandy says, "I know how to get the mass of it. Is that what this is all about? I thought we were arguing about boiling or ovening it." Apparently she knew all along what to do with the mass of the precipitate in terms of how it might help with the math. But she didn't recognize that the class was stumped. This is another reason why Debbie's comments were so crucial to helping the class move forward.

This video was long. But the last two minutes were extremely rewarding and fun to watch. This class is on its way.

SOLUTIONS WCI PROJECT—DAY 2, PART 2

Teacher's Introduction—SOLN-2B

This video shows the students finally getting into lab and implementing their procedure during the second half of the second day of the Solutions project. Each group is responsible for taking one of the six solid mixtures of potassium iodide and sodium carbonate and reacting it with a calcium chloride solution. They have then decided to filter out the calcium carbonate and use its mass to help determine the mass of each of the original solids. The class recently performed a percent yield lab in which they reacted iron (III) nitrate with sodium hydroxide and filtered out the precipitate. The lab handout is shown in Figure 5.2. This percent yield lab was done two weeks before the Solution WCI Project. The students make references to this lab as they try to remember which equipment to use and how to use it. The camera is focused on one of the six class groups while students are in lab.

Figure 5.2

Handout for What Is the Percent Yield? Lab

Video—Watch the SOLN-2B video on the DVD labeled "Video Cases for Chapters 4–5." This video takes the remaining 45 minutes of class and compresses them into approximately 21 minutes so that you can visualize what was described.

What Is The Percent Yield?

Objectives:
1. To realize the importance of a balanced chemical equation when forming a desired quantity of products.
2. To model a precipitate reaction at the particulate level.
3. To learn to calculate percent yield of a product.
4. To determine appropriate reasons for the numerical value of the calculated percent yield, applying lab technique and particulate models as evidence.

Technique: Filtering/washing

Safety Background: The chemicals for today are 0.200 M iron (III) nitrate [$Fe(NO_3)_3$] and 1.00 M sodium hydroxide [NaOH].

Task: Given the reactants 0.200 M $Fe(NO_3)_3$ and 1.00 M NaOH, form exactly 0.250 grams of the precipitate formed from this reaction without wasting any chemicals!

Pre-Lab Planning: Write out a plan that shows how you will complete the task. Show all applicable information. Any calculations needed should also be included.

Post-Lab: Answer in your journal unless otherwise noted.
1. Show a balanced chemical equation with phases for the above reaction. What type of reaction is it?
2. Show how you calculated the volume (in mL) of each reactant that you used in order to obtain 0.250 g of the precipitate formed from this reaction.
3. What problems or adjustments arose during the lab? How did you deal with them?
4. What was your percent yield? Show all work. Discuss the reasons for your percent yield.
5. Model this reaction at the particulate level.
6. Write a conclusion for this lab in your journal.
7. Type up your responses to #1-6 to be turned in on Feb. 9th.

Teacher's Analysis—SOLN-2B

I am pleased to see the students finally getting back into lab. They definitely needed the time they took to work through the content piece of this lab. And recall that Debbie saved the day before the lab began. It was the turning point for this project.

As they work to implement their lab plan, I am pleased to hear references to the procedure we used in our percent yield lab a couple weeks ago. One student questions how to fold filter paper. Others want to know if using deionized water as a means of getting excess material from beakers to the filter paper is acceptable. Still others want scrapers (rubber policemen) to aid in the transfer of the precipitate from the beaker's inside surface to the filter paper. Even though the students had not requested rubber policemen on their materials list, I decide to get a bin of these items out when I hear a student refer to them by their proper name. Many students were happy about this. All these connections to this previous lab are fantastic. They're applying skills and knowledge gained from a previous experience to this one without any input from me.

At one point in the video, I decide to walk around to get a better sense of just how well the groups are implementing the plan developed by the class. In doing so, I make the impromptu decision to ask a few questions about content. I hope this will get students to think about what's happening during the lab rather than to blindly follow procedural instructions and to not know why they're doing what they're doing. It should be noted that I didn't find this necessary in one of my other classes but did in a third. So I was able to provide guidance in character as needed for each particular class. I am disappointed that the group the camera is focused on takes a long time to identify what the white precipitate is; my journal notes, however, indicate that four out of the six groups were able to easily make this identification.

I do notice some interactions between students and Kima (me) during the first half of this video. At one point, Kim asks about my tie-dyed lab coat. She says, "Really, you didn't do that yourself?" I said, "Nope." And Frank jokes, "No, she just messed up one day in the lab and..." When they say this, I think they don't remember that this counts as one of their five questions. Later in the video, they are discussing who can come in during a free period to weigh the filter papers with precipitate. They then try to figure out how many questions they have left. Eventually, they just make the assumption they have at least one left and that they need to use it to get some overtime.

At one point Frank comes up to Kima and says, "You didn't give us our paper towels." He makes a statement rather than ask a question. I've always found these moments fun. Because I spend so much time during first quarter setting up a safe, positive class climate filled with trust and challenge, I find that I rarely have to deal with students trying to buck the system or destroy the role-play environment set in front of them. Instead, they work within the guidelines and sometimes come up with very clever ways to solve their problems. After Frank makes this statement, I don't need to comment. There are times when something like this happens when I would just stare at the student or answer by saying, "That's right. I didn't," just to see what happens. But I think he is clever, and this class has been working hard enough up to this point that I don't want to add another frustration. So, I decide at that moment to say, in a frustrated tone, "There are paper towels right over there." Again, this role-play and set of parameters give me the freedom to choose how to respond to him. And it was Kima being frustrated, not Ms. Gallagher. So the students blame the character for being upset, not the teacher.

The five questions the students asked during this second day of the lab, along with my responses and notes I wrote to myself for later discussion, follow. (The first two questions were asked on the previous video during the first half of this second day.) For the record, these are the questions I remembered to type in my computer. I may have forgotten one along the way, but I try to be careful about keeping track of all the parameters in a particular project and I believe this is accurate.

- "I was wondering about the water with the monohydrate in the double replacement reaction..." (Sandy asks about sodium carbonate monohydrate. She's confused about what the reaction should be both because of this hydrate, which they've never dealt with before, and because there's no water as a product. We talked through it. I gave her guiding questions to figure out. And each time she figured it out, I gave her another question. I didn't count this discussion as more than one question.)
- "Could a solute be filtered out of solution with filter paper?" (You and your company need to look that up again.)
- "Really? You didn't do [your lab coat] yourself?" (I answered, "Nope." Frank jokes that there must've been a lab accident that caused my lab coat to be tie-dyed.)
- "Can I go to the restroom?" (That will be up to your managers.)
- "Can two people come during 6/7 SRT to get the masses of these filter papers?" (After some discussion as to what "SRT" and "6/7" meant, I said yes. As Kima, I wouldn't understand the school lingo, that's why I asked them about SRT and 6/7. It's important to stay in character!)

After the lab implementation, students gather up front to discuss their lab calculations. Sandy has a template for group calculations on the board. But just as Sandy is beginning to explain these calculations, Debbie stops her. Again, Debbie feels comfortable jumping in to help. She received the positive reinforcement, the trust of her class earlier in the period. This gives her the confidence to help the larger group audience. Joe adds his thoughts, which parallel Debbie's. It's good to be a part of a team.

Once she makes the correction from Debbie and Joe, Sandy explains the calculation for how to calculate the percent composition of each of the original substances. She does a great job, especially since she just recently figured this out for herself.

And finally, the class spends the last few minutes figuring out the mechanics of the presentation and assigning chores to everyone. Keep in mind that, in some classes, students have already begun putting the presentation and report together. These classes used their time in lab to do computer work and the lab at the same time. They also had time at the end of class, while their filter papers were drying, to work on the presentation and report. This class took a bit longer to work through their lab planning and therefore has more work that needs to be done outside of class. My hope was that this presentation would be better than the one the class did for CanCo in October.

SOLUTIONS WCI PROJECT—DAY 3

Teacher's Introduction—SOLN-3A

Today is the day this class has an opportunity to redeem itself. Remember how awkward their presentation was for the CanCo WCI Project. The students obviously tried, but they didn't execute very well. CanCo was early in the year, and the students hadn't had much practice working as a class, nor had they had much feedback to use. So this video shows their presentation for the Solutions WCI Project after having five more months of experiences together and many more occasions for feedback.

The video begins before the Solutions, Inc., representative gets there. The class is setting up for its presentation. You can see that the students have named their company Solution Solvers Corporation. Within a few minutes, the representative, Dr. Miller, enters. She is given a seat in the middle and shown a commercial on a separate laptop. This company (class) created a commercial as a means to show its creativity and in an effort to appear more professional than any other company. After that, the company presents its findings from the Solutions WCI Project.

Teacher's Analysis—SOLN-3A

Watching this video, I am extremely touched by what happened before the company representative entered. Jack holds up a thank-you card and says that he'd like everyone to sign it so they can give it to Kim's parents who allowed the class to use their home on Sunday to create and put all their products together. What is moving to me is that Kim's parents had also loaned their home for the same purpose back in October and, as far as I know, no thank-you card had been sent. It seems this class now is connecting on a level beyond just being chemistry classmates. How fabulous that they thought to do this.

Before my character enters, the students discuss their efforts. Kim says they have streamlined their PowerPoint presentation by editing out all but the essential information asked for in the project sheet. She explains that this will make their presentation look more professional. She also mentions that she heard something from another class in terms of what to expect regarding follow-up questions. I always find these comments humorous because I rarely ask the same follow-up questions from class to class. In this case, however, I did use the same questions, so they got lucky.

After walking in as Dr. Miller, the company representative, I am shown to a center seat. Right away I notice that the students have prepared the room in a professional manner. They have food to offer the company representative. Every student but one is dressed professionally. Some even are wearing suits. They have printouts for me of both the presentation slides and the lab report ready and waiting at my desk, and add more printouts later. These are all improvements on the CanCo presentation.

After being seated, I am shown a commercial on one of their personal computers. This video was created by six people in class and showed the willingness of the company (class) to go above and beyond what was expected.

Throughout the presentation, I notice some content errors. As I see these things, I typically record them and formulate a question to the class at the end of the presentation. Sometimes I'll wait for our feedback day to address these issues, especially if the class makes the correction on its own during the presentation. For this presentation, here are the accuracy errors I noticed:

Video—Watch the SOLN-3A video on the DVD labeled "Video Cases for Chapters 4–5." This video takes the first 30 minutes of class and compresses them into approximately 20 minutes so that you can visualize what was described.

- The product is not calcium chlorate; it's calcium carbonate.
- They should've used 18.4 g of calcium chloride when making their solution, not 13.89 g. (The calcium chloride was a dihydrate, which was written on the bottle given to them.)
- The formula for calcium carbonate was written $CaCo_3$ instead of $CaCO_3$.
- They should have canceled out the KI on either side of their molecular equation.
- In the error analysis, there was no discussion on how those errors were either corrected or how those errors would have affected their calculations. There was also no comment on why some of the errors occurred or which data was affected by these errors. Also, using the phrase *filtering out the solution* needs clarification.
- They chose calcium hydroxide as another solution they could use to precipitate out one ion from lab. Their solubility rules sheet lists this as slightly soluble. This should've been addressed. At room temperature, the maximum concentration for a calcium hydroxide solution would only be 0.01 M. This low concentration would require too large a volume to precipitate out the entire ion.

At the end of their presentation, the students take time to add pictures and comments to support why this company should be hired rather than other companies. Again, this is something mentioned during feedback from CanCo and they choose to implement it. Good for them!

After they are finished, Dr. Miller takes a few minutes to ask them questions. Some of these questions are simply clarification for me. Sometimes a class will go through information so quickly that I miss something. For instance, this class has the volume of calcium chloride needed for each group in a chart. I simply didn't see it the first time through, but the students can immediately show it to me and explain how they got it.

I then ask them one of the questions from the bottom of their project sheet. It was about listing two other solutions that would precipitate out one of the starting two chemicals from your lab and to write the net ionic equations. They had a prepared slide to answer this question, which was wonderful. They made sure they were prepared for the information on the project sheet. As stated above, though, they should have double-checked their choice of calcium hydroxide.

I then want the class to talk through their particle model. For the most part they did well with this. My follow-up question dealing with their calculations and limiting reactants is understood well by Sandy, who gives a good explanation after I repeatedly restate the question. I even have Mary come up to clarify pieces of her drawing. It is a fairly accurate drawing, but it just doesn't take into consideration that they added an excess of calcium chloride. My concern is that only Mary and Sandy really understand it, so we would go through this together during feedback. Mary feels bad about her drawing being inaccurate, as you can hear at the end of this video. But a classmate reassures her that it is not a big deal.

Solutions is the third WCI project for this class, and it occurs at the end of February. The class has demonstrated incredible improvement over the last five months by implementing so much of the feedback it received from previous WCI assessments and projects. Given the class's growth, for the next WCI project presentation, I would throw in more twists. In previous years, some of the challenges I've thrown at a class after the Solutions project include the following:

- I might tell a class that no previous presenter can present for the next project.
- I might tell a class that no manager can be a presenter.
- I might surprise a class and choose three random presenters on the day of the presentation.
- I might go around the room after a presentation and ask every person a question after the presentation is finished.

At this point in the year, they should be ready for all these tests. And in previous years, my classes have risen to the challenge.

My favorite thing on this video is the class reaction after I leave the room. They applaud. There are high-fives. I hear heavy sighs of relief. And then they all come together to eat treats and decompress. They are still processing what happened; you can hear them talking about what just took place and commenting on some of the behind-the-scenes activity. What a wonderful bond the class has developed.

Teacher's Additional Thoughts—SOLN Video Cases

We chose not to include video for the class challenge and feedback for this unit. It would be redundant and is already explained in detail in both chapter 3 (WCI Assessments) and chapter 4 (CanCo). From this point on in the year, this class continued to improve the quality of its presentations in accuracy and professionalism. The community bond grew even deeper through the next two WCI projects, PharmChem (Kinetics) and FDA (Acid/Base), and through the remaining WCI assessments. And finally, the culminating three-week project in May, The Soap Project (Bolos and Smithenry 1996; Gallagher-Bolos and

Smithenry 2004), allowed the students to demonstrate everything they had learned through the year about safety, accuracy, and community. It gave them one last shot to show their stuff. Every year I am simply amazed at how much progress each class shows.

Another activity I do with my classes illustrates just how close these classes become and how beneficial WCI projects are to the social aspect of learning. At the end of each school year, I write my students a letter that summarizes all the experiences we've had as a class. I tell them that I'd like to have a class reunion during the following school year. So, during the spring of 2007, one year after the Solutions WCI Project, I invited all three of my 2005–2006 chemistry classes in for pizza after school one day. I asked each class to draw a picture, one picture per class, illustrating all its favorite chemistry class memories. Yes, I gave my students one more WCI project, 10 months after they finished what they thought would be their last project.

Twenty-nine students showed up for this reunion. I had had 70 students in my three chemistry classes, so it was a great turnout. The students always talk about how much they miss working together. One student said, "Chemistry really made me think, because you never gave us the answer. You made us work for it. Mostly, it was just fun to never know what was gonna happen next. I wish I could do this again because I didn't realize how valuable this experience was until now. And I miss everybody."

RESEARCHER'S ANALYSIS—SOLN VIDEO CASES

Teaching Strategy 10—Understanding Is the End Goal

In the video cases for the CanCo WCI Project in the previous chapter, you saw how each group conducted a separate lab experiment to determine how one specific variable affected the amount of can crush. In the students' presentation to Dr. McMurry, they describe the impact of each variable and then present a particulate model that explains why the can was crushed. Through the probing questions that Dr. McMurry asks, it is clear that the students' particulate model is still in a developmental phase. Holes remain in the model because it only partially explains why the can was crushed. The students know that a large pressure differential occurred when the can was flipped into the water bath, but they are not able to provide an explanation for this pressure differential that makes sense. Although they attribute the differential to the idea that the "particles" slowed down in the can when it was cooled by the water bath, they do not recognize that the pressure differential should be attributed specifically to the water vapor particles going through a phase change.

On the day after the presentation, Joan asks two questions about whether a can would be crushed given certain starting conditions. The students easily answer these questions correctly because their lab experiences have made them familiar with connecting the can's initial conditions to its crushing outcome. Obviously most of the students have built an informal model to explain when the can would be crushed; however, few of the students seem to have developed a detailed particulate model that would fully explain the can-crushing phenomenon. Using the students' answers to the two questions, Joan then spends half of a class session helping the students develop a particulate model that does make sense—one that takes into account the phase change of water.

You may be wondering why I am talking about the CanCo WCI Project when you just finished watching the video cases for the Solutions WCI Project. It is not a mistake. I wanted to begin with the CanCo WCI Project because it serves as an excellent lead-in to explaining the impact of Joan's teaching strategy of making clear that understanding is the end goal. In the CanCo Project, Joan dedicates a lot of time to ensuring that her students truly understand why the can is crushed at the end of the project. According to Joan, developing the particulate model to explain this phenomenon is one of the main reasons for doing the project. If the project does not lead to a greater conceptual understanding of chemistry at the particulate level, then the project is not worth doing. If the students finish the project with only a practical sense of how to make a can be crushed, then the project does not serve the goal of helping students learn chemistry concepts.

For me, the most interesting thing to watch during both the CanCo and Solutions WCI projects is how the students are able to collectively develop a strong understanding of the particular phenomenon under study when they are given sufficient time to do so. Some researchers propose that it should be almost impossible for students to gain such an understanding with only minimal teacher guidance (Kirschner et al. 2006); the CANCO and SOLN video cases provide evidence to the contrary. The students are able to listen critically and respond to each other's ideas in such a way that they maneuver toward a solution that makes sense. The class gradually and collectively develops its understanding as each student travels a unique (and intersecting) path to understanding. Willingly expending the mental energy necessary to make this journey is a conditioned behavior that arises from Joan's unerring focus on understanding as the end goal of any lesson, project, or assessment in which she has her students engage. Her students know they cannot just go through the motions. They have to put forth the effort to understand the chemistry content behind whatever they are doing in her classroom. As the year progresses, they accept the idea that they are responsible for ensuring that all of their fellow classmates understand the chemistry content too. If their peers do not understand something, then they need to take the time to teach it. In the Solutions video cases, the students took the time to teach in several instances. As one example, in the SOLN-1B video case, Kim makes the following announcement to the class:

[13:50]—SOLN-1B

Kim: Okay, guys, can everyone please be quiet except for the...so, guys, over their typing, go ahead and do it. If you would all come and listen to what Sandy's gonna explain, because I think right now she's the only one who understands what's going on.

Sandy then proceeds to explain how to do one of the sample problems provided on the project sheet. In this instance, not only is she taking the time to teach her fellow students how to do a given problem, but she is also relaying the information that she has learned from her recent discussions with Kima. As indicated in the dialogue below, Sandy has definitely taken on the role of teacher; the students, however, do not blindly follow what she has to say.

[14:17]—SOLN-1B

Sandy: For this equation, honestly, all the other things that we've done, you have to find a balanced equation for this lab so the products, so when you read it the mixture is silver nitrate and potassium nitrate. This is potassium nitrate, silver nitrate, um, and then it says to isolate silver with excess 1.5 molar hydrochloric acid. I think that's what it is, HCl. So all these three things are added together. That yields, um, it says there's dry AgCl precipitate so you know that the solid formed is AgCl and since it says somewhere in here to focus on double replacement reactions, then you know that somewhere there's a double replacement reaction. So we used one of our questions to ask about, um, the two things that are in the mixture and, alright, and we found out that the potassium nitrate stays the same so it's...it just doesn't react with anything, but these other two do, so it's double replacement. So that's what you get. And you know that you form 3.50 g AgCl 'cause that's what it says. So if you put that...if you change that into moles, then use the balanced equation to find the moles of $AgNO_3$. And then...

Mary: Okay, why isn't the bottom one AgCl?

Sandy: Wait, yeah, I didn't finish it. Sorry.

Kim: I was rushing you. Sorry.

Sandy: Anyways, that's not what you do, but then you put it into grams, then you get...No!
Kelly: The bottom should be AgCl.
Sandy: Oh, yeah, this is AgCl. Well, anyways...
Mary: Well, write it. Erase it.
Sandy: And then you put it into grams. So 4.15 grams. Then you just divide by 5 grams because that's the initial quantity that you have. You multiply that by 100% and you get 83% $AgNO_3$. So then that's only the first half of the problem. Oh, and that's the right answer, by the way, we checked.

The fact that Mary and Kelly find an error in Sandy's solution indicates that the students are mentally engaged. They recognize the value of having one student teach, but they also know they need to ensure that the teaching makes sense. These formal teaching instances occur several times in the SOLN-1B and SOLN-2A video cases; but the students also engage in informal interactions as they attempt to solve the problems posed in the Solutions WCI Project. The students cross paths frequently as they interact to understand, although each student's path is different. As an example, Angie's path to understanding involves walking around to each group and asking them if they know how to deal with three reactants. In the dialogue shown below, Angie walks up to a group of students, interacts with Maria who is part of this group, and then moves on to another group.

[05:28]—SOLN-1B

Angie: I don't understand because there's three reactants.
Maria: Yeah.
Angie: And we don't know how to find products for three reactants.
Maria: And it's a double-replacement reaction.
Angie: She gives us a hint it's a double replacement, but like Mary thought... Mary has written down that silver nitrate plus hydrochloric acid yields whatever because they give us...
Maria: ...that it's a double replacement.
Angie: Yeah, they give us the thing, but the silver chloride or whatever, but you can't just take the potassium nitrate out.
Maria: Because it says that it's added to the mixture.
Angie: Yeah. So I don't know.
Maria: Glad we established that.

In the above example, Angie connects the discussions of the six groups who have been told to work on the sample problem. No one tells Angie to walk around the room, but she feels the need to do so because she wants to see if others are making progress or if they are stuck on the same issue that she was. Angie's choice of traveling among the groups comes from the autonomy with which the WCI projects provide. This autonomy also enables other sorts of interactions in the classroom. For instance, at times several students gather together in one part of the room to grapple with one particular issue or problem that is important to all of them at that moment. Once they deal with the issue, they disband and move on to something else. One such informal gathering formed to debate the feasibility of using filter paper to separate dissolved ions from a solution. This gathering involved six students at a lab table in the back of the room:

[09:23]—SOLN-2A

Dan: So what we're saying is like this [pointing to filter] is not fine enough, if there's even such paper fine enough, to break away ions and trap them in here [pointing to filter] from the water molecules, whereas if we boil it we can like dispel out water by evaporation and then we'll be left with the salt for sure. Whereas we might, there's a maybe we'll be left with sodium, there's a for sure that we'll have salt if we boil it.

Frank: I like that idea.

Tom: But boiling's going to take a long time to evaporate it all completely.

Frank: But we're not having the reaction happen by adding water. Are we? The only water that is left is from our solution [pointing to volumetric flask on middle lab table]. We're just adding solute into it.

Dan: Aren't we all just taking a little bit of this for each group?

Frank: Yeah.

Dan: Right now, our goal is to pour this in there and hope that when it goes through that we're left with solute on the paper, right?

Frank: Yeah, but I don't think that we should do that.

Tom: I wouldn't worry about salt getting through this filter. I mean you can see a grain of salt, but you can't see the holes in this filter.

Joe: Salt can't be filtered because it will come out eventually. I haven't found it yet, but...

Dan: So CaCl was mixed with...

Craig: Water.

Tom: And salt dissolves.

Joe: It won't work with the filter paper. It's bonded to the water...

Mark: Then let's evaporate it.

Although it may be surprising to some teachers that these honors chemistry students entertain the possibility of using a paper filter to separate ions out of solution, the dialogue shows what they are really thinking. It reveals the conceptions that these students hold in their minds. The research into students' understanding of scientific concepts such as the one above indicates it is not uncommon for high school students to hold conceptions that are mismatched with those currently held by scientists (Driver et al. 1994; Scott, Asoko, and Leach 2007). The dialogue also illustrates how these students are not afraid to tell each other what they are really thinking. In this discussion, there is no sense of condescension. They genuinely share ideas with each other, knowing that their peers will listen and critically react in a respectful manner. They also know that they have to get their ideas out in the open if they are going to make any progress on their individual paths to understanding.

As I have said, although the whole class may be making progress in its collective understanding of how to solve the problems posed in a WCI project, each student is on a unique path of understanding. As you observed in the CanCo project, after Joan explains her particulate model for why the can is crushed, she lets the students know that it is normal for them to be at different levels of understanding:

[07:14]—CANCO-4B

Ms. G.: Questions. Some of you have it clicked. I can tell just by looking at you. And others are, like, what is she talking about?

The Solutions video cases clearly show that the students are at differing levels of comprehension throughout the project. Although it is difficult to follow the paths of comprehension for each student, because some students are less vocal than others, the students who vocalize their thoughts throughout the project provide a running inventory that illustrates their path toward understanding. Angie, Joe, and Sandy are good examples of such students. In the following paragraphs, I briefly summarize the path of only one of them during the SOLN-2A and SOLN-2B video cases to illustrate how it differs from the collective path of the class. I chose Angie's path because it clearly shows how she has internalized Joan's strategy that understanding is the end goal and then used it as a guide in her interactions with peers to further develop her understanding.

For Angie, at the beginning of the SOLN-2A video, her first focus is to help peers recognize that each group needs to take its result for mass and plug it into the equation that Sandy has written on the board. Later, when the class is debating how to do the lab procedure, Angie acts as the mediator between (1) those who think that they should mix the solution in a beaker first and then filter, (2) those who think they should just mix it in the filter, and (3) those who think they should just mix it in a beaker and boil off the water. At one point, Angie rereads the project tasks because she believes that her peers do not understand what they need to find in the lab. She then presses the class to think hard about the wisdom of the boiling option. After Debbie offers her insightful ideas and the class agrees with her, Kim summarizes the agreed-upon lab procedure. Before they go back to the lab, Angie asks, "Do we know what we're doing?" and then says, "We gotta go." When Angie joins her group in the lab, it is clear that she herself does not have a clear understanding of what they need to do in the lab. Up to this point, she has trusted that the class is on the correct path; however, now that she is in a small group, she seizes the opportunity to ask a series of questions that will help her understand what they are doing. Below I present a list of the initial questions that Angie asks as soon as they get into lab during the SOLN-2B video case:

[00:03]   Okay, so what else are we going to need? What else are we gonna need besides...?
[00:12]   Okay, but tell me what this is.
[00:43]   Okay, wait. And then what are we doing with this?
[00:46]   Is this what we're putting in there?
[00:57]   Wait, is this potassium iodide?
[01:01]   Potassium iodide and monocarbonate thing?
[02:15]   Wait. I have a question. We're mixing it in here first and then filtering it into what?
[02:28]   Are you guys mixing it in here?
[03:39]   So we're just putting it in there? We don't? Okay, we sure?

All of these questions indicate that Angie has not thought through how she and her group would be doing the lab procedure. She doesn't have a clear mental image of such things as which chemicals are which, which phase each chemical is in, and what containers they need to use. Two of her group members, however, who have a clearer understanding help Angie come to a better understanding of what they are doing. Even though it takes several minutes for them to do so, Angie's group members patiently answer each of her questions. As the following exchange shows, Rita and Kelly take the time to explain why it won't matter if they add deionized water to help transfer the precipitate to the filter:

[04:34]—SOLN-2B
Angie: I don't understand how that's gonna...
Rita: We're not measuring this stuff left.
Angie: I thought that was the whole point 'cause we were measuring the substance in the filter paper, not the stuff that gets filtered out.
Rita: Yeah. We're measuring this [points to filter paper]. The deoinized water won't like...
Kelly: It's not gonna matter.
Rita: All the...it will just add more to this [points to the filtrate] which doesn't matter.

Angie: So wait, we're not going to put that stuff in [pointing to remainder of solution with precipitate]?

Kelly: No, we are. We're adding water into here [solution with precipitate] and pouring it into here [filter]. You know what I mean?

Angie: And that won't do anything to the weight. Do you want me to go get some deionized water?

In the preceding exchange, Angie is finally convinced that using water to transfer the precipitate will not negatively affect their measurement of the precipitate's mass after it is dried. I believe that the students in this class are willing to answer patiently each other's questions because of Joan's teaching strategy in which she models how it takes time, energy, and critical thinking to achieve learning goals. Joan does not expect that every student will get it on the first go-around. Rather, she provides several opportunities for the students to come to a better understanding and expects them to take advantage of these opportunities.

After watching the students' presentation in the SOLN-3A video case, it seems clear to me that these students still have questions. It is likely that, at the end of the presentation, only a few students have a strong understanding of the answer that Sandy provides to the difficult question asked by Dr. Miller. Although this may be the case, their teacher, Ms. Gallagher, has several more opportunities in store for these students so that they will arrive at a similarly strong understanding. After all, she believes that understanding is the end goal.

In this chapter I discuss only one of Joan's teaching strategies. And this happens to be the final one of the 10 that I have discussed in the book. I hope that my analysis and presentation of these strategies will help guide you in your teaching practice. All of the 10 strategies that I have discussed in this and the last three chapters are likely instrumental in producing the learning outcomes found in the research project that I present in the next chapter. In chapter 6, I describe the results of this study by describing what the students thought about their experiences with the WCI curriculum and presenting the skills and knowledge that they gained.

REFERENCES

Bolos, J. A., and D. Smithenry. 1996. Chemistry incorporated. *The Science Teacher* 63 (7): 48–52.

Driver, R., A. Squires, P. Rushworth, and V. Wood-Robinson. 1994. *Making sense of secondary science: Research into children's ideas.* New York: Routledge.

Flinn Scientific. 2005. *Flinn Scientific Chemical & Biological Catalog Reference Manual.* Batavia, IL: Flinn Scientific.

Gallagher-Bolos, J. A., and D. W. Smithenry. 2004. *Teaching inquiry-based chemistry: Creating student-led scientific communities.* Portsmouth, NH: Heinemann.

Kirschner, P. A., J. Sweller, and R. E. Clark. 2006. Why minimal guidance during instruction does not work: An analysis of the failure of constructivist, discovery, problem-based, experiential, and inquiry-based teaching. *Educational Psychologist* 41 (2): 75–86.

Scott, P., H. Asoko, and J. Leach. 2007. Student conceptions and conceptual learning in science. In *Handbook of research on science education,* eds. S. K. Abell and N. G. Lederman, 393–441. Mahwah, NJ: Lawrence Erlbaum.

Chapter 6
The Impact and Utility of the WCI Curriculum

Although far from unequivocal, the overall picture from the research suggests that inquiry-based curricula can lead to positive student learning outcomes in terms of achievement, attitudes, and skill development (Anderson 2002). A recent meta-analysis of science education research conducted in the United States shows that student achievement is positively correlated with the use of teaching strategies that employed enhanced context (connection to prior knowledge or student interest), collaborative learning, and inquiry (Schroeder, Hofstein, and Clough 2007). In addition, research on inquiry-type laboratory experiences indicates that they help students develop positive attitudes toward science learning (Hofstein and Mamlok-Naaman 2007; Lunetta et al. 2007), acquire better questioning skills (Hofstein et al. 2005), and obtain scientific process skills related to experimental design and data analysis (Roth 1994; Roth and Roychoudhury 1993).

As you have seen in the video cases presented in chapters 2–5, Joan is quite successful at creating a holistic, yearlong curricular experience that embeds inquiry-based projects and assessments among traditional activities. Therefore, the results of the above research would suggest that her students should benefit from their experiences with the WCI curriculum. Yet how do they benefit? What do they take away from their experiences? How does the WCI curriculum affect the students' acquisition of knowledge and skills? In this chapter, I present the results of a research study (Smithenry, Gallagher-Bolos, and Kosnik 2007) that I conducted at Joan's school to answer these types of questions. Before doing so, I explain the classroom goals that Joan and I had in mind when we began designing the WCI curriculum in 1994 and our beliefs about what students are capable of doing. The explanations lay the foundation for describing how I designed the research study and what I found.

DESIGNING THE WCI CURRICULUM: GOALS AND BELIEFS

Like other teachers and researchers who have focused on the development of a "community of learners" in the classroom (e.g., Ball 1993; Brown and Campione 1994; Crawford, Krajcik, and Marx 1999; Driver, Blumenfeld, and Krajcik 1994; Lampert 2001; Marx et al. 1997; The Cognition and Technology Group at Vanderbilt 1994), Joan and I have been dedicated to reforming our chemistry classrooms so that students work on authentic inquiry-based and problem-based tasks, negotiate their understanding, and share the responsibility for teaching and learning. Since we met in 1994, we have engaged in an informal and iterative process of design, enactment, and analysis to create a chemistry curriculum that would change the social structure of the classroom. Our main goals were to increase the number and quality of interactions among our students and engage them in a solid community of scientific practice.

Early in our design process, we experimented with several teaching strategies and found one that was particularly effective at drastically altering the social dynamics of our classrooms. This teaching strategy, which we call now call WCI, is at the heart of our designed curriculum. As you have seen in the CANCO and SOLN video cases, the WCI teaching strategy involves our (1) assuming another identity through the use of teacher role-play, (2) posing a carefully designed problem, (3) informing our students that it is their job to work together as a whole class to solve it, (4) telling them what and when products were expected, and (5) then providing them with feedback after they deliver the products.

As a cornerstone to the design and implementation of the WCI teaching strategy, we firmly believed that 26 high school students were capable of working together as a class to tackle a well-defined problem and find a solution acceptable to the whole class. We also believed that our students would make a genuine and dedicated attempt to solve the problem with minimal teacher intervention if given the chance to do so. Over the years, as we have embedded increasing numbers of WCI projects and assessments into the traditional curricular framework, our beliefs have been confirmed. When we turned the typical classroom structure on its head as we enacted the WCI approach, we observed a dramatic increase in the amount of student talk and student-student interactions as students took charge of the classroom. We saw our students deciding when to hold a class discussion, when to break into groups, when to go into the lab and collect data, and when to reconvene. We saw that our students took ownership of a project as they devised

164

their own experiments and decided who did what. We found that they were capable of and interested in accepting the responsibility for dealing with the issues that normally develop in the social process of working together as a community.

These informal classroom observations indicated to us that we were successful in enacting the WCI approach in our classrooms; however, we did not have any formal evidence to suggest how the students were affected by their experiences with the WCI curriculum. We did not know how the WCI curriculum affected the students' acquisition of skills and knowledge. Determining the impact of the WCI curriculum provided the impetus for conducting the research study described below.

RESEARCH STUDY DESIGN

Research Questions

When I set out to conduct research in Joan's classroom, I had two main goals. My first goal was to create a set of engaging video cases about Joan's teaching practice that would be useful to other science teachers. If you are reading this book from start to finish, then you have already viewed these video cases. My second goal was to determine how the WCI curriculum affected the students who experienced it. During the two school years from 2005 to 2007, I attempted to achieve this second goal by conducting a research study on the impact of the WCI curriculum on the students' acquisition of knowledge and skills. My study was guided by the following specific research questions:

- How does the WCI curriculum compare to a more conventional chemistry curriculum?
- How do WCI students score on a traditional chemistry assessment in comparison to a similar group of students who experienced a more conventional curriculum?
- Which aspects of the curriculum do WCI students perceive to be most useful in helping them acquire knowledge and/or skills?
- What types of skills do WCI students think are acquired as a result of the curriculum?

Research Participants

The main subjects of my research study were students who were enrolled in honors chemistry between 2005 and 2007 at a suburban high school in the midwestern United States. During the 2005–2006 school year, two teachers, Joan and Mr. Keno (pseudonym), each taught three of the six honors chemistry courses offered at the school. During the 2006–2007 school year, Joan taught only two honors chemistry courses while Mr. Keno taught the remaining four. There were no significant compositional differences in race, gender, or age among the two teachers' students during either year. On average, 72% of the students were white and 25% Asian-American; 50% were female; and 71% were in grade 10 and 29% in grade 11.

Both teachers hold state certification to teach chemistry but differ in their amount of teaching experience and training. At the beginning of the study, Joan had taught for 16 years in seven school districts, held a bachelor's degree in secondary education and a master's degree in curriculum and instruction. Mr. Keno had taught for a total of three years in two school districts, held a bachelor's degree in chemistry, and had completed two years of scientific research in a graduate program before earning his teaching certificate in secondary education.

As ascertained through classroom observations and informal interviews, during both school years of the research study, Joan fully enacted all elements of the WCI curriculum while Mr. Keno did not. The previous statement may seem to imply that Mr. Keno was a traditional teacher who only lectured and did the occasional lab, but this was not the case. On the contrary, Mr. Keno was keenly interested in reforming his teaching practice and was experimenting with the incorporation of more student-centered and inquiry-based activities into his lessons. At the time of the research study, however, the data from my classroom observations and interviews suggested that Mr. Keno's teaching practice was more conventional than Joan's practice. Of particular note, Mr. Keno reported that teacher role-play was a strategy with which he was uncomfortable and one that he did not wish to use.

Research Methods

For this study, I used a combination of quantitative and qualitative methods to gather the data to answer the research questions posed earlier. Below, I describe the particular methods that I used to gain an understanding of (1) how the WCI curriculum was structured, (2) how it affected students' acquisition of chemistry knowledge, and (3) how students perceived their experiences with the WCI curriculum and what they thought they had learned from it.

The Structure of the WCI Curriculum. I asked Joan to keep a detailed, daily journal of the various activities that occurred during the entire 2005–2006 school year. I used the entries in this journal to analyze the structure of the WCI curriculum and compare it to that of the typical chemistry curriculum currently enacted in the United States (Smith

2002). This analysis allowed me to develop several graphics like the one already presented in chapter 2 (Figure 2.1).

Students' Acquisition of Chemistry Knowledge. During the first year of the study, I measured how the WCI curriculum affected student achievement. I did so by administering to 113 students the same achievement test at the beginning and at the end of the school year. Of Joan's three classes, 99% ($n = 66$) of the students took both the pre- and posttests; of Mr. Keno's three classes, 94% ($n = 47$) took them. The test consisted of 30 multiple-choice questions selected with a stratified random sampling strategy from the 1991 ACS-NSTA Cooperative High School Chemistry Examination. This particular exam was chosen because the chemistry department at this school had previously purchased a classroom set that had been used until a few years before as the course final exam. After the post-tests were administered to the six classes (and not before), I gave both teachers the opportunity to review the test and indicate which items they had covered during the past year. Of the 30 questions, Joan selected 22 and Mr. Keno selected 20, with 18 in common. Two different student scores are reported in this chapter. The first score includes all 30 items while the second score contains only those 18 items discussed above.

Students' Perceptions of the WCI Experience and Outcomes. I used qualitative methods to determine the perceptions the students held about their experiences with the WCI curriculum and what they thought they had learned from these experiences. In the first semester of the 2005–2006 school year, I conducted four semistructured interviews with 11 of Joan's students who are shown in the video cases. During the second semester, I conducted four more interviews with 10 students. In total, I interviewed 14 out of the 26 students from Joan's class, with seven of these students interviewed in both semesters. The students volunteered for these interviews and attended as either pairs or trios. The interview questions included:

- How does this class compare to other science classes that you have had in the past?
- What are the most important things that you think your teacher wants you to learn?
- What are the most important things that you have learned so far?
- How do you feel about working together as a whole class?
- What aspects of this class help you to learn the chemistry content/concepts?
- In what ways has the teacher's feedback been useful (if at all)?
- What do you find frustrating about this class?

The student interviews conducted in the second semester were videotaped and transcribed. I read over the resulting transcripts several times and then divided the student responses into units that conveyed a holistic thought or idea. Approximately 300 units of information were then printed and placed onto index cards. I sorted these index cards into categories using the constant comparative method (Glaser and Strauss 1967). Once all the cards were sorted, I went through an iterative process in which I went back to the data, checked the validity of each category's definition against its content, resorted and/or redefined the categories based on confirming and disconfirming evidence (Erickson 1986). After several iterations, I summarized the contents of each category into a theme. To make further sense out of the resulting themes, I then looked across all of the themes to seek out possible connections. This process yielded a flowchart model that connected all of the themes. During the early part of the second semester of 2007, I conducted a member check by presenting the model with illustrative quotes to 12 of Joan's previous students. Two of these 12 students were among those who had been originally interviewed in 2006. I asked the members to comment (through a questionnaire) on how well the model reflected their perceptions of the WCI curriculum. I then made a few minor adjustments to refine the model to include the feedback that did not fit with the original model.

Based on the results of my interviews with the WCI students, I postulated that these students' experiences were different from those of their non-WCI counterparts in Mr. Keno's classes. I also hypothesized that the WCI students might have obtained a different set of skills because of their experiences. To test my ideas, I designed a Likert-scale survey that contained statements related to the themes developed from the interview data obtained from the WCI students. During the latter part of the second semester of 2007, this survey was administered to the honors chemistry students who were enrolled in Joan's two classes ($n = 48$) and Mr. Keno's four classes ($n = 99$). To complete the survey, students were asked to read each statement and respond with either "strongly agree," "agree," "neutral," "disagree," or "strongly disagree." The responses to each statement were compared between the two student groups and subjected to a chi-square analysis to determine if there were significant differences at the $p = 0.05$ level. To better meet the criteria of the chi-square test, counts for the strongly agree and agree categories were collapsed into one agree category. Counts for the strongly disagree and disagree categories were also collapsed into one disagree category. Thus, for each statement, a chi-square analysis was done on a 2 (WCI, non-WCI) × 3 (agree, neutral, disagree) table. Unless otherwise stated, the effect sizes for each of the significant differences reported in this paper were determined through a Cramer's V calculation. The strength of these effect sizes ranged from moderate (0.21) to strong (0.54).

RESEARCH RESULTS

The Structure of the WCI Curriculum

The analysis of Joan's journal allowed me to create the visuals presented in Figures 2.1, 6.1, 6.3, and 6.4. As shown in Figure 2.1, the WCI projects occurred periodically and were related to a variety of topics that were covered throughout the entire school year. These projects accounted for about one-third of the classroom time (see Figure 6.1) and were embedded among other activities that traditionally occur (such as lectures, demonstrations, and verification labs). When compared to the traditional chemistry curriculum (see Figure 6.2), the WCI projects replaced much of the time that is traditionally allotted to lecture and discussion (Smith 2002).

Figure 6.1

Distribution of Time Spent on Various Activities in the WCI Chemistry Curriculum

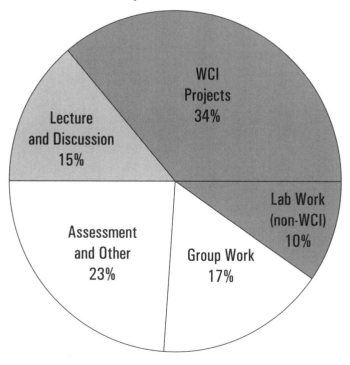

Figure 6.2

Distribution of Time Spent on Various Activities in the Traditional Chemistry Curriculum

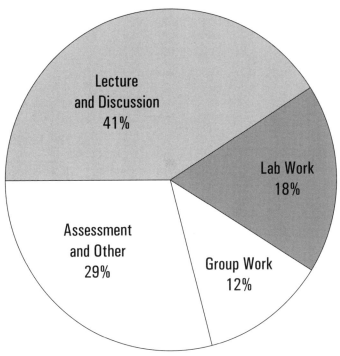

As you have already seen in the video cases, the entire WCI curriculum is based on the cyclical model that contains three steps (Figure 6.3). First, the students take part in traditional activities in which they have the opportunity to learn the concepts and skills they will be expected to apply in an upcoming WCI project or assessment. Second, students are challenged to work as a whole class to apply the recently covered concepts and skills in solving a problem. Third, at the end of the project or assessment, the students reflect on their WCI experiences and receive feedback from the teacher on how to improve their ability to operate safely in the laboratory, obtain accurate results, and work together effectively as a community. The cycle begins again as they learn more concepts and skills that will be useful in the next, more challenging WCI project or assessment. As depicted in Figure 6.4, a typical WCI project lasts four days and has the phases illustrated.

Figure 6.3

Cyclical Nature of WCI Curriculum

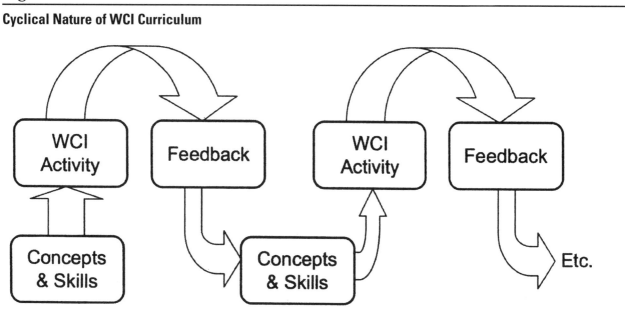

Figure 6.4

Phases of Typical WCI Project

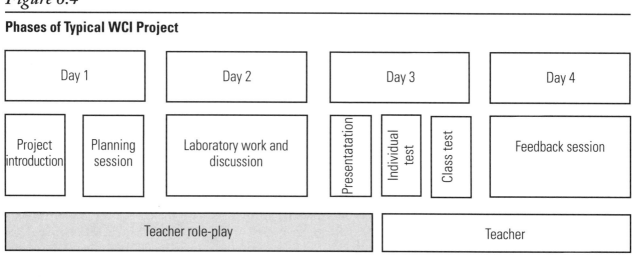

The Impact of WCI on Chemistry Knowledge Acquisition

Out of the 30 items on the pretest, the WCI students answered 9.8 ± 2.6 correctly; non-WCI students, 9.7 ± 2.6. These pretest scores indicate that there were no significant differences between the two student populations in terms of initial achievement. Out of the thirty items on the posttest, WCI students answered 18.3 ± 3.6 correctly; non-WCI students, 16.0 ± 3.1. These posttest scores indicate that the WCI students scored significantly higher (unpaired t-test, p < 0.001) than the non-WCI students, with a medium-effect size (Cohen's d = 0.50).

To check that the difference in scores was not due to a difference in the content of the two teachers' curricula, the scores were reanalyzed (as discussed in the methods section) using only those 18 items that both teachers commonly covered. Out of the same subset of 18 items on the pretest, WCI students answered 5.6 ± 1.8 correctly; Mr. Keno's students, 5.4 ± 1.8. Out of the 18 commonly covered items on the posttest, Joan's students answered 12.0 ± 2.5 correctly and Mr. Keno's students scored 10.7 ± 2.6. Even when the students were scored on the items that contain content covered in both classes, the WCI students still scored significantly higher (unpaired t-test, p = 0.01) on the posttest, though the effect size (Cohen's d = 0.36) was smaller.

Given that the differences in content coverage do not explain the differences in achievement, one might wonder if there were differences in the students' interest in science or perceptions about their teacher's ability. An analysis of the 2007 student survey data indicates there were no significant differences between these two student groups' attitudes toward the teacher, the class, or the interest they had in becoming a scientist. Both groups strongly and similarly agreed that their particular teacher knew how to teach well (92% for Joan's class versus 84% for Mr. Keno's—the order in which the percentages given stays the same throughout this chapter), expected that all students could understand the material if they tried (90% versus 90%), and respected the students (93% versus 96%). Both groups similarly disagreed with the statement that their teacher did not care if they learned (92% versus 94%). In terms of the students' attitudes toward the class, both student groups similarly disagreed that they did not enjoy the chemistry class (69% versus 77%), that they found the class to be uninteresting (81% versus 78%), that they disliked science before taking the class (58% versus 53%), or that they disliked science after taking the class (75% versus 82%). Finally, the groups did not significantly differ in the percentage of students who were interested in becoming scientists (25% versus 17%). Taken together, these similarities described above suggest that both student groups viewed their instructors to be equally effective at teaching and creating a positive classroom environment that was interesting and enjoyable.

As my research study involved only two teachers with different amounts of teaching experience, I do not make the claim that the WCI curriculum is responsible for the differences in achievement. Only a larger research study with more teachers and students would allow me to identify the true cause of this achievement differential. I do believe it is plausible to claim that, when an expert teacher spends almost one-third of curriculum engaging her students in WCI projects and assessments, this unconventional use of time does not negatively affect the scores of the WCI students on a traditional assessment. Put another way, the WCI students acquire a similar amount of chemistry knowledge as those students who did not engage in the time-consuming WCI activities.

Students' Perceptions of the WCI Experience and Outcomes

In general, by listening in the interviews to what the students had to say about their experiences, I learned that the students perceived the WCI curriculum as different from any they had experienced before and that they attributed this difference to the teaching strategies Joan used. I also learned how these students viewed the impact that these teaching strategies had on the interactions between students within the classroom and the development of skills that they deemed useful in the future. More specifically, my analysis of the coded student interview data revealed that the students' perceptions could be divided into seven major themes. In addition, by looking across all seven of the themes, I found they were connected to one another either in a linear or cyclical fashion. The connected themes are shown in the flowchart model presented in Figure 6.5. Each of the blocks in the model contains a title and represents one of the seven themes. The arrows between the blocks represent the direction of flow between themes.

Once this flowchart model was developed, I found that the seven themes could also be divided into two main categories. The first category contains themes that center on the strategies that the teacher uses to create the WCI learning environment. The second category consists of themes that were more closely related to the impact that these teaching strategies had on the students. In the flowchart model, the teacher-related themes are shaded in gray and the student-related themes are not. In the following sections, each theme will be discussed according to its place in the flowchart and its connection with the next theme. For example, I start by discussing the theme of "teacher role-play" and its relation to the next theme of "self-sufficiency."

Figure 6.5

A Model of the Students' Perceptions of the WCI Experience and Outcomes

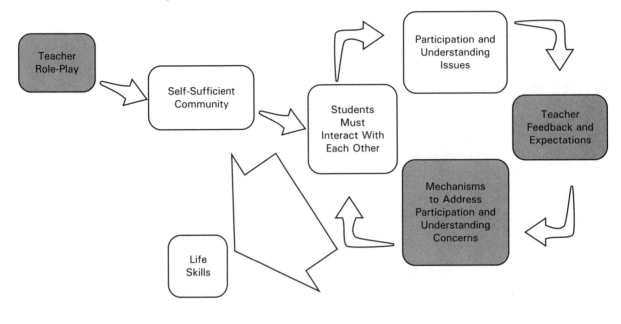

Teacher Role-Play and Self-Sufficiency. As depicted in the flowchart in Figure 6.5, the students viewed Joan's use of role-play as a key starting point for what made the WCI classroom environment different from any they had experienced. By having their teacher take on the role of another character in the room and be unavailable as the teacher, the students found that this teaching strategy forced them to become more self-sufficient as a classroom community. They felt that it encouraged them to be independent from the teacher and to do things for themselves.

> Yeah, she can't help us. Like we'll associate Ms. Gallagher with, "Oh, she's the teacher. She can help us." But if she is in a different name, or different person, we can't really get help from her...or limited help from her as in this case.

> When I was a freshman, when I heard from people who've taken this class before, they were saying how, "Oh, Ms. Gallagher will put on this secret identity and won't answer any of your questions." I was like, "Why would she do that?" I thought it was really stupid. But when we do these projects, it helps, because we need to think on our own.

The notion that the WCI students experienced a unique classroom environment in which they had to act in a self-sufficient manner is further supported by the data obtained from student surveys. Compared to the non-WCI group, significantly more WCI students agreed that their teacher made them write their own experimental plans (90% versus 42%), did not tell them how to solve a problem (88% versus 43%), and made them work together to figure out things without the teacher's help (95% versus 65%). In addition, significantly more WCI students disagreed that their teacher would always answer any questions (56% versus 9%) or did most of the talking during class discussions (69% versus 43%). Taken as a whole, these significant differences provide strong evidence to support the idea that role-play affects a sense of self-sufficiency within the WCI classroom.

Although the students realized that Joan's role-play helped them to think on their own as they took charge of the classroom, they explained that being self-sufficient as a community could be frustrating. Their frustrations were related to the perception that there were times during the WCI tasks when they felt that there was too much to figure out on their own or that they just needed more help.

> Some of the questions we do ask her [and she won't answer], we should [be able to] figure them out for ourselves. But some of them, we need help with.

> Sometimes it's just really frustrating to try to do everything on our own.

These frustrations were confirmed through the survey data in which 54% of the WCI students wished the teacher would offer them more help, while only 30% of the non-WCI students agreed with this statement. Interestingly, in comparison to the non-WCI students, fewer WCI students (42% versus 85%) disliked it when the teacher would not answer their questions. Also, fewer WCI students (33% versus 68%) preferred the teacher to just tell them what they needed to know for the test. These last two differences indicate that the WCI students may be more comfortable being self-sufficient and thinking on their own, even though they found the process to be challenging. This comfort level with self-sufficiency may be related to the differences in the amount of thinking and type of thinking reported by both groups. Indeed, more WCI students felt that they did more thinking in the class than in previous science classes (96% versus 70%) and were expected to think creatively (92% versus 60%).

Students Must Interact With One Another. Just as the teacher's role-play forced the students to act in a self-sufficient manner, they reported that being self-sufficient led them to increase the number of student-student interactions. In comparison to other learning environments they had experienced, they realized they had to interact with other classmates if they were going to be successful at accomplishing a given task in a WCI activity.

> I do like how independent it is now. You have to use the other students around you.

> There's a lot more stuff we have to do ourselves than in classes past. There's a lot of stuff where we have to interact with other people inside of the class.

> It's a class that requires you to be more involved with the actual classmates.

The perception that the WCI students were encouraged to interact with one another is further confirmed by the survey data. In comparison to the non-WCI students, more WCI students disagreed that their teacher would be the first source for help when they were confused (73% versus 50%). In addition, significantly more WCI students disagreed that the data collected in the laboratory was not important to other students (85% versus 52%) or that it was not important to listen to other students' thoughts and ideas (81% versus 56%). Taken together, these three statistics suggest that the WCI students were more likely to engage in student-student interactions in which the purpose was to learn something or share newly gained knowledge.

Interestingly, these students emphasized that the increased focus on interactions between students allowed them to get to know one another better (in comparison to other classes they were currently taking). These interactions also allowed them to form a strong sense of community within the classroom.

> I got to know more other people than any other class.

> I like the class. I like the people in it. Like I love our chemistry class, and I like the teacher.

These ideas were confirmed in the survey data in which significantly more WCI students knew the names of all of their classmates (81% versus 46%) and felt as though they were part of a community (79% versus 44%) in comparison to the non-WCI students.

Participation and Understanding Issues. Because the students had to interact with and rely upon one another to successfully solve a problem as a whole class, they gained a heightened sense of the levels of participation and levels of understanding among the students in the classroom. In terms of participation issues, the students shared concerns about the low level of participation of a few students in the class. The general feeling was that the number of these "low-participating" students was low and had decreased during the course of the school year.

> I think that there's always going to be those people who just like fly by in classes and do as well as other people without trying. But I think it has gotten like a little better. Like some people talk more. I think there's like six people [who don't talk].

> There's probably like three people [who may not feel like they can contribute], or one or two I guess. Like less than 10% [of the class], but a significant amount where it shouldn't be there.

Taken together with the idea that the WCI students know one another better, the above quotes suggest that they are mindful (and perhaps critical) of their classmates' actions. This mindfulness may cause the WCI students to feel less comfortable in participating or sharing ideas. Indeed, fewer of the WCI students (46%) agreed that most of their classmates felt comfortable participating in the class in comparison to the non-WCI students (83%). In addition, more of the WCI students agreed that most of their classmates did not feel comfortable sharing ideas (21% versus 7%). Although these two statistics support the idea that WCI students felt less comfortable about participation and sharing ideas, another interpretation may apply. In comparison to the non-WCI students, the WCI students may simply be better assessors of their peers' comfort levels, given that they knew each other better. The WCI students may have developed a more accurate sense of their peers' feelings and did not naively assume that the majority of their classmates were equally comfortable.

Overall, in the interviews, the WCI students postulated that some of their classmates were not participating fully because they were too shy or because they did not care enough. These fairly straightforward ideas offered to explain the differing levels of participation within the WCI classroom were in contrast to the more complex picture that emerged around the issues of understanding. This complexity lay in the WCI students' perceptions that participation and understanding are intertwined. On one hand, as illustrated in the quote below, if students do not understand something, then they must participate in order to understand. In this case, participation is the means to understanding.

> Let's say somebody doesn't understand something and, instead of asking someone else for help, they just say, "Oh, I don't understand it. I'm not going to do it. I'm not going to participate." That'll be basically the worst thing that could happen. Which isn't so bad in the long run, because there are another 25 students that are doing it. But that person, that'll be bad, because they themselves don't learn the information.

On the other hand, the students recognized that there were times when only a few students in the classroom really understood the concepts during a WCI project. As you have seen, this type of situation occurred in the video cases several times, especially in the Solutions WCI Project. During these instances, the students discussed how it was important for those particular students to explain the concepts to the rest of the whole class so that everyone could then participate. In this case, understanding was a means to participation.

> When we do figure [the problems] out, sometimes it's just a few select people in the class that understand it.

> All it takes is like one person to really understand it. Then if they are right, all of us will get it.

The idea that a two-way relationship exists between understanding and participation was more prevalent among the WCI students in comparison to the non-WCI students. Significantly more WCI students agreed with both statements that "you must participate if you want to understand" (85% versus 54%) and "you must first understand the material before you can participate" (67% versus 36%).

Teacher Feedback and Expectations. As can be seen in Figure 6.5, the four themes on the right-hand side of the diagram form a "feedback loop" that oscillates between two student-related themes and two teacher-related themes. As discussed above, the first two themes are related to the student's perceptions of how they must interact with one another in the WCI projects and how these interactions heighten their awareness of the differing levels of participation and understanding among the students. The third and fourth themes in the feedback loop relate to the students' perceptions of how the teacher strategies and expectations help the classroom community learn how to improve its interactions and the level of understanding and participation among its members.

As mentioned earlier and indicated in Figure 6.3, Joan conducts feedback sessions with her students after each time they work together as a whole class. These feedback sessions, as well as the expectations that she holds for her students, represent the third theme in the feedback loop. In these feedback sessions, she gives the students the opportunity to reflect upon and discuss what went well and what could be improved. After the students share their ideas, she provides her own feedback and advice on the ways she believes each community could improve its performance. Students felt that this feedback enabled them to learn from their previous experiences and apply that knowledge toward becoming a more productive and organized community in future WCI tasks:

> We got feedback back from her and she told us what we should've done, and that helped us with future labs, future class tests, and stuff like that. So we learned from our mistakes basically.

> [The feedback] does help, 'cause people can look back on their journals, and the next time we do a class assessment, it's like, "Oh, last time we didn't do that, so we should do this now."

> It's useful because I think it makes people want to try harder for the next time.

Although all of the students agreed that the feedback was useful in the beginning of the school year, some felt that it was less so as the year progressed. These students believed that this later feedback provided by Joan was too generic and not personalized enough for their needs. In addition to the feedback sessions, the students also referred to how Joan held high expectations throughout the school year that each individual student would participate in the community's work and would be willing to help other students in the class fully understand the concepts discussed.

> In my math class, we're never expected to talk to other people. Like there's people in that class who sit and do nothing. They are not expected to work with other people. Although in this [chemistry] class there are some people who don't do anything, but they are expected to. They should be. But in math, they are fine. They are not doing anything wrong when they don't speak to other people.

In comparison to the non-WCI students, a greater proportion of the WCI students agreed that their teacher paid attention to who participates (85% versus 54%) and expects that all students will participate (90% versus 68%). In addition, more WCI students (98% versus 77%) disagreed with the statement "we are not expected to learn from each other." These differences suggest that the WCI students did experience a classroom environment in which all of the students were expected to participate and help one another learn.

Mechanisms to Address Participation and Understanding Concerns. The students indicated that the feedback sessions and the teacher's expectations provided them with specific ideas for the mechanisms that they could use to address their concerns about participation and understanding. The students discussed how these classroom mechanisms helped them improve upon the dynamics of the classroom environment and enable more students to participate and understand at higher levels. Of particular note, the students frequently discussed how useful it was to use Joan's suggestion that they have classroom managers during WCI work. They felt these classroom managers were very effective in allowing the class to organize its work. For example, in response to a question about which mechanisms the class would use to solve a new problem posed as part of a class test, one student explained the role of the class managers:

> The leaders decide what we're going to do. And then we do it and we find the answer. All the people in the class do it. So the leaders will come up to the board. They'll read out the sheet out loud. We'll have our minute of silence to figure out what we're going to do; then the leaders will split us up into groups or will lead us as one big group. It doesn't really matter as long as we get the answer. But the leaders don't participate in getting the answer. They participate in seeing like if we do what we're supposed to do, and if we do it on time. We're the ones that actually get the answer. Oh, yeah. And then we reconvene and we write down the answer.

As is evident from the above quote, Joan had provided her students with a clear scaffold that allowed them to manage the classroom mechanics when they were working without the teacher's help. The WCI students also tended to expand upon this general framework, employing mechanisms that they themselves developed.

> I think we did good today, because the problem, no one really understood or knew how to do it, except for one person. And we figured that out, and we're like, "Well, you write it out and then you'll explain it to everyone."

In addition to thinking of ways to get everyone to understand, the WCI students also identified mechanics that would increase student participation both inside and outside of the classroom. As evidence, in comparison to the non-WCI students, significantly more WCI students (85% versus 28%) agreed that they were expected to think of ways to get everyone to participate. A greater percentage of the WCI students

(92% versus 68%) also indicated that they had met with other students outside of class time to work on assignments.

Life Skills. When the students were asked what they had learned from their WCI experiences, they talked about how they were learning "more than just chemistry." In Figure 6.5, I labeled these learning outcomes as "life skills" because the students referred to them in terms of their lives outside of the school setting, especially their future careers. They were appreciative that the class had taught them how to (1) communicate better, (2) work more effectively with other students, and (3) develop skills that would be useful in the future.

> I've learned communication a lot better, and how to listen to people. 'Cause before the class managers, if I had an idea, I just wanted to say it. And I didn't always want to listen to other people's ideas. I just wanted to kind of go with my own. But I think I've learned how to listen a lot better.

> When we are [working] for a company or something like that, I'll be making reference back to those skills that we learned here.

> I think when we're older, if we are doing a presentation, I think some of these things will come back and pop back into our heads and [we'll] be like, "Oh, yeah. Ms. Gallagher taught us that." At least we'll think and remember it better, because it's something we don't do in other classes.

The idea that the WCI students experienced a classroom environment that led to the development of life skills is strongly confirmed by an analysis of the survey data. In comparison to the non-WCI students, significantly more WCI students believed that the class was worthwhile because it developed life skills (83% versus 50%) and that they would use these skills in the their future careers (73% versus 27%). In terms of specific skills, more WCI students (73% versus 37%) felt the class had taught them how to listen to other people's ideas. A greater percentage of the WCI students disagreed that the class had not helped them to communicate better (77% versus 43%) or had not taught them how to be a better team player (85% versus 57%). Finally, more WCI students (85% versus 58%) believed the class had taught them how to work more effectively with other people. All of these differences indicate that the WCI curriculum has a marked effect on the types of skills the students take away from their experiences.

DISCUSSION

The findings just outlined suggest that the students who experienced the WCI curriculum gained a different set of skills and acquired a similar level of chemistry conceptual knowledge in comparison to their non-WCI counterparts. The results also indicate that the WCI students believed the teacher's role-play, feedback, and high expectations were critical in bringing about these outcomes. In the next few pages, I discuss and interpret these results through the lens of two structural models I have developed to represent the WCI classroom and the traditional classroom. I bring meaning to these structural models by invoking the theoretical concepts of Lave and Wenger's "community of practice" (Lave and Wenger 1991; Wenger 1998) and Vygotsky's "zone of proximal development" (Vygotsky 1978). My hope is that these structural models will provide teachers with a theoretical foundation for bringing the WCI approach into their practices.

Structural Models of the Traditional and WCI Classrooms

I present two structural models in Figures 6.6 and 6.7. In the traditional model (Figure 6.6), the large circle represents the traditional classroom space in which the teacher and students typically operate. Within this space, the teacher is in charge of the classroom and guides what the students are doing. In comparison, the WCI classroom model has a world within a world design. The inner world is created when the teacher assumes another identity (denoted in Figure 6.7 by the dotted circle around the teacher) through the use of role-play. By assuming another role in the classroom, the teacher adds a new social boundary and creates the non-traditional WCI world in which the students are forced to take charge of their environment and work together. The inner circle that surrounds the students represents this new boundary. It is largely an impervious boundary, but there are some holes in it. These holes allow some interaction between the role-playing teacher and the students; it is the teacher, however, who sets the parameters and controls the number and type of interactions. It is important to note that, without the inner boundary present, the WCI classroom looks just like the traditional classroom.

The WCI curriculum is not a blend of the two structural models presented in Figures 6.6 and 6.7; rather it is a curriculum that oscillates between the two structural models. Every so often, multiday WCI projects or single-session WCI assessments are embedded (Figure 2.1) into the traditional curricular framework so that students periodically experience (approximately one-third of the time) the WCI structural

Figure 6.6

Structural Model of the Traditional Classroom

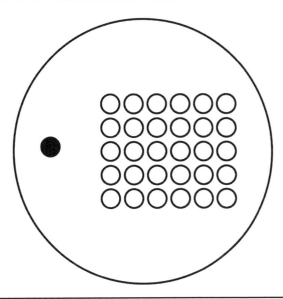

Figure 6.7

Structural Model of the WCI Classroom

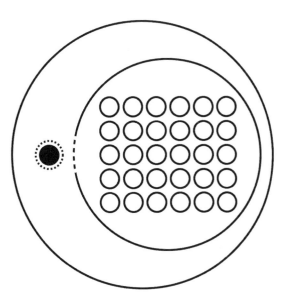

model. After each WCI activity, the students receive feedback (Figure 6.3) on their efforts, knowing that their teacher will re-erect the inner boundary in a future WCI activity. As the students cycle between these two structural models, the teacher continually reminds her students that the end-of-the-year goal is for them to be able to operate within the WCI model with minimal student-teacher interaction.

Differing Communities of Practice Produce Different Learning Outcomes

Lave and Wenger contend that learning is situated within the context of a "community of practice" in which an individual participates (1991). They propose that the type of knowledge and skills that an individual acquires is related to the social structure of the community of practice in which the learning occurs. Therefore, individuals who are engaged in different communities of practice should experience different learning outcomes. In the traditional classroom, the community's practice is largely focused on having students learn the chemistry concepts presented by the teacher. The teacher is in charge of the classroom's activity and structures the ways in which the students should interact with each other. In the WCI classroom, the community's practice is more complex. The students are expected not only to understand the chemistry concepts but also to learn how to structure the classroom environment so that they can successfully apply their chemistry knowledge and collectively solve the problem posed by their teacher.

Lave and Wenger's idea of situated learning is borne out in the differential learning outcomes that were found between the WCI and non-WCI student groups. When one group of students (WCI) was afforded more opportunities to practice working together to accomplish a common task, significantly more students in this group reported having learned how to listen to other people's ideas, to communicate better, to be better team players, and to work more effectively with other people. Interestingly, even though this same group of students spent less time engaged in the practice of the traditional classroom, they acquired a similar level of chemistry conceptual knowledge in comparison to the non-WCI students.

Similar differential learning outcomes were reported in a mixed-methods research study that compared the impact of reform and traditional mathematics classrooms (Boaler 2002). In the reform classrooms, students were presented with ill-structured problems. They were then given ample time to solve these problems and discuss their mathematical ideas with classmates and the teacher. In contrast, students in the traditional classroom experienced the same daily routine in which they

184

were presented with a lecture on a specific mathematics concept, provided with several worked-out examples, and then asked to start work on a lengthy set of homework problems. The students in the reform classrooms outperformed their traditional counterparts on achievement measures and were also able to relate their mathematical learning to contexts outside of the classroom. In contrast, students in the traditional classrooms were able only to relate their learning in the context of what might appear on the next test.

The differential learning outcomes reported in Boaler's study align well with the differential learning outcomes found in my study and support the idea that differing communities of practice lead to different learning outcomes. The WCI students, who experienced a differing community of practice for one-third of the time, acquired a unique set of skills in addition to learning a similar amount of chemistry knowledge. This outcome suggests it is possible to design effective science curricula that embed inquiry elements into a traditional framework in which students move back and forth between two different communities of practice. In this type of oscillating curriculum, Joan and I believe that it is imperative that the two communities of practice be related to each other. The knowledge and skills learned by students in the WCI community of practice need to have meaning in the traditional community of practice, and vice versa (see Figure 6.3).

The Power of Role-Play

Our findings indicate that it is the teacher's use of role-play that erects a new social boundary in the classroom and brings her students into a new community of practice. These findings suggest that role-play can serve as a powerful tool because the teacher can draw upon it to control when, how, and to what extent her students move between the traditional and nontraditional communities of practice. By altering the parameters of the role-play assumed, the teacher can tailor the amount of freedom her students experience and thus differentially change the community's practice. This ability to differentiate is useful given that no two classes of students are alike and that the teacher will need to increase the complexity of the WCI projects as the year progresses.

What about teachers who, like Mr. Keno, may feel uncomfortable with the use of role-play in their classrooms? Does this mean that they cannot enact the WCI environment in their classes? The WCI structural model implies that it is vital to erect the new boundary within the classroom for students to take charge and gain ownership of the posed problem. Joan and I tentatively propose that it may not be absolutely necessary for a teacher to role-play to erect this inner boundary. It may be feasible for the teacher to set clear parameters (e.g., specifying the types of questions that the teacher will answer or limiting the number of questions that can be asked) for interacting with students during a WCI project. These parameters must be designed to send a clear message to the students that they are in charge, not the teacher. This message should also nurture the idea that the students must interact with one another.

Our experience in the classroom has shown that, if a teacher does not stick to the original parameters (with or without role-play) and steps in to take over when the students meet a rough spot, the inner boundary is quickly dissolved and the students relinquish ownership of the problem. Once this boundary is removed, the traditional classroom model returns and it is very difficult to re-erect the inner boundary because the students now know that the teacher will intervene when things do not go smoothly. The students interpret the teacher's intervention to mean "business as usual." Given that the students have been conditioned with years of experience of having the teacher in charge of the traditional classroom space, their natural inclination is to revert back to this default state if given the opportunity.

Although it might be possible for a teacher to bring about a WCI environment without using role-play, Joan and I expect that this teacher would likely find it difficult to effectively maintain a distinct boundary between the teacher and the students. Without the role-play, students may continue to perceive the teacher as the traditional authoritative figure who should be expected to answer most of their questions or step in when they need help. This perception may undermine the teacher's efforts to create a new boundary in the classroom so that her students take charge.

More Horizontal Interactions

I believe that the oscillating nature of the WCI curriculum allows students to access a wide array of interactions. In both the traditional and WCI classrooms, the structures allow for both vertical teacher-student and horizontal student-student interactions to occur, but the ratio between the occurrences of these two types of interactions is different in each classroom. In the WCI classroom, the students talk more often to each other rather than to their teacher. Thus, the frequency of the horizontal interactions is much higher than that in the traditional classroom. As the students move into the WCI classroom environment, they gain access to a greater range of horizontal interactions that are not available to students who experience only the traditional classroom.

This wider range of horizontal interactions implies that the students may also have an increased amount of possible "zones of proximal development" (ZPD) available to them. Vygotsky defined this zone as the distance between what an individual is able to do independently and what an individual can do with the help of others who are more capable (1978). I interpret this definition to have several implications. First, it implies that learning is a social process because it involves interactions between individuals who are less capable with those who are more capable. Second, it suggests that both the less and more capable individuals must actively participate within the ZPD for the less capable individual to learn and construct knowledge. Last, it indicates that learning cannot be a passive process; learners cannot simply be receptacles that are filled with knowledge. In the social constructivist tradition, I use these implications to interpret the ZPD as an intellectual space where an individual constructs knowledge through a socially mediated process that involves active interactions with others who are more capable. In the classroom setting, I assume that ZPDs can occur between two students (horizontal interaction) and between a teacher and a student (vertical interaction).

In the WCI classroom, a student who has a question or wishes to learn something has access to a large number of students who may be more capable and able to enter into a ZPD. In the video cases, you witnessed how students often asked questions of one another and invited other students to engage in a ZPD. The students engage with their peers when the need arises. The teacher does not set up the ZPDs in advance in a collaborative group activity or a pair-share; rather the students structure these ZPDs when appropriate. This management of ZPDs by the students may represent a new way for dealing with the difficult task of providing scaffolding to all of the multiple ZPDs that can exist within a classroom (Davis and Miyake 2004). Typically, the teacher is regarded as the main person in the classroom who is responsible for distributing scaffolding across the class in order to manage the multiple ZPDs (Puntambekar and Kolodner 2005).

We propose that the increased number of possible ZPDs available in the WCI classroom may have helped the WCI students to engage deeply with and make sense of the chemistry concepts they encountered in the traditional classroom. This engagement in more ZPDs may be one explanation (among many) of why the WCI students were able to acquire a similar level of chemistry knowledge in comparison to their non-WCI counterparts. This connection between student-student interactions and achievement is supported by the research on peer collaboration and cooperative learning in the classroom (see Tudge 1990). It also aligns well with the results of other researchers who have found that a student-centered (inquiry-based or context-based) science curriculum has a positive impact on student achievement on traditional measures (Bennett, Lubben, and Hogarth 2007; Schneider et al. 2002; Schroeder et al. 2007; Sutman and Bruce 1992; Winter and Volk 1994; Yager 1999).

Student Participation

Although the fraction of students who participate vocally increases over the course of the year, some students remain nonvocal. A review of the video data during the CanCo and Solutions projects indicates that these nonvocal students are not off task. Indeed, these students often nod in agreement or disagreement, turn their heads to face whomever is speaking, and appear to be participating mentally in the whole-class discussions. Both the vocal and nonvocal students appear to be engaged in what Hatano and Inagaki call "collective comprehension activity" (1991). Indeed, the activity that occurs during the WCI projects and assessments appears to meet the four parameters that Hatano and Inagaki propose are necessary for collective comprehension activity.

First, as shown in the video cases, there are ample opportunities for horizontal interactions to occur among the students. Second, because the whole class is asked to work together, a third-party audience exists to which ideas can be presented. Third, the students have access to an outside authority as they test their ideas through experimentation in the laboratory. Last, as suggested by the interview and survey data, the WCI students perceive that the teacher expects that every student participate and understand the chemistry concepts involved in the WCI project. This expectation emphasizes to the students that the true goal of the WCI activities should be about helping each other to acquire individual knowledge, not just about solving the problem, getting a high mark, or making a strong presentation. Because the above four parameters are met during the WCI projects and assessments, it follows that the majority of the students, whether vocal or nonvocal, are intellectually participating in the classroom community's work.

The Community's ZPD

In the designed WCI curriculum, Joan expects her students to get better and better at working together as a self-sufficient community. This expectation implies that, at any given moment, she believes her whole class is capable of accomplishing only certain tasks on their own and not capable of accomplishing other tasks that are more complex. Interestingly, the WCI students seemed to share this belief, implied by their perception that Joan's postproject feedback was useful in terms of becoming better at completing future projects. Realizing that the students recognize the inner world in the WCI classroom as a place to learn skills leads to the idea that the whole class could be thought of as having a community ZPD. Hedgegaard put forth a similar idea as a result of her research conducted in a Danish elementary school (Hedgegaard 1996). Each time Joan pushes her students into the WCI inner world, she brings them into a new ZPD in which the task that they are to complete is more difficult than the last one. She supports them in this new community ZPD with scaffolding that comes in the form of the project sheet, the parameters she sets in her role-play, and the feedback provided during the last project. Over the course of the year, the students start thinking of themselves as a community and recognize that everyone must participate and understand if the community is to be successful. Although it may be that the teacher is the only person who initially expects that the whole class will act as a community, at some point the students internalize this expectation and it becomes engrained in the community's practice as evidenced in the students' perceptions of the WCI curriculum.

Acquiring the Collaborative Skills of Scientists

By listening in interviews to what the students had to say about their experiences with the WCI curriculum, I was able to identify a set of themes that are presented in the flowchart model. Of particular interest to me is that the WCI students reported having developed a set of "life skills" as a result of their WCI experiences. Through the survey data, I was able to confirm that significantly more of the WCI students believed that they had learned these life skills in comparison to the non-WCI students. I propose that this differential exists because the WCI students were engaged also in a community of practice in which these life skills were part of what was practiced. They were not only engaged in the practice of learning chemistry content knowledge, but they were engaged in the practice of learning how to work together as a community to accomplish an assigned scientific task in the WCI projects. I believe this second community of practice led the WCI students to report the learning of skills, such as communicating better or working more effectively with other people. These skills, which are highly social in nature, match well with those skills that scientists use when they construct knowledge as a member of a research team.

The overlap between the skills that the WCI students reportedly acquired and those that scientists use indicates that the students participated in a practice that resembles an authentic community of scientific practice. The authentic nature of the WCI students' practice is illustrated in the video cases. The WCI students work together as a large team in which they dialogue with each other. They engage in iterative and nonlinear debates as they plan their work. They seek answers, which are neither obvious nor known beforehand, to a posed problem in the project sheet. They design their own experiments to find out these answers.

They later summarize, present and defend their results to an outside audience. According to the student-interview and survey data, the WCI students felt that they had to become a self-sufficient community (apart from the teacher) in which all of its members tried to interact with one another, participate in the community's work, and understand what was going on. These traits are similar to those that ethnographers have found when studying how scientists work together as members of the scientific community (Knorr-Cetina 1981; Latour and Woolgar 1986).

SUMMARY

When Joan and I initially designed the WCI curriculum, we wanted our students to experience periodically what it is like to be a member of a scientific community, acquire some of the skills necessary to construct scientific knowledge, and still learn the chemistry concepts typically found in the traditional chemistry curriculum. The findings from my research study indicate that the enactment of the WCI curriculum does lead to these goals. Joan's students learned a sufficient amount of chemistry knowledge and acquired a set of collaborative skills that are related to effectively carrying out scientific work. These findings are in alignment with the claim by Lunetta, Hofstein, and Clough that "through the collaboration, reflection, and discussion associated with investigation, students [...] can begin to glimpse the collaborative nature of an expert scientific community" (2007, p. 407). They are significant because they indicate the knowledge and types of skills that we can expect students to learn from curricular activities that simulate scientific practice. What is more, the results hold importance because they are rooted in the students' perceptions and suggest "what students take away [from] or how they are changed by" (Ford and Forman 2006) their experiences in the WCI classroom.

REFERENCES

Anderson, R. D. 2002. Reforming science teaching: What research says about inquiry. *Journal of Science Teacher Education* 13 (1): 1–12.

Ball, D. 1993. With an eye on the mathematical horizon: Dilemmas of teaching elementary school mathematics. *The Elementary School Journal* 93 (4): 373–397.

Bennett, J., F. Lubben, and S. Hogarth. 2007. Bringing science to life: A synthesis of the research evidence on the effects of context-based and STS approaches to science teaching. *Science Education* 91 (3): 347–370.

Boaler, J. 2002. *Experiencing school mathematics: Traditional and reform approaches and their impact on student learning.* Mahwah: Lawrence Erlbaum.

Brown, A. L., and J. C. Campione. 1994. Guided discovery in a community of learners. In *Classroom lessons: Integrating cognitive theory and classroom practice,* ed. K. McGilly, 229–270. Cambridge, MA: MIT Press/Bradford Books.

Crawford, B. A., J. S. Krajcik, and R. W. Marx. 1999. Elements of a community of learners in a middle school science classroom. *Science Education* 83 (6): 701–723.

Davis, E. A., and N. Miyake. 2004. Guest editors' introduction: Explorations of scaffolding in complex classroom systems. *Journal of the Learning Sciences* 13 (3): 265 – 272.

Driver, R., H. Asoko, J. Leach, E. Mortimer, and P. Scott. 1994. Constructing scientific knowledge in the classroom. *Educational Researcher* 23: 5–12.

Erickson, F. 1986. Qualitative methods in research on teaching. In *Handbook of research on teaching,* ed. M. C. Wittrock, 119–161. New York: Macmillan.

Ford, M. J., and E. A. Forman. 2006. Redefining disciplinary learning in classroom contexts. *Review of Research in Education* 30:1–32.

Glaser, B. G., and A. L. Strauss. 1967. *The discovery of grounded theory: Strategies for qualitative research.* New York: Aldine de Gruyter.

Hatano, G., and K. Inagaki. 1991. Sharing cognition through collective comprehension activity. In *Perspectives on socially shared cognition,* eds. L. B. Resnick, J. M. Levine and S. D. Teasley, 331–348. Washington, DC: American Psychological Association.

Hedegaard, M. 1996. The zone of proximal development as basis for instruction. In *An introduction to Vygotsky,* ed. H. Daniels, 171–195. New York: Routledge.

Hofstein, A., and R. Mamlok-Naaman. 2007. The laboratory in science education: The state of the art. *Chemistry Education: Research and Practice in Europe* 8 (2): 105–107.

Hofstein, A., O. Navon, M. Kipnis, and R. Mamlok-Naaman. 2005. Developing students' ability to ask more and better questions resulting from inquiry-type chemistry laboratories. *Journal of Research in Science Teaching* 42 (7): 791–806.

Knorr-Cetina, K. D. 1981. *The manufacture of knowledge: An essay on the constructivist and contextual nature of science.* Oxford: Pergamon Press.

Lampert, M. 2001. *Teaching problems and the problems of teaching.* New Haven, CT: Yale University Press.

Latour, B., and S. Woolgar. 1986. *Laboratory life: The construction of scientific facts.* Princeton, NJ: Princeton University Press.

Lave, J., and E. Wenger. 1991. *Situated learning: Legitimate peripheral participation.* New York: Cambridge University Press.

Lunetta, V. N., A. Hofstein, and M. P. Clough. 2007. Learning and teaching in the school science laboratory: An analysis of research, theory, and practice. In *Handbook of research on science education,* eds. S. K. Abell and N. G. Lederman, 393–441. Mahwah, NJ: Lawrence Erlbaum.

Marx, R. W., P. C. Blumenfeld, and J. S. Krajcik. 1997. Enacting project-based science. *The Elementary School Journal* 97: 341–358.

Puntambekar, S., and J. L. Kolodner. 2005. Toward implementing distributed scaffolding: Helping students learn science from design. *Journal of Research in Science Teaching* 42 (2): 185–217.

Roth, W.-M. 1994. Experimenting in a constructivist high school physics laboratory. *Journal of Research in Science Teaching* 31 (2): 197–223.

Roth, W.-M., and A. Roychoudhury. 1993. The development of science process skills in authentic contexts. *Journal of Research in Science Teaching* 30: 127–152.

Schneider, R. M., J. Krajcik, R. W. Marx, and E. Soloway. 2002. Performance of students in project-based science classrooms on a national measure of science achievement. *Journal of Research in Science Teaching* 39 (5): 410–422.

Schroeder, C. M., T. P. Scott, H. Tolson, T.-Y. Huang, and Y.-H. Lee. 2007. A meta-analysis of national research: Effects of teaching strategies on student achievement in science in the United States. *Journal of Research in Science Teaching* 44 (10): 1436–1460.

Smith, P. S. 2002. *2000 National survey of science and mathematics education: Status of high school chemistry teacher.* Chapel Hill, NC: Horizon Research.

Smithenry, D. W., J. A. Gallagher-Bolos, and C. Kosnik. 2007. Student perceptions of community inquiry in the chemistry classroom. Paper presented at the American Educational Research Association, Chicago, 2007.

Sutman, F. X., and M. H. Bruce. 1992. Chemistry in the community–ChemCom. *Journal of Chemical Education* 69 (7): 564–567.

The Cognition and Technology Group at Vanderbilt. 1994. From visual word problems to learning communities: Changing conception of cognitive research. In *Classroom lessons: Integrating cognitive theory and classroom practice,* ed. K. McGilly, 157–200. Cambridge, MA: MIT Press/Bradford Books.

Tudge, J. 1990. Vygotsky, the zone of proximal development, and peer collaboration: Implications for classroom practice. In *Vygotsky and education: Instructional implications and applications of sociohistorical psychology,* ed. L. C. Moll. Cambridge: Cambridge University Press.

Vygotsky, L. S. 1978. *Mind in society: The development of higher psychological processes.* Cambridge, MA: Harvard University Press.

Wenger, E. 1998. *Communities of practice: Learning, meaning, and identity.* New York: Cambridge University Press.

Winther, A. A., and T. L. Volk. 1994. Comparing achievement of inner-city high school students in traditional versus STS-based chemistry courses. *Journal of Chemical Education* 71 (6): 501–505.

Yager, R. E. 1999. Scope, sequence and coordination: The Iowa Project, a national reform effort in the USA. *International Journal of Science Education* 21 (2): 169–194.

Chapter 7
Summary

After 15 years of collaboration, we (Dennis and Joan) agree there is one fundamental constant in our work together as educators—teaching is a journey, not a destination. We are constantly striving to determine how best to reach our students, regardless of age, socioeconomic background, gender, experience, or motivation. We know that this goal is simultaneously increasingly draining and indescribably rewarding, but the outcome is more than worth the effort.

Teachers know there is a huge time commitment involved with writing, implementing, and assessing new approaches for the classroom. But they also know how important it is to continue to grow as educators and improve their practices. Our goal with this book is to share our journeys together thus far and, we hope, to inspire others to evaluate their practices and take them to the next level with their students. Ultimately, we hope that teachers will value the idea of the WCI approach and decide to let go of their students' hands by giving them the opportunities and guidance that will help them develop a self-sufficient classroom community of learners.

We were lucky to teach together in the same building for one year. In that year, we developed a lifelong friendship, as well as a professional relationship that exponentially stretched our growth potential. In essence, through our collaborations we have been able to bridge the gaps among research, education, and industry. Our stories in this book aim to show the benefits of meshing these three worlds by writing and implementing authentic projects and assessments in order to give our students a realistic understanding of what a community of scientists might experience together. We continue to improve our teaching strategies and explore new ones to provide more opportunities for whole-class inquiry experiences for our students.

As we said, the original idea of the WCI approach was borne of Dennis's work as a scientist and his experience in his high school chemistry class and Joan's reflections on watching her daughters grow and conversations she had with her husband, father, and brother. It seemed natural to us to try to develop a self-sufficient scientific community of learners based on our life experiences. Reassurance that our methodology is beneficial arrives continually through parental and student feedback letters. We have had dozens of educators approach us with success stories once they've taken the risk of allowing students to depend on one another.

There is a large volume of brain-based and social science research that further acknowledges that education needs to move in the direction of WCI. James Surowiecki, for instance, a historian and journalist, proposes that a crowd of people is often much wiser than any one person in the group, in fact smarter than the smartest person in the room (2004). We see evidence of this each time our students struggle through a task together. Their problem-solving strategies and their collective cognitive diversity are two fundamental reasons why a classroom community is better able to accomplish our challenges than any individual in that classroom. For similar reasons, scientists engage in a larger community to ensure that their work draws upon the benefits found through collaboration.

We want to emphasize that it is not necessary for a teacher to connect with a professional scientist or an educational researcher to constructively implement the WCI methodology. All that is required is the belief that the process and outcome is worth it. Once you make the mental shift as an educator that you believe in a student-centered, inquiry-based science classroom in which students rely on one another to solve problems, the rest will follow. We do think there are a few tangible actions that will help you as you start this journey.

1. *Do not try to change your curriculum all at once.* If you plan with the end in mind, you probably can incorporate small pieces of the WCI approach throughout the year without taking on an overwhelming task. Having an idea of what you want your students to take with them as they leave your classroom at the end of the year will help guide you in your curricular changes. Use these thoughts as a guide for the feedback you share with students for any curricular changes you make. For instance, perhaps you will add a small WCI assessment at the end of each unit one year, along with implementing one or two WCI projects each semester. Carefully plan the feedback for each WCI activity so that your students can grow in the direction of your year-end goals as the year progresses.

2. *Find another teacher to collaborate with.* This is essential. You don't need a scientist. Just find someone who shares your belief in the WCI approach, and you will have a wonderful time creating new lessons for your students. It helps to have someone walk this journey with you. Plus, it illustrates that you believe in learning communities as you're trying to practice what you teach. This book focuses on chemistry, but, if you find someone with whom you can talk through your ideas, WCI can be modified to fit

into any science content area—including biology, Earth science, physics, and environmental science. We know several teachers who have successfully adapted the WCI approach in other subject areas. Just think through how to modify our ideas to fit your student demographics.

3. *Record everything.* This will help you build your curriculum and not have to reinvent the wheel month after month, year after year. If you have an idea, write it down. If there's something you want to change with an activity, record your modifications. If you felt something went well or poorly, reflect on it in writing. You will save yourself much time in the future if you record things as you go.

We will continue to modify and improve our WCI approach to science education to ensure that it nurtures the growth of the whole child and provides all our students with lifelong skills and a fundamental appreciation for thinking like scientists. As we do so, we will continue to enjoy the journey by handing over classroom decisions to our students. When our students (and yours) reflect on their class experiences in years to come, we hope their thoughts affirm that they indeed owned their education. Their success and growth belongs to them because they trusted their teachers enough to dive in and learn from the experience of working with one another.

REFERENCE

Surowiecki, J. 2004. *The wisdom of crowds: Why the many are smarter than the few and how collective wisdom shapes business, economies, societies and nations.* New York: Doubleday.

Index